SILENT
NO MORE

Dear Joan,

Peace,

Erika Nora
July 10, 2013

SILENT
NO MORE

Personal Narratives of German Women who Survived
WWII Expulsion and Deportation

ERIKA VORA

To order additional copies of this book, contact:
Xlibris Corporation
1-888-795-4274
www.Xlibris.com
Orders@Xlibris.com
87772

CONTENTS

ACKNOWLEDGEMENTS...11

PREFACE..13
    Historical Context 15
    Organization of the Book 19

ROMANIA...21
Brief History of Romania and Deportation of Ethnic Germans..........22
    Romania and World War II 23
    Germans in Romania...24
    Deportations of Germans to Russia.................................25
    Deportations of Germans to the Bărăgan Grassland of Romania.....27
    Deportations of Germans from Romania 28

Personal Narratives of Ethnic Germans Deported from
Romania to Russia..35
    Elisabeth Maltry...37
    Elisabeth Rudlof...51
    Anna Schauer...71
    Eva Doggendorf..85
    Anna Frombach 97
    Anna Riedl...109
    Juliane Becker 117
    Anna Nover..125
    Katharina Valentin..131
    Magdalena Kasznel 133
    Elisabeth Braun...137
    Franz Engel 141
    Helmut Graf...147

Personal Narratives of Ethnic Germans Deported to
the Bărăgan Romania 151
    Magdalena Reb...153
    Anna Dewald 167
    Elisabeth Mann 171

Life of Ethnic Germans in Communist Romania 175
    Franziska Graf.... 175

YUGOSLAVIA.. **180**
Brief History of Yugoslavia and Ethnic Germans in Yugoslavia........... 181
    Yugoslavia and World War II 181
    Germans in Yugoslavia.. 182
    The Treatment of Germans 183

Personal Narrative of an Ethnic German Deported from
Yugoslavia to Russia... 185
    Magdalena Kubrikov 187

Brief History of Czechoslovakia and Ethnic Germans in
Czechoslovakia 202
    Czechoslovakia and World War II.. 203
    Germans in Czechoslovakia 205
    The Expulsion of Germans 206

Personal Narratives of the Expulsion of
Ethnic Germans from Czechoslovakia... 211
    Josef Antoni 213
    Maria Antoni... 221
    Isolde Zaschke.. 225
    Elisabeth Siebert 247
    Traudel Schüttig... 263
    Regina Schnell.. 271
    Frau Wimbersky 281
    Isabella Müller... 293

The Perspective of a Local Bavarian on the Flood of Refugees 303
    Elisabeth Eckl.. 303

GERMANY.. **309**
Brief History of East Prussia and Silesia, Germany and
the Expulsion of Germans... 310
    East Prussia, Silesia and World War II 312
    Flight and Expulsion of Germans from East Prussia..................... 312
    Flight and Expulsion of Germans from Silesia 314

Personal Narratives of the Flight from Silesia, Germany.................... 317
    Ruth Hoffmann.. 319

Elfriede Laske..341
Erna Böke...347

Personal Narratives of the Flight from East Prussia, Germany.............351
   Herta Pflug 353
   Irene Borger 367
   Irmgard Pautz 373

Brief History of Pomerania, Germany and the Expulsion of Germans 377

Personal Narrative of the Flight from Pomerania, Germany.............379
   Frau Berghof...381

POLAND **388**
Brief History of the Warthegau, Poland 389
   Flight and Expulsion of Ethnic Germans...........................390

Excerpts of a Personal Narrative of the Flight from
the Warthegau, Poland 393
   Leokadia Wenzel...393

AUTHOR'S NOTE **415**

EPILOGUE...**417**

REFERENCES **419**

APPENDIX 1...**429**

APPENDIX 2...**431**

For the millions of women, children and the elderly who were victims of flight, expulsion and deportation during WWII and the years that followed.

And for my daughters Davina and Ariana who are my pride and joy.

ACKNOWLEDGEMENTS

Writing this book has been an arduous journey which could never have resulted in its birth without the help, support and encouragement of so many people to whom I am eternally grateful.

My deepest thanks go first and foremost to the thirty four women and men who graciously shared their powerful stories with me. It was not easy for them to share their compelling experiences without risking recurring nightmares and emotional pain. Without them breaking their silence this book would not have materialized.

This book would have not been published for a long time without the enormous help of my husband Jay. With the patience of a saint, he worked with me through every stage of this book. His never failing support, encouragement, advice, creative ideas, and editing and technical expertise rallied me on to complete this project. It is Jay who created all the maps, photo lay-outs, and the book cover.

I owe my deep gratitude and many thanks to Franziska and Helmut Graf, the much loved leaders of the Senior Association of Banat Swabians in Ingolstadt, Germany. It was they who encouraged the Banat Swabians to share their traumatic experiences with me; it was they who arranged for the many audio interviews and six video interviews which Helmut Graf graciously taped for me. I particularly thank Franziska for diligently providing missing information about the interviewees throughout the process of writing this book. I also would like to thank Egon Schuster, former Director of the Nieschbach Home in Ingolstadt for hosting me and supporting my many interviews at the Nieschbach Home.

I remain grateful to the wise counsel of my friends and editors of this book, Judy Litterst and Jan Braun, for their loving and generous gift of time in editing the entire manuscript. Their excellent editorial comments, helpful suggestions and creative ideas were invaluable. Many arms full of thankful hugs go also to our daughter Davina who expertly edited portions of the book, providing helpful suggestions and insightful questions which greatly improved the final version.

I owe a deep gratitude to Maria Mödl from the Cultural Affairs office in Ingolstadt, and to Elisabeth Eckl, Isolde Müller, Erna and Siegfried Hoffmann, Reverend Koehler, and my sister Lilli and brother-in-law Egon, for introducing me to several interviewees.

My heart-felt gratitude and thanks go to Dr. Molefi Kete Asante at Temple University, for his wise counsel and enthusiastic encouragement. He pressed upon me that the lived history of these authentic witnesses must be told to complete our understanding of WWII.

Many warm thanks go to our daughter Ariana and son-in-law Alan who presented me with the complete set of all five German volumes of the Schieder team's invaluable documentation of the expulsion of the Germans in East-Central Europe. It was of great help to me in my research.

PREFACE

The great humanist Albert Schweitzer said that to be expelled from your home is a most cruel offense of human rights (Weber, 1998. p.7). What does "home" mean? What does it mean to have a homeland? What does it mean to be thrown out of your homeland, a place that you and your ancestors called home in a land in which your ancestors toiled for generations and centuries? What does it mean never again to be able to go to the resting place of your loved ones where you found solace? What does it mean to be forced to leave behind your familiar church or temple, school, neighborhood, neighbors and friends, never to see them again? How does it feel to be thrown out on the frozen streets with a little baby in your arms while desperately holding on to your other small children, suddenly homeless and without any rights? How does it feel not to be able to feed your little children who, like you, starve and freeze on the dangerous streets during a bitter cold winter? How does it feel to be torn away from your helpless child? How does it feel to see death all around you and to constantly fear being attacked any minute? Yes, what does it mean to be thrown out of a place which you called home, where you felt safe?

The powerful narratives of the women in this book answer these questions. These women have broken their silence and found the strength to share the trauma of their flights from the Russian Red Army, their expulsion from their homeland, their deportation to Russia's *Gulag* (forced labor camps or death and hunger camps), and their deportation to slave labor in Romania's Bărăgan grassland. Their plight was so unbearably brutal that three men, who bore witness to the unspeakable cruelties German women and young girls had to endure, felt compelled to share their eye witness reports in this book. The survivors in this book are only thirty of the fourteen to fifteen million civilian German women, children, and the elderly who were robbed of their homes and all their rights and brutally expelled from their ancestral homeland during World War II and the years that followed.

More than sixty years have passed since their expulsion, but deep wounds of sorrow continue to fill the hearts of all these women. They carry deeply carved emotional scars that will last as long as they live and relive that horror of their lives over and over again in their thoughts and nightmares. In spite of their immense pain and sadness, they did not point fingers; they did not blame; they did not turn bitter. They would rather have liked to forget, but many are still struggling to overcome their lived nightmares. In the words of one survivor, "Once you have seen what I have seen, you can never forget it."

We are hardly informed about the psychological and social pain of expulsion, deportation, mass rapes, terror, slave labor, separation from children, and loss of children and families, which German women had to suffer during World War II and the years that followed. Those living in Romania and Yugoslavia were forbidden by their communist governments to even mention any of their gruesome experiences under Russian and Romanian communist rule. Any whisper of the slightest atrocities they had experienced was considered an offense against the communist government and severely punished. Most German victims of flight and expulsion tried to cope with their tragic odysseys by keeping it silent in their hearts. Many have taken this pain to their graves. It is high time to hear the voices of those who are still alive to tell their tragic tales so that all voices can be heard in relation to the war that shook the world and so that those millions of women and children who tragically lost their lives will not be forgotten.

Historical Context

Germans migrated centuries ago to eastern and central Europe, often at the invitations of the rulers. They lived in that area and contributed greatly to the economy, agriculture, industry, arts and architecture. During the nineteenth and twentieth centuries, many countries were formed and re-constituted in East-Central Europe because of numerous wars and the emergence of many new empires, such as the Ottoman Empire, the Austro-Hungarian Habsburg Empire, the German Empire, as well as the Napoleonic War and World War I.

The end of World War II and the collapse of the German Third Reich in 1945 brought major losses of German territories (see maps of Germany 1914 and 1950 in Appendix 2). Poland's post-war borders were shifted all the way west to the rivers Oder and Neisse, deep into German territory within about fifty miles of Berlin. A large part of Germany became post-war Poland. The German states of Silesia, Pomerania, a section of the state Brandenburg, and a large portion of East Prussia became part of Poland. The rest of Germany's East Prussia, with the old capital of Königsberg, were annexed to the Soviet Union (Exhibition, 1998; Kleindienst, 2001; Magocsi, 2002). The Germans who lived in all these provinces were dispossessed and forcefully expelled (Kleindienst, 2001, Magocsi, 2002, Reuth, 2007).

Before the war ended, it is estimated that 300,000 to one million German women of prime age, including teenagers, were deported to *Gulags* [forced labor camps] in the Soviet Union where they had to do extremely hard labor for many years (Cwikla, 2008, p. 139). These treacherous deportations of ethnic German civilians from South East Europe to the Russian *Gulag* started already in December 1944, and the deportations of German civilians from eastern Germany started in February, 1945, as soon as the Soviets marched in. The Red Cross reported that twenty-five to thirty percent of the deportees died in those *Gulags* (Cwikla, 2008, p. 139).

Millions of people of German descent lived outside the borders of Germany. They were called *Volksdeutsche* [ethnic Germans]. All Germans who lived in Germany were called *Reichsdeutsche* including those in the eastern provinces of

Silesia, East Prussia, and Pomerania. Twelve million Germans from these eastern provinces were expelled, deported, tortured or killed (Jungk, 2005; Knopp, 2004). Millions of ethnic Germans throughout eastern and central Europe, notably in Czechoslovakia, Poland, Yugoslavia and Hungary suffered the same tragic disaster. Between fourteen and fifteen million Germans fled or were driven out of their homes by force (Von Darnstädt and Wiegrafe, 2005; Kent, 2003). More than two million German women and children were killed or were not able to survive (Knopp, 2004).

The fate of these millions of German people who lived in Central and East Europe may be regarded as "a classic case of ethnic cleansing on a grand scale" (Barwich et. al., 1992, 1993). For example, in November 1944, before World War II ended, all ethnic Germans who had lived for centuries in Yugoslavia were declared "enemies of the people" by the government of that country (Scherer et. al., 1999, p. 131; Wildman et. al., 2001, p. 31). Even those Germans in Yugoslavia who were critical of Hitler's regime were stripped of all civic rights, totally dispossessed, and expelled.

A similar fate fell upon the ethnic Germans in Czechoslovakia when President Beneš called for the "liquidation" of the Germans. In his own words, "The Germans in our republic must be liquidated . . . to cleanse the republic" (Glassheim 2000, p. 473-4). His ambitious German expulsion campaign completely destroyed the large one-thousand year-old German community because of their ethnicity. It purged effectively 28.8% of the national population of Czechoslovakia (Schieder, 2004, Vol. 4/2). In Poland, where the German population was thirty million, which accounted for one third of Poland's total population, the communist party chief Wladislav Gomulka started and completed a successful hate and ethnic cleansing campaign, "We have to throw them out . . . We demand the expulsion of the Germans" (Meyer, 2005, pp.155-156).

World War II spread ethnic cleansing, death and devastation throughout most of the world. It brought about the greatest mass migration of the twentieth century (Schieder, 1961; Bade, 2000; Münz, 1985; Naimark, 2001; Ther and Siljak, eds. 2001). More than twelve million Germans fled or were expelled from all the German provinces east of the rivers Oder and Neisse, i.e., Silesia, East Prussia, and Pomerania (Jungk, 2005; Knopp, 2004) which became part of Poland. According to the Potsdam Agreement of the victors (Churchill, Roosevelt and Stalin), these German people were to be expelled so that Poland could legally occupy all those German provinces and move those Poles who were living in the Russian occupied territories of Poland to the German provinces. As a result, wild and violent expulsions of German descent people took place. In the winter of 1944/45, all these states east of the rivers Oder and Neisse became the "land of the dead" where the streets were covered with dead German women and children, where plunderers robbed the refugees of their very last possessions, and where rapists took German girls and women as their loot (Jungk, 2005; Knopp, 2004). "It is not an exaggeration to say that in some villages, especially those located further east, there were more people dead than alive after the Russian Red Army had moved in" (Grube & Richter, 1980, p. 67).

During that bitter cold winter of 1944/45 the streets of Poland and the far eastern regions of Germany were filled with German civilians, mainly women, children and the elderly, who had to leave everything behind and flee westward, trying to escape the approaching Russian Red Army. They fled on foot or by horse and wagon while carrying with them only the bare essentials to survive (Grube and Richter, 1980; Knopp, 2004). Many carried a baby. Suddenly homeless, they were totally defenseless on the icy streets. Since their husbands and fathers had to fight in the war, they were alone and defenseless. There were no laws to protect those German women, children, and the elderly, no police they could contact, no judge to cry out to against the gross human rights violations (Jungk, 2005). My eighty year old great grandmother, my grandmother, my mother carrying a baby in her arms (me), and my three sisters were among these unfortunate millions of people. More than two million women and children did not survive the unspeakably gruesome conditions of the flight (Knopp 2004).

The Russian Red Army was inspired by Stalin's propaganda, exemplified by the following excerpt from a pamphlet distributed to millions: "After you kill one German, kill another—for us there is nothing more fun than German bodies" (Reuth, 2007, p. 10). Even mass rape of German women was encouraged by the Soviet regime as a rightful loot of the Russian Army (Reuth, 2007). There is no verifiable data on the exact number of rapes, not to mention that many women and young girls were raped over and over again (Anonymous, 2003). Mass rapes of German women by Soviet soldiers continued long after the war was over (Weidner, 2008). Researchers of the Russian archives and German hospital archives gave an estimate of about one million German women raped in Berlin and its surrounding areas, and two million German women in the eastern parts of Germany (Weidner, 2008). The pictures of the women who were raped or killed were put on posters and displayed everywhere (Reuth, 2007). Every German girl and every German woman learned to expect rape at any time.

Many homes were burned and plundered, and civilians in German cities were literally slaughtered, as in the city of Nemmersdorf in East Prussia (Reuth, 2007). An eye witness reported that in Nemmersdorf, "Women were found naked, their hands nailed to barn doors like a cross. Inside of the homes, we found seventy two women and children, and an old seventy-four year old man, all of them dead, murdered like beasts, except for the very few who were shot in the neck" (Reuth, 2007, p.9). For the German women and children living in Poland and the eastern provinces of Germany (Silesia, Pomerania, East Prussia), the Russian Red Army was associated with unspeakable horror (Knopp, 2004). A similar fate befell ethnic Germans living in Czechoslovakia, Yugoslavia, Romania, and other European countries. All these fourteen to fifteen million German civilians, mainly women, children and the elderly, who were forcefully expelled or deported by the victors from their *Heimat* [home and homeland] were, "Hitler's last victims" (Lemberg & Franzen 2002, p.1). However, little has been written in the English-speaking world about the lived history from personal narratives of the survivors.

At long last, ethnic German survivors who were deported from their homes in Romania and Yugoslavia to slave for years in the Russian *Gulag* and the Romanian Bărăgan, and who were strictly forbidden to talk about it for more than four decades during communist rule, tell their heart-rending stories in this book. Ethnic Germans whose families lived for centuries in Czechoslovakia share the pain of their dispossession and expulsion from their homes and land. German refugees who fled from the Warthegau region in Poland, which bordered on Germany, and from the eastern German territories of East Prussia, Silesia, and Pomerania tell of their terror trying to flee from the approaching Russian Red Army and the years of hardship that followed. All these civilian women were not only the victims of Hitler's war but had to pay the highest price of revenge against the Nazis because they were of German descent.

Organization of the Book

The book is organized into five sections, each covering different regions and countries in East-Central Europe from where the women in this book were expelled or deported. It includes Romania, Yugoslavia, Czechoslovakia, the Warthegau region in Poland, and the provinces of East Prussia, Silesia and Pomerania in Germany. To help the reader understand the context of the narratives, each section begins with a brief history covering that particular country or region and the settlement and expulsion of Germans. The brief histories are followed by narratives of personal experiences of German survivors.

The powerful narratives of thirty women survivors and three men who bore witness to the gruesome atrocities done to German girls and women are the main portion of the book. All these thirty three survivors have provided detailed and graphic accounts of the grim fate of the ethnic German civilians, particularly women and children. The last narrative is that of my courageous mother who fled with four children (I was the baby in her arms) from our home in the Warthegau region in Poland. It is a brief excerpt from my book, *The Will to Live. A German Family's Flight from Soviet Rule* (Vora, 2010). In addition, the personal narrative of a native Bavarian woman is also included to shed a light at the chaos that existed in bombed and destroyed post-war West Germany, which had a daily influx of countless German refugees from its lost eastern provinces and ethnic German expellees from East-Central European countries.

This book attempts to preserve the human history of this tragic period. Each of the powerful narratives is based on my personal interviews which were audio-recorded, and some of them also video-recorded, except for two written personal narratives offered to me for inclusion in this book. Almost all interviews were in the German language which I translated into English.

Here are the compelling narratives of witnesses at a time in history when the world was turned upside down. How fortunate we are to still be able to hear their voices. Each woman speaks in the first person. Many were reluctant to share their lived narratives because they had suppressed it for so long and the memory hurts too much. Only after I had shared my own German family's odyssey of flight and expulsion from the Warthegau region in Poland were the women willing to break their silence. Before they opened their deeply carved wounds, they needed to trust me to understand what they had endured, so that I would not just hear a mere eye witness report. While they were telling their tragic tales, most women shed many tears, as it was extremely painful for them to talk about the trauma which changed their lives forever.

ROMANIA

Brief History of Romania and Deportation of Ethnic Germans

In 1856, at the Treaty of Paris, the principalities of Walachia and Moldavia were removed from exclusive protection by Russia and Turkistan. In 1861, Walachia and Moldavia were united (Bobango, 1971), and the newly born state was called Romania.

When World War I started in 1914, King Carol sympathized with the Germans. Since Romania's economic interests were with Germany, Romania remained neutral and did not join in World War I. After King Carol died in 1914, he was succeeded by King Ferdinand who ruled from 1914 to 1927. On August 18, 1916, Romania joined Russia, Great Britain, Italy, and France in World War I (Matley, 1970).

When the Austro-Hungarian Empire collapsed at the end of World War I, the armistice of Nov. 11, 1918, gave Romania vast territories from Russia and the Austro-Hungarian Empire. This doubled the size of Romania. The areas acquired included Bessarabia, Siebenbürgen [Transylvania] which was heavily populated by ethnic Germans, and the Austrian dukedom Bukovina (see map of Romania in Appendix). This more than doubled the size of Romania and the new "Great Romania" was a totally new state structure (Krallert, 1943, p. 17). Siebenbürgen was the most important of the new territories, in terms of its economy, size and population, and it became a main province of the new Romania (Schieder, 2004, p. 5 E). The Banat, a Hungarian area with a high ethnic German population, was divided with Yugoslavia.

When King Carol II was crowned in 1930, he transformed the throne into a royal dictatorship. In 1938, he abolished the democratic constitution of 1923. Romania was reorganized along Fascist lines in 1940, and the Fascist Iron Guard became the nucleus of the new totalitarian party (Nagy-Talavera, 1970). On June 27, the Soviet Union occupied Bessarabia and northern Bukovina. King Carol II dissolved parliament, granted the new prime minister, Ion Antonescu, full power, abdicated his throne, and went into exile (Hillgruber, 1954).

Romania and World War II

In June 1940, Soviet troops marched into Romania and re-occupied Besserabia and northern Bukowina. Later that year, Romania joined Germany and went to war against Russia to reclaim those territories. On August 20, 1944 the Soviet Army invaded Romania. On August 23, 1944, General Ion Antonescu was toppled and arrested by King Michael I of Romania who joined Russia and declared war on Germany (Hillgruber, 1954). At the end of the war, Moldavia became the Republic of Moldova. Northern Transylvania returned to Romania, but Besserabia, southern Dobruja and northern Bukovina were not recovered. While the Soviet Red Army was still stationed in Romania, the Communist Party gained control over Romania. In 1946, Soviet-style communism was established in Romania. On April 13, 1948, Romania adopted a new constitution based on that of the Soviet Union. The Romanian government nationalized farmland, industry and banks, and it took control of religion (Vucinich, 1952).

Germans in Romania

One of the largest groups of Germans was in Siebenbürgen [Transylvania] which was a part of Hungary before becoming a part of Romania after World War I. They were called Siebenbürger Saxen [Transylvanian Saxons]. The other large German settlement in Romania was in the Banat, which was a part of the Habsburg Austro-Hungarian Empire and became Romania after the Habsburg Empire collapsed. The Germans who settled in the Banat came predominantly from the southwest regions of Germany and are referred to as Danube Swabians or Banat Swabians (Mackintosh, 1963).

The Transylvanian Saxons were one of the oldest German ethnic groups in Southeast Europe. They had lived in this region since the middle of the 12th century when the Hungarian King, Geisa II, urged Germans to come and settle in his kingdom. In 1224, King Andreas II wrote the *Golden Freedom Letter* in which he assured political, territorial and religious autonomy to the Saxons who settled in Transylvania (Schieder, 2004, p.7E; Kopeczi 2001). Over the centuries that followed, the Transylvanian Saxons enjoyed their political independence. They built many thriving German cities, schools, churches and communities while continuing to speak their German language and follow German culture. In1550, after Martin Luther had established Protestantism, they were free to practice the Evangelical Lutheran religion and built Evangelical Lutheran churches in a predominantly Catholic area (Teutsch 1907-1926). Even when Transylvania was transferred from Hungary to Romania after World War I in 1918, the autonomy of the Transylvanian Saxons did not change.

The German population in the Banat region is younger than that of Transylvania. After the Peace Agreement of Passarowitz in 1718, the administration of the Austrian military actively recruited and encouraged German farmers and skilled workers to come to the Banat. Germans were recruited to develop this predominantly swampy region, to work in the mines, to practice their individual crafts and to settle in the Banat. They were welcomed, promised free land, six years of tax free living, technical and material assistance from the state to build their own homes, and authority over their own land in the Banat (Bosch, 1995; Grothe, 1932). Many Germans could not resist this attractive offer and came from various parts of Germany to settle in the Banat. The German settlements continued over the entire 18th century (Bosch 1995). The largest waves of German settlements took place during the reigns of Karl VI (1711-1740), Maria Theresia (1740-1772) and Emperor Josef II (1772-1790).

After the collapse of the Austro-Hungarian Empire, the Banat Germans came under Romanian rule. The predominantly German villages, farms and German skilled workers, professionals and academics east and northeast of the cities of Temeschburg and Arad were now under Romanian rule. About one third of the population of the city of Temeschburg was of German descent. In 1930, the city of Temeschburg had a total Austro-Hungarian population of 91,580, with 24,217 Romanians, 27, 807 Germans, and 27, 652 Hungarians (Schieder, 2004, Vol. III, p. 9 E).

At the end of World War II, many actions were taken by the new Romanian government against the ethnic German population in Romania from August 24 to 27, 1944: German telephone connections were cut; weapons, radios, transportation vehicles (e.g. cars, trucks, bicycles) and even sewing machines and cameras were confiscated. All ethnic Germans in Romania were forced to register at the police station of their hometowns. They received a special passport which indicated their ethnicity and obliged them to be ready to report to the police at any time within two hours when ordered to do so. Germans were not allowed to leave their villages or towns, and they were not allowed to take the train or other transportation anywhere (Schieder, 2004, Vol. III, p.62E).

Deportations of Germans to Russia

During the autumn of 1944, the Germans in Romania were registered according to age and profession and put on a list for deportation purposes. The first deportations took place during the nights of January 10 and 11, 1944. In the cities of Bucharest and Kronstadt where all telephones were disconnected, all city exits were guarded. The first groups of Germans were deported in cattle-trains to Russia. Within just one week, 75,000 Germans of prime age were taken from their homes and streets and deported to forced labor camps in Russia (Barcan and Millitz, 1977, p. 39). If the young people on the list were not home, their parents or younger siblings were transported in their place. The transport in locked-up cattle-trains lasted two to six weeks. The sub-human conditions were so unbearable that quite a few people died during the transport (Lay, 1995, p.1).

When the survivors finally reached the much feared Russian *Gulag* (forced labor camps in Russia), they were freezing, starved and dirty from that long, ice-cold ride. Stiff from the over-crowded, weeks-long cattle-train ride, they were forced to walk in deep snow and minus forty-degree Centigrade temperatures toward their barracks. At the camp they were forced to do hard physical labor under dangerous conditions in coal mines, on railroad tracks, on street construction, on deforestation, and in *Kolchoses* (large Soviet government-collected farms which the government had taken from individual farmers). Nearly 11,000 Danube Germans died in the Russian *Gulag* due to starvation, over-exhaustion, and illness (Landsmannschaft, 1983, p.45; Klier, 1996).

Only a few, who were so severely ill that they could not work any more, were transported back to Romania. However, between 1946 and 1948, the severely ill deportees were no longer transported back to their homes in Romania but to the Soviet-occupied zone of East Germany, which became the German Democratic Republic (GDR) in 1949. Most of them never saw their homes again (Lay, 1995). Those women who were deported to the GDR and tried to return to their children and loved ones in Romania risked their lives to cross the many borders of East Germany, Hungary and Romania. Under constant danger, they crossed forests at night and walked some 2000 kilometers or 1250 miles in order to be re-united with their children. Many died on their dangerous flight home (Weber, 1998).

When the rest of the emancipated survivors of the Russian *Gulag* finally were set free after five years and returned home to Romania, they were not allowed to mention anything about the *Gulag* or their forced labor. Any whisper about deportations or labor camps was considered to be defamation of the Soviet

Union, strictly forbidden and severely punished. This law of silence was enforced until the Communist Soviet regime broke down at the end of 1989-90 (Weber, 1998).

After surviving the brutalities in the Russian *Gulag* and finally returning home, the deportees had to face yet another shock. They had no idea that their families had been totally dispossessed since 1945. According to the Land Reform Law Nr. 187 of March 23, 1945, all German homes and farms, including farm animals and farm machines, land, and any property, were taken away from all ethnic Germans in Romania (Bundesministerium, 1997, pp.85E-91E). Individuals had to share their homes with Romanians who were moving in from different parts of Romania and considered themselves masters in those German homes; or they had to pay rent for their own homes while the Romanians were their landlords; or they were simply thrown out on the street. Dispossession and mistreatment of Germans in Romania continued in the years that followed (Landsmannschaft, 1983).

Deportations of Germans to the Bărăgan Grassland of Romania

The word *Bărăgan* evokes for tens of thousands of Germans immense horror and suffering. It was the Romanian *Gulag* (Geier 1994, Freihoffer, 1981). Many Germans who returned after five years of forced labor in Russia came home to Romania only to be victims of another deportation into forced labor for another five years. This time, the Romanian communist regime deported entire families to the Bărăgan grassland of Romania, the former Romanian-Yugoslavian border. A total of 9,413 Banat Germans were forcibly deported to the Bărăgan and 629 of them died during the sub-human conditions of their forced labor there (Weber, 1998, p. 52). Unlike the deportations to Russia, the Bărăgan deportations victimized not only Germans but also Serbs, Hungarians, Bulgarians and other ethnic minorities living in Romania (Marinessa et.al., 1994). One fourth of the total number of Bărăgan deportees were German (Weber, 1998, p. 49). The Bărăgan is located in the barren, most eastern unpopulated region of Romania where the summers are extremely hot and the winters extremely cold. It is described as "a God forsaken land where nothing grows but thistles" (Istrati, 1987, pp.1-11). The communist Romanian government forced the deportees to create farmland in that bare and barren region and to build villages, so that the region might be populated.

Left homeless and defenseless against the harsh environment, the deportees managed to build eighteen villages with their bare hands during their five years of slave labor under starvation, ill-treatment and sub-human conditions. Many did not survive these hard conditions and died there, never to see their homes again. When the survivors finally returned home after five years of slavery and starvation, they were not allowed to mention anything about their Bărăgan deportations in communist-ruled Romania. Just like the Russian deportations in 1945, any whisper of the Bărăgan deportations was strictly forbidden in Romania for four decades, until the end of communist rule (Weber, 1998).

Deportations of Germans from Romania

Introduction by Franziska Graf
Chair, Senior Association of Banat Swabians in Ingolstadt

Our ancestors moved from Germany to the Banat region along the Danube River and settled there along the Danube region of the Banat in Romania centuries ago. That is why we are called the *Donau Schwaben* or *Banat Schwaben* [Danube Swabians or Banat Swabians]. Before our ancestors settled there, that region was a desert area. Thanks to the diligent and hard work of the Banat Swabian Germans, beautiful, fruitful villages were built in the Banat region. The Banat had one of the highest standards of living in Europe before World War II. It was the Wheat Chamber of Europe. But later, under communism and the Romanian dictator Ceausescu, the people in Romania had to endure hunger. They sold their potatoes piece by piece. Never before have we heard of such a thing in our region.

The forced deportation of Germans from Romania, first to Russia in January 1945 and later to the Bărăgan grassland of Romania in 1951, were the most painful and traumatic events in the many centuries-old history of the Banat Swabians.

The tragedy began during the night of January 15, 1945, when in all communities in the Banat region of Romania Germans were forced out of their beds and homes. The women who were between eighteen and thirty-two years of age (some even younger), and the men who were seventeen to forty-five years old were taken away from their homes by Romanian and Russian forces and deported, like cattle, in cattle-trains to Russia. Actually, it was mainly women who were transported because the men of that age group had to serve in the war. Mothers were, by force, torn away from their children. Many of them had small children. If there were no grandparents, those children had to be quickly left with neighbors, hoping that they would take care of them. One can hardly imagine the immense separation pain of the mothers. The worst was the uncertainty about the future of their children. The young mothers, who had to leave their little children behind in the care of strangers, were constantly plagued with the question, "What will happen to my children?"

Nobody knew where the deportees were taken. Some died before they were fetched and deported. Whenever individuals defended themselves, they were simply shot, like Kübler Hans, for example, in the Jahrmarkt region. Many committed suicide in their despair, like Ella Dienstl from the Temeschburger city district Fratelia, who suffered such extreme despair when she was torn away from her little son that she shot herself in the ladies room of the local Roxy-Kino (movie house) which was the building where the Germans were brought and held captive.

Once collected, the people were shoved into cattle-trains without even the most primitive hygiene facilities and had to sit there for weeks in the freezing cold. Many did not survive the severe water shortage, lack of food and freezing cold, dying in the cattle-trains during the long treacherous transport to Russia. Those people who were taken directly from city streets and had no chance to retrieve warm clothing or any food were the first to die during the transport.

Many died during the first year in the Russian *Gulag* (forced labor camps) due to starvation, freezing, hard labor, contagious diseases, treachery and tyranny. One of the most feared Russian forced labor camps was the Death Camp Makejewka. Many people suffered from typhus, rash eruptions, ulcers, fatigue, and most of all, starvation.

The survivors' time of grief and sorrow in the Russian *Gulag* lasted five long years during which they were not allowed to receive a message from their loved ones at home. Mothers were constantly worrying what happened to their young children. Those mothers who survived the Russian *Gulag* and returned home found that many of their children did not recognize them any more. That was the ultimate pain. There was also the shock to find out that they had been dispossessed and had lost their homes and all their properties.

But that was not the only shock. When those survivors finally returned home from Russia, skinny, hungry and overworked after those treacherous five years of slave labor, many of them were once more deported in June 1951. This time entire German families were put in cattle-trains and by force deported to the barren, tree-less grassland of the Bărăgan in Romania. The Bărăgan was a desert-like barren region of Romania where the summers were extremely hot and the winters extremely cold. On that fruitless and empty land, nothing grew other than thistles. That's where the cattle-trains transported the German Banat Swabians. They were left there in the wild with no protection from the harsh environment, no housing, no shade, and no roof over their heads. Only the sky was their roof.

The first thing the deportees did was to dig holes in the ground for protection from the extreme heat in the summer and extreme cold and snow storms in the winter. They had to do hard slave labor under the most inhumane conditions and were not allowed to leave. Most of them were kept there for five years. Those who survived were finally released and returned home but were not allowed to talk about whatever happened to them. The subject of deportation and slave labor, whether in Russia or in the Baraga, was strictly taboo under Communist rule. The omnipresent Secret Police made sure that no one talked. Only after the fall of the dictator Ceausescu were the survivors of the deportation allowed to speak about their years of suffering and sorrow. It is, indeed, a wonder that they survived. Their faith gave them the strength not to give up hope. In their misery, many became poets, like Frau Anna Frombach (whose poem will appear later in this book). To keep the death rates low, the Russians sent a transport of the most seriously ill back to the Banat in Romania. Many of them died during the transport, while for others death waited until they got home. Very few of the seriously ill deportees survived.

When the first deathly ill people, skeleton-thin, and closed in rags arrived back home from labor camps in Russia or the Bărăgan, they resembled skeletons more than living human beings. Now the church was faced with another challenge: how to find desperately needed medication, food, and clothing for these unfortunate people. For that reason, the *Heimkehrerhilfswerk* [Home-comer's Help Organization] was started under the leadership of Sister Patricia Zimmermann. With the help of repeated contributions of money and clothing, it was possible to help a few of these unfortunate returning deportees.

It was only during the first year of the deportation to Russia that those with life-threatening illnesses were transported out of the Russian forced labor camps back to their homes in Romania. In 1946 and 1947, the Romanian administration refused to accept back into the country those people whom they deported to the Russian labor camps in 1945, even though they had been living in Romania for generations. That's why the transports of the ill and wounded had to be directed to Frankfurt an der Oder (a city in Russian occupied East Germany). Those who survived had to wait for many years until they could see their family members and loved ones again, unless they risked crossing various borders illegally to go home to Romania.

We know of one group of Swabian Germans who tried to escape from the GDR and was shot at the border. One of them pretended to be dead and was able to escape to tell his story. Otherwise, one would not know that those desperate people somehow tried to make their treacherous way back home and died either on the way or shortly after arriving home.

It was not until a year after the signing of the Paris Peace Treaty on October 2, 1947, and its ratification in the Romanian Parliament on August 23, 1947, that the Republic of Romania accepted back into Romania the German Romanian deportees who were released from Russian forced labor camps. The last survivors were set free after five years of slave labor in Russia and transported back home to Romania.

Many of the women who were very young and single when they were deported never married. Those poor girls, during the best years of their youth, they had to slave in Russia. When they returned, they resembled sheer skeletons. They looked so bad, it was painful to look at them. Most weighed about 40 kg or less. They had experienced death, suffering, tyranny and starvation all around them. There was no trauma therapy at that time; there was no mention of post traumatic stress. As a matter of fact, under communist rule, they were strictly forbidden to even mention the forced labor camps in Russia and the Bărăgan. They had to deal privately and silently with their trauma the best way they could and start a new life all over again with absolutely nothing but their lives.

The grief, sorrow and suffering of the deportees and their families can only be imagined. Of the forty thousand ethnic Germans from the Banat region in Romania who had to labor night and day in Russia to make good what Hitler had done, about twenty five percent died. In his speech on the fifty-year anniversary of the German Romanian forced deportation to Russian labor camps, Dr. Michael Kroner said, "The expulsions and deportations cannot be justified with blame and atonement, they remain a crime against humanity, who-ever committed them" (Banater Post Nr.3, 1995).

A man named Josef Nieschbach (after whom the senior home for Banater Swabian deportees in Ingolstadt, Germany, is named) started a charity for those children who were orphaned when their mothers or parents were deported. He and a Benedictine nun, Sister Begades, located the children, gathered them, and the two of them took care of these children.

It was a terrible time of grief, leaving deep scars which still do not heal today. Every year in January, we hold a memorial service here in Ingolstadt, Germany, to remember those *Leidenszeiten* (times of suffering) and what those poor unfortunate people had to endure for no other reason than being of German descent. We had nothing to do with Hitler; we were born and lived for generations in Romania. But we were of German descent and, therefore, had to pay the highest price for Hitler's evil deeds.

That is how it is: always the innocent have to suffer. Many people are still haunted by nightmares. Some try to free themselves by writing down their painful memories, like Katharina Valentin and Anna Nover. I think no historical writing can make such an impression or better reveal the true distress of the people at that time than their lived experiences and eyewitness reports.

Personal Narratives of Ethnic Germans Deported from Romania to Russia

Elisabeth Maltry, née Glassmann
Born August 24, 1927, in Jahrmarkt, Banat, Romania

"They pushed us all (men and women) into a train which was meant for cattle. There was no window, no light, no lavatory, no food, no water, nothing. When they closed and locked the doors, it was so dark, one could see nothing . . . On our way, they threw some old goat meat into our compartment. They threw it at us, as if we were caged animals."

ELISABETH MALTRY

Interviewed in July 2009 in Ingolstadt, Germany

I was seventeen years old when, on the fourteenth of January 1945, my peaceful and protected life changed forever. My father, who was employed at City Hall, knew what was going on. He knew that German people would be deported to Russia for slave labor. He also knew which German people were on the list to be deported. Therefore, he had to swear on his life to the Romanian officials that he would not tell anyone that German people were being dragged out of their homes and deported into Russia. My father would not tell anybody, not even our very closest family members, because he had sworn on his life not to tell. He merely said to me, "You hide!" I thought, however, that I was far too young to be deported.

The entire night between the thirteenth and fourteenth of January 1945, my father was standing outside our house. He knew they would come to drag Germans away from their homes and transport them to Russia. At four o'clock in the morning, there was a knock on our door. My aunt called frantically, "Agnes, Agnes, you are still lying in your bed, and they have already taken my children away." We quickly jumped up. A short while later, my father came and told us in a worrisome tone that I needed to hide quickly even though I was not on the deportation list. However, that was only what he assumed; I was actually already on the list.

Oh, what to do? I hurriedly got dressed, and within a few minutes they arrived, two military men with guns, one Russian and one Romanian. They asked for me right away, called my name, "Elisabeth Maltry." My Mom started to cry bitterly, and so did I. Never, in my entire life, will I ever forget that moment. As the two military men took me away, they also cried with us. Yes, they both cried, even the Russian. The Russian and the Romanian armed men both looked back and cried. "I beg for forgiveness, the Russian said, "I, too, have children at home." The Romanian nodded his head and said he, too, was truly sorry. But it all did not help. I needed to leave. Then they brought me to a large crowd of people. That was something I also did not know. Two or three days ago, they had evacuated Germans living on the last street in our village, and all the homes of the Germans living on that street were now empty. Most of the people who lived in those homes on that street were taken away. It was like a ghost town.

They brought us into a big hall, men and women together. It was a catastrophe. We were there for three days, sleeping at night on the bare floor. On the last day, my Mom came and brought me a suitcase. I still remember it, as if it were yesterday. Among other things in that suitcase were hand-knit sheep wool stockings. I said, "Mom, please take those wool stockings back. I will not wear them; they scratch too much." With tears in her eyes, she insisted, "My child, you will be glad to have them. They will keep you warm." She was right. Later I was happy and thankful to have those knit wool stockings.

Three days later, all of us who were taken from our homes (all Germans) were forced to climb on trucks. Many people were watching in the street. It was like an exodus. My Mom stood there with her little child in her arm, her tears rolling down her cheeks. People called out names of their loved ones who were driven away and cried bitterly. All the lamentation did not help. The trucks drove through the city to a big railroad station. There was already a train waiting for us. They pushed us all on to the train which was meant for cattle. Men and women were pushed together into this cattle-train. There was no lavatory, no window, no light, nothing. When they closed and locked the doors, it was so dark one could see nothing; one could see nobody. We could not look out. Our train compartment was locked from outside, and we were literally locked up in the dark.

There were some men among us who had small pocket knives. They cut a hole in the wood wall of the compartment, so that we had a glimpse of light and so that we could look out a little and see where we were going. I don't remember completely, but I think we might have stayed that whole night in that cattle-train before the train moved. We thought that the German people who were left behind would not allow us to be transported; they would save us. We had talked ourselves into hope, like holding on to a straw. In reality, they couldn't do anything. They were helpless.

When the train started to leave the station, we could hear our fellow people cramped into that miserable compartment crying in the dark. The train kept rolling on for a long time. Finally, it made its first stop. We had arrived in Iase. They opened all the doors. We were in the middle of nowhere. It was bitterly cold. Nobody went outside, except for those who desperately needed to relieve themselves. I will never forget how they had to run back to get on the train in the middle of nowhere. The train continued to run for fourteen long days and nights. There was no water, no food, no chair or couch to lie down. We were freezing; we were starved; we were unkempt; we were scared.

On our way, they threw some old goat meat into our compartment. They threw it at us, as if we were caged animals. We did not quite know what to do with it. But hunger hurts, and every one of us ripped up to the bones that old meat the best way we could, just to have something, anything in our stomach. Now, what to do without a lavatory? It was a despicable condition, beyond any human dignity. I was seventeen years old. Another girl was sixteen, and we were about fifty to sixty people, men and women, tightly cramped like animals in that cattle compartment. It was a catastrophe. We were on that train under those horrid conditions for more than fourteen days.

Then the train stopped. The sign at the station read "Sabaroschi." We thought we had arrived at our destination. Here in Sabaroschi, all the men were ordered to get off the train while the women had to remain on the train. There were men with their daughters. They did not transport women who were over thirty-two years of age. So the wives were not with most men, but quite a few men had their daughters with them. Here in Sabaroschi, the fathers were tragically separated from their daughters. No pleading helped. It was heart breaking to witness the lamentation of those agonizing father-daughter separations. Nobody knew why and what was to happen next.

The train with the women continued for another eight to ten days until we arrived in Novotroitzki. It was the second of February, 1945. Novotroitzki is not far away from Stalino. We were ordered out of that miserable train where we were cramped for about two weeks under abominable conditions. Now we had to walk in knee-high deep snow. It was bone chilling cold, minus forty degrees Centigrade. We had to take our little bundles or our little suitcases, or whatever we had, on our shoulders and walk a long way in that deep snow and deep freeze. Russian children stood on the roadside. They shouted hateful swear words and nasty Russian names for Germans. They threw snowballs and other objects at us, all because we happened to be of German descent. We were half frozen, but we had to continue to walk through that deep snow for quite a long time. It was treacherous.

Then they brought us into a big barn which previously housed horses. Upstairs there were some wooden carts which were to be our beds (without any slightest piece of bedding). I slept upstairs. There was one oven, a little stove oven, in the middle of that cold barn. However, there were plenty of rats in that horse barn; and now the rats had human roommates. Now they had the company of so many people living together with them in that horse barn. To protect us from the rats, every one of us carried a stick whenever we had to go to the outhouse. So we constantly heard and said, "Shh, shh" to drive the rats away.

Next to me was a girl named Helene, who had a severe bone illness. They had transported everyone who was on their list, regardless of whether that person was sick or even pregnant. Helene was very sick, but they took her from her home and family, and transported her in that cattle-train to that God-forsaken place. That poor girl was in no condition to work. So she stayed inside the entire day. She slept in the bunk under me. Once, in the middle of night, she shook my bunk, woke me up and said, "Look! Look!" She was pointing at a swarm of rats. We counted them; there were fourteen of them. Yes, we had to sleep with at least fourteen rats in that old barn. There was no water to wash ourselves or our clothes, no toilet, no food, nothing. But, there were plenty of rats.

I had to spend three long and painful years there. It was most difficult, extremely hard labor and constant starvation. I would still not have been able to go home after these three years, had it not been for an unexpected event. Two people from our group died. So they ordered another girl and me, I was the youngest, to do back-breaking work on the old railroad track. At night, whenever a freight train came, we were forced to get out and empty that train. We were to unload everything off the train, no matter how heavy the load was. It was extremely hard physical labor, and we dropped exhausted on our bunks when we returned. Every morning, even after having worked all night emptying railroad cargo, they always looked for us and ordered us to go back to do all our regular day work. Those Russians did not have an ounce of empathy. They forced us to get up again whether we had any rest or not, whether we could still crawl or not. So when they came, we covered ourselves up with our blanket, pretending to be asleep. We were so exhausted and did not want to get up and start that hard labor all over again without any sleep. However, sleep or not, we were forced to get up and continue working.

One day in 1948, a German woman from Siebenbürgen, now called Transylvania (another German region in Romania), came with a Russian physician. She called out loud, in German, "Whoever is here in this barn, speak up." I did not make a sound. Then she called out, "Come down from your bunk. You will not be sorry. I will say it one more time. Do come down. You will not be sorry!" I was scared and wondered what that was all about. Finally, the girl next to me and I both did come down. The Russian physician asked us how old we were. We told him, and he said, "Oh, the youngest in this camp." We were lucky. We were released, and our horrible years of slavery in Russia were over. However, instead of transporting us back home to our families, we were transported to the Russian occupied communist sector of East Germany which a year later became the German Democratic Republic (GDR). The Romanian government did not want those Germans that were deported to Russian labor camps to come back to Romania. They refused to let them back into Romania, even though that was their home. That is why we were transported to the Russian-occupied communist ruled sector of East Germany.

I could tell you volumes about what was happening there. They dumped us at a former concentration camp in the city of Frankfurt an der Oder. On one side was a Russian, and on the other side was an East German guard. The Russian counted how many people we were, and the German wrote it all down. There were so many people; it was such a big camp. Then they brought us into a large room. On the first day, a tall man came. He announced in the microphone, "Come and get your food ration." They brought food from somewhere. Not having eaten for a long time, all the starving people literally fell over the poor man who carefully rationed that precious food. All of us were mere skin and bones. I was so skinny; I weighed forty-one kilogram [less than 80 pounds].

Later, they brought us from Frankfurt an der Oder to a camp in Magdeburg in East Germany. There we had physical examinations and were deloused and hosed down with cold water to make sure we were clean. There was no privacy. It was awful. But more awful were our hunger pains. We got rations of bread. One loaf of bread was to last us for two days. It had to be carefully rationed so that no one got a little bit more. But that evening we ate every little crumb of that loaf of bread even though it was to last us for two days. We were so very hungry. We were fourteen days in that camp in Magdeburg.

I remained in East Germany for four months. There I could be in touch via mail with my Mom, who always wrote,

"Come home; please come home." At that time, many people from back home in Romania tried their luck to escape secretly from East Germany and somehow make their way to Romania. I got those pleading letters from my Mom. What could I do? Romania did not want us and would not let us back into the country any more. However, we tried our best to make our way somehow. Since Romania, like East Germany, was at that time also under communist rule, it was relatively easy to cross the East German border into another communist country. However, it was life-threatening to cross the border into West Germany, which was a free democracy.

On the first day when we came out of the Magdeburg camp, they wanted to separate the three of us from our home town. But we had earlier promised each other that the three of us would stay together, no matter what. We had heard that it was possible to go to Romania via Austria. So we believed that we could try our luck and do just that some day somehow.

When the three of us went to church in Magdeburg on Sunday, the pastor noticed us, talked with us, and was very moved by our plight. Next Sunday, in his sermon he talked about the tragedy of us poor Danube Swabian German girls from Romania. The people who were in that church and listened to his sermon were so moved that many had tears in their eyes. The pastor said he wished that none of us women would leave the church without being invited by someone for lunch after the sermon. Across from me was a woman with a boy who was about fifteen or sixteen years old. He saw the people all looking at me. His mother came immediately to me and said, "My son said I should take you with me." So I went with them, and I shall never forget these good people.

The name of that woman was Agnes, the same as that of my dear mother. Her husband lost his life in the war. Her brother, whom we met in her home, had lost both of his legs in the war, and her sister had died of typhus at the age of seventeen. They gave me all the clothes of that departed seventeen year old girl. I could not believe it. Now I, who had nothing else to wear but the same old clothes I wore since I was taken away from home four years ago, I had now so many dresses. I did not know what to do with them all. That East German family was most generous and gracious. They even offered for me to stay with them. Since we worked in a farm further away from where they lived, they paid for my train ticket to their town every weekend. They even picked me up from the train station. Oh, they were such kind people. I shall always be thankful to them, always.

Again, I got a letter from my Mom saying, "Come home, please; come home!" Her letters were touching, and I got so very homesick. Then I received the address of my father's cousins who were in Marktl am Inn. It was the address of a camp where all the released prisoners of war gathered. I found out that two other women had gotten the same address. One woman got the address from her husband and the other from her cousin. So all three of us stole across the border to that camp.

Oh, there was such misery in that camp. The German prisoners of war were all wearing civilian clothes. They had no place to live after they were released from their prison camps. They had literally nothing. So they made, with their old bullet-hole blankets, a little tent for themselves, and that was where they lived.

One of them already had a job for me in Marktl am Inn. There were three convents in the city, and Catholic nuns gathered children who had lost their mothers and fathers during the war. The nuns gave those children, four hundred boys in all, a home in those convents. I got a job at the convent to work as a medical assistant. There were twelve of us who worked there, each at a different job. Some worked in the kitchen, the others some place else. I was the assistant to a nurse. They treated me so well there, so very well. When they noticed that I was so starved and that I eagerly ate anything that I got with such zest, they fed me even more.

In the meantime my Mom would write again, "Come home; please come home. I would so much love to see you." Of course I was also very homesick and wanted to see my dear Mom whom I missed so very much. So I decided to leave Austria and go home to Romania. But the well-meaning nuns kept on saying, "You will not go to the Romanians who don't want you. Just think about it; they were the ones who ripped you away from home and deported you into slavery to Russia. Don't worry about your mother; she will get along just fine. She still has your younger sister. You must think of your future." I thought of my little sister who was two years old when I was deported, and how my Mom held her in her arms and cried. I heard the nuns urge me, "Stay here, your future is here." This was well-meaning advice and made total sense. However, I missed my Mom so much and had such a bad case of homesickness that I could not stand it any longer. So I decided to somehow risk my way home to Romania to my mother. That was on a Sunday. By Thursday, the nuns did not persuade me any longer to stay. They gave me their blessings and said reluctantly, "Go home, go home with our blessings."

The journey home to Romania turned out to be quite an ordeal. We three friends from home were on the road for fourteen days. There were other people going our way. The train went as far as to the Austrian/ Hungarian border, near Schalding bei Passau, no further. So we decided we would do the rest of the journey on foot. We had to walk all the way to Vienna. In Vienna, there was a huge ballroom where, thanks to the help of Caricas donations, food was given to the poor, the displaced, the homeless, refugees and prisoners of war. All these people came together there in that big ballroom in Vienna. So I entered that huge ballroom, found a table, and whom did I see? Standing right there in front of me was Susanne Schneider. Susanne was a dear friend of mine from home. She said, "Don't be afraid, everything will work out." I was so surprised and so happy to see her. Now I had new courage to go on. Her loving words, "Don't be afraid, everything will work out" gave me so much courage and hope. The mere sight of Susanne had given me new strength. Oh, I was so very happy to see her!

Later, we three women from home went on foot as far as Schalding bei Passau. It was still in Austria, and everything was still written and spoken in German. However, across the border in Hungary, it was a different story. Oh, there we had a hard time; none of us could speak Hungarian. We had a little bit of Hungarian money and wanted to take a train. But we could not communicate with the Hungarians. We did not know the Hungarian word for railroad station. Desperately, we talked with our hands and arms until someone figured out what we were trying to say and pointed us in the direction of the railroad station.

We traveled all across Hungary by train until we arrived at the Hungarian/Romanian border. At the border city of Hegyeshalom we saw for the first time uniformed Hungarian border police. A kind Hungarian border guard told us he would bring us across the border. He said to us that he knew the area very well. We should not go across that particular border crossing to Romania. He would show us a better and safer way. He said, "On the left side is Arad, and on the right side is Curtici. Always make sure that you stay on the left side, not the right. Left is safer because on the right side is the border police." That kind man took us to his home. There we got goulash to eat. Oh, it was so delicious. We could also sleep for a few hours, and it felt so good to be able to sleep.

In the middle of the night we left to cross the border. It was dark, and we thought we might be lost. There was a little house, and we crawled behind a corner of that house. Oh my goodness, somehow we were back exactly where we had started. Yes, indeed! Instead of keeping left, we must have gone right in the dark. From the corner of that house, we saw two people. One of them saw us. All the time people were coming, day and night, they tried to cross the border, which was illegal.

Well, a border guard saw us, and we needed to return. However, this time, we said we would definitely make sure to stay on the left side, always left, as we had been advised. Then as we looked, what did we see? We had arrived in Curtici. Since I was the youngest in our little group trying to make our way home, they always sent me to look, "Go see what is written on that sign. What's written on it? " they asked me. I went around behind the railroad track. It was dawn. I read on the sign the name of the city, "Gross Curtici." That is exactly where we did not want to be. Oh, my God, what now?! We looked through a window of the house and saw an old woman in her traditional Romanian costume lying on a bench. I ran right back to my friends and said, "This is no good; we are in Curtici."

Now what to do? We got to get away, we got to get away! All of a sudden a wagon came along. It was carrying two layers of fowl, and a woman was on it. She was probably going very early in the morning to the market. That kind Romanian woman on the wagon motioned us to come and said quietly that we should walk along the other side of the wagon because the Romanian border troops would see us right away from where we were, and we might lose our lives. But, she said, if we walk along side of the wagon on the other side, they might not see us. We were so very lucky to come across that wonderful woman who most likely saved our lives. Exactly as she told us, we ran and ran and ran along side the wagon, on the side where the Romanian guards could not see us.

At that time, no one could drive across the Hungarian/ Romanian border. One could only go along the border, but not across it. So we ran and ran alongside the wagon, and all of a sudden we heard a train stopping. So we quickly got on that train and admitted to the conductor that we had no tickets. He grinned a little. He already knew what was going on because that happened every day. "You don't need to worry, I know where you are coming from", he said.

Oh, I did not tell you earlier that in Budapest, we met someone who had crossed the border from Romania to Hungary and he had Romanian money. We had Hungarian and Austrian money. So we gave all our Austrian and German currency to him in exchange for Romanian money. Now, we were able to give the conductor some of the Romanian money. He was happy and told us that when we get out of the train, we should not get out on the right side, but to make sure to get out on the left side. He said, "On the left side, there will be women who will bring you to their pastor. On the right side will be the police who will bring you into a prison or shoot you." That good man knew everything that was going on there and was so kind to give us that advice. We followed his advice. We made sure to exit the train on the left side. Just as the conductor had said, there indeed were women who brought us to a pastor. The pastor's house was filled with crowds of people. The good pastor took everyone in. He asked where we came from and where we wanted to go.

He was genuinely interested in our well being and asked us to please let him know when we arrived safely at our destination.

Oh, I cannot tell you exactly how we got home or I will never stop crying. But I can tell you that when we arrived in my home town at nine o'clock in the evening, there were no more trains that day any more to my home town. So I had to take a taxi. The taxi driver already knew what was going on because he drove so many people who faced the same conditions day in and day out. When we passed by the familiar neighboring Hungarian community, we all cried. Then we passed by our familiar big well. It was such a beautiful well. We were so moved that we all cried at the sight of that familiar well near our home town.

I was the first one to get out of the taxi. The taxi driver stopped when we reached my village. He said we should not worry, he would not report us. I was so filled with emotion to see familiar streets, familiar buildings, and familiar ground again. I cried so much. Yet, I could not leave the taxi, could not leave the women with whom I had experienced so much hardship together. I sat inside the taxi. One of the women got out and walked down a little hill and ran to our house, knocked at the gate, and called, "Agnes, Agnes!" That was my mother's name.

It was nine o'clock at night, and my mother, awakened from the first phase of her sleep, was a little disoriented. She did not have any idea that I was coming. So now, in her nightgown, she came running out of the house. My grandfather was the first to reach the taxi. He had to carry me out of the taxi; I could not move. My whole body shook; I was not capable of getting out of the car. They helped me get into the house. My Mom asked the other women and the taxi driver to come in. She tried to pay the taxi driver. However, since she had no money, she gave him wheat, or corn, or such things. Then the taxi driver drove the rest of the women to their villages. That was on the 19th, my *Namenstag* [name day]. My name is Elisabeth, and on my name day, *Elisabeth,* I arrived home in 1948 after nearly four years of forced deportation, slave labor and starvation in Russia's feared labor camps, after escaping from the GDR and risking the dangers of crossing several dangerous borders illegally in order to return to my family in Romania. It was like a dream to me, like a miracle, to see my mother again, to be home again.

However, then I learned how many terrible things had happened to the Germans in Romania, so much hardship and so much tragedy [she had tears in her eyes]. There is so much more to tell, but I will end now. I have talked enough. All these experiences are too painful to talk about and impossible to forget.

Elisabeth Rudlof, née Heimerl
Born October 26, 1921, in Alt-Sadova, Banat, Romania

"To help us work and not despair, we made up songs and sang them. They were very sad songs depicting our slaving life, exactly as we had to endure it there in Siberia's forced labor camp. We sang our sad songs while working to help us keep on going."

ELISABETH RUDLOF

Interviewed July 13, 2009, in Ingolstadt, Germany

It was the weekend of the 14th of January 1945. I had come home from a neighboring town where I worked and lived as a housekeeper. That weekend, my girlfriend came home with me. When it was time for us to leave home in the evening, my sister asked me to stay a little while longer. She wanted to sing a song for me. We all liked to sing then, especially young people. So my friend and I decided to stay overnight and leave early the next morning.

At two o'clock at night, there was a knock at the door. At lightening speed, we hid in the basement. There were three men, a watchman and two policemen who had come to search for us in the middle of the night. After searching the entire house, one of the men said in Russian, "No, there is nobody here." So they asked the neighbor if he had seen "those people." The neighbor said that we had to be there somewhere in the house. He asked the three men, "Did you look underground in the cellar?" The men started to search the cellar. They lifted the lid, and found us. They took all three of us away immediately, just the way we were. I was wearing my Sunday clothes. Even though my sister was sick, bed-ridden with high fever, they took her anyway. Of course the Russians would come in the middle of the night and do everything so secretly. That way, nobody could escape them.

They brought us to the schoolhouse, which had become a camp. There were many German people in that school house. We had to stay there until Tuesday, when they brought us to another school building in Alt-Sadowa, which is close to the main road and close to the train station. We had to stay there from Tuesday until two Saturdays later. During those twelve to fourteen days, my aging mother came to see us once in a while. My sister, who was with me, was ill and still had a very high fever. Her temperature was so high that her whole body shook. A German woman, Hilda Stauber, gave her a blanket to cover her body. However, that didn't help to stop my sister's shaking.

On Friday an officer came, most likely a physician, and called out loud, "Those women who are pregnant, and those who have a sexual disease, don't be embarrassed or ashamed, just come up and say so. You will not need to be going on the trip." Nobody seemed to have a sexually transmitted disease. One woman was pregnant. It was exactly that woman who had given my sister that blanket. Even though my sister was seriously ill, she was not released. She was not spared.

I could speak a little Russian. Let me briefly digress and tell you how it came that I could speak some Russian: In the Romanian household where I worked and lived, there was a Russian commando for the last few weeks. During that time the Romanian family for whom I worked gave me a private room, so that no harm would come to me at the hand of the Russians. We all knew that many German women were raped by Russians. It was common knowledge that Russians would go searching for German girls and women. For example, my friend, who was with me, had a little house with two windows close to each other. The Russians came, and since the door was locked, they broke a window. She quickly jumped out of the other window and ran into a neighbor's house. Her mother was very ill and was lying in bed. The Russians did not care; sick or not, no matter what age, she was a woman; and the Russians raped her. Her bed was upside down, the covers were torn. There was blood on the floor, and my friend's mother was dead. That happened much earlier when the Russian Red Army had marched into Romania.

It was during the time when a Russian commando was stationed in my Romanian employers' household that I learned to speak some Russian, which came in handy in that schoolhouse after I was taken away from home. Now we were in that schoolhouse with many other Germans, and I tried to translate for them whatever the Russian officer said. I had heard that whenever the Russians heard the words, "typhus" or "malaria", they ran away as fast as they could. But earlier, when the Russians came and were looking to rape women, they did not care if the women had typhus or malaria or whatever disease. They had only one goal in mind, to rape German women and girls. They did not ask if you were sick or not. In the hope that they would not transport me, I told the Russian officer that I was infected with typhus and malaria. But my desperate lie did not work. Two Saturdays later, after we were kept there for about two weeks, they put us all in rows, and all around us were Russians with their guns. We formed about three or four long rows. In between each row, and all around us, were armed Russians to make sure not one of us would run away.

My father was already old then and in poor health. He had raised fifteen children. My twin sister and I were the youngest. When they brought us to the schoolhouse, a Romanian woman was shouting, "Germans, go to the devil, to Russia." But we did not say a word. When we passed by on the street from the schoolhouse to the railroad station, my mother rushed toward us, but they hit her so hard that she fell down. Quickly she stood up tall and screamed my name, "Elsa! Elsa!" She placed her hands on top of her head lifting her hair and in despair called out loud again and again, "Elsa! Elsa!" Again and again, my mother's desperately called "Elsa! Elsa!"

I will never forget that as long as I live. All the many hard years when I was in Russia, I heard my mother's desperate cry," Elsa! Elsa!" It will always ring in my ears, and my eyes still see that painful gesture with her hands on top of her head. My father was walking in front of the wagon. He had to carry the luggage which my mother quickly put together for me, my sister and my girlfriend. Yes, she had to come too. Mother gave me my father's pants. They were old but they were warm linen pants, which she had sewn herself. At that time, women did not wear pants, but my mother wanted to quickly give me something to keep me warm.

When we arrived at the railroad station, we were ordered to get onto dark cattle-trains that were waiting for us. Surrounded by police and guns, we had no other choice but to climb up on that cattle-train. Even cattle had it better in that cattle-train than what we had to endure. Cattle could at least stand up. For us, there were wooden planks laid from one end of the cattle box car to the other, to make sure that a maximum number of people could fit into it. As many people as possible were pushed on the top plank and as many as possible on the bottom plank. The wooden planks were laid like bunk beds, one on top of the other, except that they were no beds, just wooden planks. They shoved people into cattle box car. In the smaller box cars, they shoved thirty people. In the bigger twenty-ton box cars, like ours, they shoved sixty people. Of the sixty people in our box car, there were thirty from Alt-Sadova and thirty from Reschitza. Earlier, when they gathered the men, they told them to bring along saws, shovels, and so forth. Now we feared the worst. Now we knew where they would bring us. They said we had to pay for what Hitler did. However, we had nothing to do with Hitler. Our crime was that we were Germans, even though we were living in Romania for generations.

Once we were all inside that cattle-train, they slammed the door shut and locked it. There was no way out. There was no window. It was dark. One could not look out. We could not see where we were. With a little saw, the men made a hole in the ground for our human waste. We were, after all, sixty people there, men and women all together. So whenever a woman had to follow nature's call, we took a big scarf and held it in front of her, and whenever a man had to go, we did the same thing. The train did not stop until we came to Lugosch. We stayed in Lugosch for a whole day until another train came from Karansebesh and brought more people who were transferred to our cattle-train.

After we were in that horrible train for four weeks, we arrived in Adjund, which was on the border between Romania and Russia. When we stopped in Adjund, Russian soldiers came and knocked on our compartment. The door was opened from outside and the Russians said, "Don't you need wood to keep warm?" They took eight people with them to presumably fetch firewood. But from those eight only three came back. Five of them escaped. The name of one of those men who escaped was Becker; another was Mr. Jung. All of them ran away. They ran so fast that the railroad watchman did not see them. Miraculously, they were not caught. God knows what happened to them. There was another man from Alt-Sadowa. His name was Franz. He, too, ran away in that deep snow. Where he landed, I don't know. But he did manage to escape that unbearable cattle-train ride which transported us into slave labor.

In Adjund, we were all ordered to get off the train. We had to walk across the border to Russia. There we were put into another cattle-train because the Russian train tracks are wider than the Romanian train tracks. They now shoved one hundred and twenty people in each of the big compartments and sixty people in the smaller ones. Again, there was no toilet, no water, nothing. There was no stove to keep us warm. It was bitter cold. We shivered; we were half frozen. I was twenty-four years old, and my whole body shivered, that's how cold it was.

Day and night, for six long weeks after we were taken from home, we had to endure that miserable cattle-train ride. We were wearing the same clothes which we wore when they had taken us away. For six weeks we could not wash up, we could not brush our teeth. We were pressed together like sardines. Long after we passed by Stalingrad, they had already disconnected some of the wagons from the train, but not ours. Our cattle-train rattled on passed the Ukraine. Now and then one person was allowed to go out and fetch some water, of course under strict armed supervision. Yes, one person per wagon only, with one pail of water for sixty people.

One night it was so unbearably freezing cold we could hardly stand it. We were not prepared for the Siberian winter. We had no proper clothing; they had snatched us from home, just as we were. Those people whom they had picked up directly from the street had nothing with them, no warm clothes, only their Sunday clothes. One of the girls with me was captured right from the street. My mother gave her something warm to wear at the last minute. Most of us had no idea that we would be captured.

Many people died during our miserable six-week-long cattle-train transport. In our compartment a man from Holzberg choked to death in his own vomit. He could not endure those unbelievably gruesome conditions. That poor man had a sixteen-year-old son with him in that cattle-train. He was even a year younger than the minimum age that German men were to be transported. We felt so sorry for that poor young boy who lost his father. Now we were with his father's body in that sardine-like cramped cattle-train. When the train finally stopped and they opened our box car, they took the body out, and we never saw it again. While the train had stopped, a few people left the compartment to go to the toilet at the railroad station. One of the men reported that he saw that they had undressed the body of that dear man from our compartment, took the clothes and left the totally naked body there on the floor. Yes, that's how the Russians did things, yes, yes, the Russians.

We were locked up and held captive in that freezing cold cattle-train. What could we do so that we would not freeze to death and end our lives in that miserable cattle-train? It was a group effort. All the people from the lower row climbed up on the top wooden plank, each very close to the other. We were all lying sideways in a row, so that we would all be squeezed next to each other, our feet and bodies touching for warmth. We formed a row in front of us and next to us, to the left and to the right. Now we were sitting literally smashed together like sardines, so that nobody was able to move at all. Then we took all the blankets we brought and put them over our heads. We all crawled under the blankets, body to body, so that we could warm each other with our bodies and that not too much cold air could come between us under our many blankets. But we were so tight together that we could not move at all. That was a big problem. Sitting there night and day, my left foot swelled up so severely, it was huge. It was so huge [she was motioning the size of a bowling ball], red and hot from inside, and so painful that I thought I would die. A girl from Salinow, who was squeezed next to me, kindly offered me her hand, so that I could put my foot in her hand. That was how we sat all those weeks until we reached that horrible labor camp in Russia. When we arrived there, my foot looked dangerously huge, red, and it was hot from within.

All those weeks in that awful train, we were not only freezing, but we were starved, thirsty and severely dehydrated. When our box car finally was opened and we came into the daylight, how did we look? Dirty, unkempt, stiff, and yes, we smelled badly. The women and young girls had lost their periods. I still had my period when I was at home, but in that cattle-train, and during all the years in slave labor in Russia, I lost my period. I never got it back until I returned home. No woman had her period there in Russia, with the exception of those very few who had it a little easier than we, who did not have to do extremely hard physical labor and who had the opportunity to get a little more food. Those few women got their periods now and then but not regularly. But those were very few.

Well, let's come back to when they finally opened our box car and we saw light. We had arrived at a huge railroad station and were ordered to get out of the cattle-train. Those who had weak hearts fell on the floor like flies. Yes, they dropped on the floor just like flies. It was bitter cold, a deep freeze, and very high snow was piled everywhere. You could see nothing else, far and wide, but high snow. Then they brought us into another cattle-train. The physician, who was with us, understood a little Russian. And when we finally landed where we were supposed to be, they positioned us all in a row like in a march and threw our baggage in a car. Then we had to ride quite a bit in a truck until we reached the camp. But they left me in the cattle-train because I was unable to move. I said to my brother-in-law, the brother of my husband, who was also deported with me, "Johann, please stay with me so that I am not all alone here." He did stay with me, and later they brought us with a car into the camp. They brought me right into a room which they called "hospital." Well, it was actually only a small empty room. There they gave me some water, and I remained in that "hospital" room for three weeks. I was unable to get up, and I certainly could not stand on my legs. The others did not need to start working until three weeks later. When they started working, I had to get out of the "hospital" room. During those three weeks of rest there, my foot got better.

After three weeks they put me, together with the others, into a truck, and brought us eighteen kilometers [a little more than ten miles] away into a forest to cut trees. There, we had to cut trees with plain little hand saws. Two people per hand saw had to cut the bottom of the tree until the tree fell. We had to put the thick branches on a pile. The thin branches were cut in half and stacked in a pile until the pile was exactly one meter and ten centimeters high. That was the norm, one meter and ten centimeter high. It had to be very neat and exact. Whoever was not able to meet those exact requirements would get no food. Well, that little crumb of bread we got was old and green anyway. It would have been considered not edible under normal conditions. For six long months in that camp, we got nothing but that rancid old bread and a little sauerkraut. Nothing grew in that wasteland where they had dragged us.

Those people who were not able to work as they were supposed to were forced to stand on a wooden plank and were beaten over and over again. Then they had to stand along a wall on that plank all night long in that freezing, ice-cold winter. There were men standing there who were weak from their hard labor. They were ill; they could hardly stand up, but they had to stand there on that plank of wood the whole night long in that bitter cold. The Russians didn't care if the men were too weak or too sick to work, whether they were capable of standing there or not. They had to stand there all night long. I cannot even begin to describe what kinds of horrible things the Russians did with all of us poor people. Words fail to describe those atrocities. They were too horrific to describe and impossible to forget.

We all had to do extremely hard physical labor under the most horrible conditions. Our empty stomachs growled; we were so starved. We hardly got any food. Once in a while they gave us some mushrooms. Those mushrooms were so slimy, horrible and green that we did not eat them. So they put them in our water-soup. Those green slimy things were swimming in that watery soup, and we were supposed to eat that. But we were so starved that we closed our eyes and swallowed it. Many people got very sick. It was horrible.

After the tree cutting in the forest was finished, we had to go to work in the village. I had to work with brick tiles. It was hard work. Nothing grew there except birches, and the birches have that gum which oozes out. We took that gum and ate it. It was delicious, like sugar. That gum from the tree was our main nourishment. The Russians brought us to work in different places to do different kinds of labor. When we worked in the forest in the summer, we tried, whenever we had a chance, to pick and eat the mushrooms which were growing on those trees. We were so very hungry.

Men and women worked along side of each other. However, other than working together, they were separated. They were not allowed to sleep in the same room, even when they were married. The women had to sleep with the women and the men with the men. Men and women were also not allowed to walk together. That was actually quite good. No sexual harm came to the women in my group. I must say that our Russian guards did not do any sexual harm to anyone of us. At least I had not heard of any. I have heard plenty of it from victims of rape who were brought to our camp from other places, like Poland or the far Eastern regions of Germany.

There was one young fourteen year old girl whom they had brought in May after the Russian Army had marched into Eastern regions of Germany. That young girl was very sick. She had syphilis and was full of pus, all over her body. She told us what had happened to her. During the day, the Russians forced her to walk for about thirty kilometers while continuously beating her, until she could not walk anymore. When she fell to the ground, they told her that she had a choice, either to stand up and walk or they would kill her. That was during the daytime. At night, they brought her somewhere to a building or barn. There the Russians came, up to twenty five men, and raped that poor little girl over and over again. That little girl was so terribly sick, so infected with syphilis that the pus was constantly pouring out of her entire body. She lived for a couple of weeks after they brought her to our labor camp before she died. Yes, that's how it was.

There was another woman who was brought to our camp later, and she told us what had happened to German women in the far Eastern regions of Germany and Western Poland: "The girls who were with their mothers, they screamed and hid behind their mothers. But there was no help, no way to hide from the raping Russians, not for them and not for their mothers." That woman told us that during the day gangs of Russians beat them, and during the night they raped them. They raped girls, they raped mothers, they raped grandmothers; it did not matter to the Russians, as long as she was female. That woman told us that it was not just one Russian, but a gang of Russians, one after another after another. The Russian Red Army marched into Poland and the far Eastern regions of Germany and could do with the German women and children whatever they pleased. The German women who were transported to our Russian labor camp from Poland had terrible tales to tell about the Poles as well. They reported that the Poles were very brutal toward the Germans as well and told us horror stories, but not necessarily of rape. We felt so sorry for the women from far Eastern Germany and Poland who were so terribly violated by the Russians. I must say, rape did not happen to us Germans in Romania, thank goodness, and thank goodness it did not happen in our forced labor camps in Russia. At least we were spared that.

But oh, so many people died in the labor camp, so many young people. Somehow I was able to survive. I really don't know how. I don't know why I was spared. Perhaps those of us who were used to hard labor on the farm as children, we had an easier time during forced slave labor in Russia. But those that grew up in the city fell down like flies and died. I grew up on a farm and had to work hard from early childhood on. We were fifteen children, and my mother and father were poor. We all had to work. I was only six years old when I had to start working.

At the camp, there was a man from Reschitza with his wife. One day, he looked at my leg, shook his head and said to the Russian guards, "No, that woman, with that condition, cannot cut trees; she can hardly walk. She may be able to stand for a little while or walk perhaps a little bit. But she cannot cut trees and stand more than knee-deep in that high snow." Well, his concerned words did help. They gave me another job inside. Now I was to clean rooms and do other work inside the camp. In order to do that, I had to carry water in a bucket from far away. I had a long thick stick which I put on my neck, and on each side of that stick, I carried a bucket of water. In the evening, the cutters unloaded the wood. There was a huge oven. I placed the buckets of water next to the oven, so that they could wash themselves a little bit in the evening when they came back exhausted from cutting trees all day long.

Luckily I had a little wash basin from home to bring along when the Russians deported me. I don't know who gave it to me. That little wash basin was of great value and great use to all of us. The tree cutters used it to wash up after working hard all day. Of course they were very careful to use water extremely sparingly. Not far from us was a pond and near that pond was a hut. Inside that hut there were buckets. Every two weeks they sent those people who were not working on tree cutting to that hut so they could wash themselves. I was so happy that I was allowed to heat that hut. That was good. I could also wash my clothes there, what very little clothing I had. That was how we lived there until May 1946. It may have been the month of May, but there was still a lot of snow on the ground, and it was still cold. At that time some of us were transported to the *Kolchos* [huge areas of government owned land which the Russian communists had taken away from individual farmers and made government property]. There in the *Kolchos*, I recovered a little bit. They brought only sixteen of us to the *Kolchos*. We all slept in one room and were even able to go to a nearby town.

Next to the *Kolchos* lived Russians who had a little vegetable garden. Well, our people were starved and suffered hunger pains. So one day they said to me they would go at night and steal a little bit to eat from that garden. I said to them, "Please, do not steal any vegetables from those poor people. Those poor Russians don't have anything themselves. Second, look at those poor people; they don't live much better than we do. They are not much better off than we are. They have a small room with one oven. On that oven they cook, and next to that oven, their children sleep. Third, if you are caught, you risk your head being literally cut off."

However, when our people had such bad hunger pains that they really could not stand it any more, they dug a potato or carrot from a garden. Hunger hurts; it hurts terribly. Those poor starved people who raided that Russian garden were mercilessly beaten, and some of them were even killed for digging out that little potato or carrot. The Russians had no mercy.

Yes, for sure, the Russians had no mercy. They had designed a special torture for punishment. It was a wooden structure, smaller than the size of an outhouse. On all of the four wooden walls, the Russians had hammered in long sharp nails from the outside. Those forced laborers whom the Russians wanted to punish for whatever reason, were forced to stand inside that structure. There was no room for them to move or turn around. They could not lean on anything. If they tried to lean against the wall or even move the slightest bit, the sharp nails would tear their skin, and they would bleed right away. Whenever a man had to stand there all night after a full day's hard physical labor, without being able to move the slightest bit in that freezing cold, he screamed the most desperate screams. Oh, did he scream! There are no words to describe that kind of a scream. It was a scream of unbearable pain that I will never forget, never. You could hear that scream from far and wide. We could hardly bear hearing it. When a part of your body freezes up, it hurts like crazy. Having to stand there for a whole night or more in the deep freeze of the Siberian winter, without ever being able to move, one can easily freeze to death, and many did. Oh, I can still hear those loud screams [she covers her ears].

I know how it hurts to have a part of your body freeze up. Once, it was so ice cold that my chin froze because I had to work outside without sufficient protective clothing in this bitter cold Siberian deep freeze. It was so painful that I thought my chin would fall off. No matter how much I tried to protect my chin with some cloth, the pain was excruciating. It did not help that I was forced to work outside and had to continuously subject my poor frozen chin to the bitter cold. Oh, I will never forget that excruciating pain [she covered her chin with her hand].

In the *Kolchos*, we worked in the fields, sorting potatoes and then planting them. After the potatoes had grown a little bit, we took a few out of the ground and ate them just the way they were. That was how hungry we were. That *Kolchos* consisted of large land, about sixty to one hundred hectares of land and a huge cellar, which was bigger than a large barracks. Therefore, it was difficult for the guards to keep a watchful eye on all of it. When harvest-time came, we had to work extremely fast to put everything together as fast as possible, and yet winter came so early we had to shovel those mountains of snow from the fields and hurry up and pick the cabbage from the fields so that it could get into the cellar as soon as possible. Well, after two or three days, that cabbage was spoiled and smelled. Who could have known that the cabbage was spoiled already when we picked it up from the earth frozen stiff! Nevertheless, we had to pick it and bring into the cellar.

It was good to work in that huge cellar. Here is why: Everything was underground; only the roof was above ground. Inside the cellar there was an oven, and we were able to heat it. What a luxury! We had brought the huge mountain of potatoes into the cellar for storage. Those potatoes saved us from starvation, and here is how: The potatoes which are frozen under the earth are not at all bad to eat. When you press them hard, they become like dough. They are not even dark; they are light. We squeezed the dough out of the potato, put it on the oven and warmed it up. That's how we ate it, and what a feast it was for us. Russians ate that too. There were plenty of potatoes in the *Kolchos.*

Out of all the hard labor we had to do in different places, we would have preferred to work in the Kolchos. However, after our work in the fields and inside the cellar of the *Kolchos,* we had to go back to tree cutting in the forest. After that we had to work in a peat bog factory. That was extremely hard and dirty work. We looked totally black from the peat bogs when the day was done. It was much harder work than in the *Kolchos,* and no chance for sneaking in a potato or two. There was a long conveyer belt in the peat bog factory. We had to take the containers of peat from the conveyer and put the empty containers back on the conveyer. Then we had to take the black peat, break it into a particular shape, and dry it. When it was dry, we had to put it in a high pile. Oh, that was very hard on our hands, and our poor hands hurt like crazy. We had to break the peat into pieces with our bare hands. As a result, our hands were raw, bleeding, full of blisters and constantly hurting. We had no gloves, no protection, and no time to let our bleeding hands heal. We had no choice. With our raw, bleeding hands, we had to do what we were ordered to do or we would be horribly punished. There were always the watchful eyes of our Russian guards, just waiting for any small reason to punish us.

The conditions were so intolerable that many people died. The Russians came at night and took the bodies away. Everything happened in the darkness of night so that we would not see how many people had died. There were Russians especially employed to pick up the bodies and drop them somewhere. In that deep freeze of the Siberian harsh winter, when the ground was solid as a rock, one can only imagine what happened to those bodies.

To help us work and not despair, we made up songs and sang them. They were very sad songs depicting our slaving life, exactly as we had to endure it there in Siberia's forced labor camp. We sang our sad songs while working to help us keep on going. Yes, we made up those songs and sang them. They were songs about our daily tortured lives, about our hard labor, about our hunger, about our sorrow, about our tears, about our pain, and about our dead. I don't know all of them any more. I remember some lines of some of the songs. One song we sang to the tune of the famous German folk song, "*Wo die Weser einen grossen Bogen macht* [Where the river Weser makes a wide curve]."

Below are two slave songs which were translated into English. The original German lyrics are in Appendix 1.

Slave Song 1

Where the land's animals drive across the world,
Where the world is nailed tightly with wooden planks,
Where under tears one eats rotten water soup,
Where one sees no table and no chairs,
And all night long at lice and bug bites stares,

Where the land's animals drive across the world,
Night and day on tracks in cattle wagons ice cold,
Across frozen roads and streets,
Across sticks and stones,
There for us is no wine, no beer,
Only thirst and hunger are the rulers here.

Where the green tents are waiting
And precious water rare,
Where you find no food and drink,
Where you cannot buy or get anything,
You are forced to save all your money
(They did not have a penny)

Where you build houses out of dirt,
Where you are stuck up to your knees
In deep snow, coal and soot,
Where out of every crack
Lice and bugs are crawling,
There is the homeland of the bugs and lice,
There is also my "home" where I shiver on ice.

Slave Song 2

As soon as you lie down
And all sleep quietly,
There crawl from all four corners
Bugs and more bugs galore.

Many a girl sits gallantly
With the bug squat in her hand,
And then the cracking sound begins
Oh, how it cracks in the *Kolchos.*
Then the night is quickly over.
All night long we fought
The busy bug maneuver.
When at the break of each dawn,
A new bitter hard shift begins,
Yes, that is our life, day in, day out.

At the big cleaning and washing-up
There are loud screams from everyone.
The faucet was turned on as far as can be
But no water came out of any you could see.
Now what to do?
Instead of water, use your own spit;
You may get spit clean too.

Then Kucken comes again,
Now eat real quickly,
Crumbs of bread and two teaspoons of soup
Yes, that is our coop.
And the bread is wet as can be
It looks just like pigs' feed, see.
What's the big deal anyway with pigs' feed?
At lunch we will get two spoonfuls of broth
With worms in it, that's our meat to eat.

There were so many other songs we made up and sang in our sorrow, just to be able to cope. Someone who did not have to live through those times of hell may say, "Yes, yes, that's awful," but in reality, that person can never, ever imagine what it was like to live through that hell. It is impossible to understand. I say to myself now, "I could not live through it again. How was it possible that I could survive all that? "

After three years of slaving away in that camp, I got very sick. I got a very bad thrombosis condition on my leg. So I was transferred to another camp where I was for eight months. My condition was so bad that in July of 1948 I was finally released and sent back home to Romania with the transport for severely sick people.

When the Russians released us from the labor camp, they gave us release papers. We had to go to the police to be cleared, and then we were transported to Romania. We were in an intermediate camp for three days where we got our dismissal papers. Here they started giving us good food so that we would not look so starved and malnourished. One tall young woman, who was twenty-five years old and strong when we were taken away from home, weighed a mere twenty five kilograms [fifty pounds] when we returned. She used to be a beautiful, healthy and strong young woman. Now she truly looked like a skeleton, but she was still alive.

When I got home, my mother could not stop crying. They had heard nothing from me, not a word; they had received no mail, nothing all these years. They had thought I was dead. My mother was overjoyed to see me alive. But she cried so much. Oh, how very much she cried. When I came home, I found out that we were dispossessed. Everything had been taken away from us. All of our possessions, our land, my mother's things, they were all gone. We were truly dispossessed. It was all taken away from us by Romanian people living in our own village, not by strangers. I said, "Mama, why do you cry, why do you cry so much? I am alive, I am here, and I am not naked. I still have the clothes I am wearing." Oh God, it was such a terrible time.

But that was not all. There was yet another painful surprise I had to accept, another bitter pill I had to swallow. In 1943, the year before the deportation, I got married. When I came back from Russia five years later, my husband was gone. He had another woman. He did not hear from me all those years, and he thought I was dead. I was told that he always wrote, "Come home, please come home!" He had never received any mail from me, and his mail never got to me. How would it have been possible for me to return home? I was imprisoned in this forced labor camp in Russia and could not escape. Since I was deported in January 1944 while the war was still going on, I was a prisoner of war, as stated in the official "prisoner of war card" (photo below). As a prisoner I was allowed to write and send that card to our home in Romania from the Russian labor camp. I was seldom allowed to write but forced to say that "I was well." No, my husband never received any of my cards. Thinking that I was dead, he left Romania for Germany and never came back to Romania. He was not able to come back because the people who came illegally across the border were brutally punished. Romania became a communist ruled state, and there was no such freedom to cross borders from the West to the East.

Prisoner of War Card

Finding out that my husband was gone and that my family was dispossessed was not the only bad news I had to swallow after returning home from Russia. There was another challenge for me to face, another bitter pill to swallow. I could not get a job because of my thrombosis. Nobody wanted to hire me because of my bad foot. My foot was always bloody red and swollen. Only many years later, after returning to Romania from my Russian slave labor, and after being able to leave Romania and come to Germany where I got proper medical care did my foot give me some relief. However, I hardly got any pension. The Romanian government gave a pension based on the number of years worked in Romania; that did not include the five years of slave labor in Russia. The occasional work that I got after returning from my slave labor in Russia was too sporadic for any pension and lasted only short periods of time.

Ten years after I returned home from Russia, I got divorced and married a man who had suffered the same fate as I. He, too, had been transported to Russia and was a survivor of those despicable forced labor camps there.

Now I am old and living here in Germany. My second husband has already died. I am getting only seventy-three Euros [about 100 U.S. dollars] of pension a month. But I also get a pension from my second husband. From my first husband, I get no pension because he left when I was in the Russian forced labor camp, and then we got divorced. My second husband had been working for thirty-three years, and, therefore, I receive three hundred and twenty Euros [about 430 U.S. dollars] pension per month. Well, and if I would not live here in this Nieschbach Home for Banat Swabians, I would not know how to survive. I cannot thank that good woman enough who brought me here. I never had it as good in my whole life as I have it here in this Nieschbach Home.

Anna Schauer, née Bleiziffer
Born April 16, 1921, in Sankt-Anna, Banat, Romania.

"At the last minute, my mother gave me a rosary to protect me . . . .
We felt so forlorn and helpless. Somehow, the rosary had given us hope and strength to
endure."

ANNA SCHAUER

Interviewed in July 2009 in Ingolstadt, Germany

It was in January 1945. One of our elderly neighbors had been very sick. My father said that there must have been something wrong because when the neighbor's son came home from school, he found the windows of his home nailed shut with wooden planks. How was that possible? Nobody knew what was going on. Next day was the funeral of our old neighbor. We lived at the end of the village. There was no wagon available to carry the body. So we carried him on foot with other men for about twelve kilometers. That's how far the burial place was. When we passed by the church and the school someone said, "Look, there are so many windows of so many homes nailed shut with wooden planks. Something is wrong here." We buried the body and went home.

In the middle of the night, on January 14, there was a knock at the door. It was a woman from the village whom we knew. She said, "Be quick, hide right away, hide, quickly! If they find you, you will be transported to Russia. They are looking for girls and young women to transport to Russia; hide, hide." Well, where should we hide? My father said he would go outside and keep a look around the house, and I should hide quickly in the backyard when they came.

That was exactly what happened. At about seven o'clock in the morning, my father looked out, and there they came: armed men. I put on warm clothes and ran out into the garden. We had a large garden. The snow was deep, and it was cold. I ducked down, made myself as small as I could and sat there in the deep snow shivering like a bundle of fear. The men went inside the house.

They searched the house, looked everywhere inside and around the house, couldn't find what they were looking for and left.

On their way back, they took my cousin Diana who lived not far from us. Her mother ran to us crying and asked whether we knew where Diana was. We did not know but had a good idea. Then it was quiet for a while. We had Romanian friends in town, and they said that I should come to their house to be safe from the Russians because the Russians did not search Romanian homes; they only searched German homes and took away only German girls and German women. Our Romanian friends came to get me at night in the dark so that nobody would see us, and I hid in their home. They always said: "Be quiet! Don't be seen and they will not get you. We are Romanians, and they will not come searching in our house."

But what did the Russians do? The Russians could not find me at our home, so they took my poor mother away from home. My mother was such a pretty, well built woman, so they took her. Now my father ran to the neighbor's home where I was hiding and said, "Anna, you have to come home. They took Mother to the school house." Oh my, oh my! So I rushed to the school house to get my mother out. Thank goodness, they let her out. But now I was the captive! At the last minute, my mother gave me a rosary to protect me. Yes, yes, that's how it was. That school house was turned into a camp and filled with Germans who were fetched from our town and surrounding villages by armed Romanian and Russian officers. We were held captive in that building until January 24th.

Then they made us climb up into the box cars of the trains that were used for cattle and shoved us in, just like cattle. There was no window, no light; there was no heating, no bunk to sit on, nothing. We were treated like cattle. The doors were locked up, and the cattle-train left our town and deported us far, far away.

When, after a long treacherous ride the train finally stopped, we were in Iase, at the Russian / Romanian border. Under armed supervision, we were ordered to get off the train, which was running on Romanian tracks and get onto another cattle-train, which was running on Russian tracks. We needed to change trains because the Russian tracks were wider than the Romanian tracks. Oh, we cried; we cried and cried bitterly.

We knew where these Russian tracks were leading. As we were crying, one of the Russians yelled at us with great contempt, "Hitler, Hitler!" We said, "We had nothing to do with Hitler." After we were all shoved into the cattle-train, we rode for two weeks in that cattle-train until we arrived in Marganetz. There, in Marganetz, the Russians said, "No, you won't stay here. You'll go further; you'll continue on!" Dear God, where would they take us? The miserable train ride continued. Finally, the train stopped, we got out in the middle of nowhere, and they led us into a big military hall. All of us cried. The more we cried, the more the officer continued to shout, "Hitler, Hitler!" He said something in Russian, but we could not understand Russian, and he could not understand German. But "Hitler, Hitler," he could say; and he shouted it in a most contemptuous way.

In that military hall, they counted us and assigned each of us to do hard physical labor. Then an interpreter came; her name was Reichmann. She said, "You are here because Hitler destroyed everything, and you are here to build it up again." It was bitter cold. The snow was so very high. Those shoes we were wearing could hardly protect us from that deep snow. We were in the middle of nowhere. There was nothing but deep snow around us. We had to go out every day in that deep snow and do hard physical labor. I thought of my rosary that my Mom had given me just before we left and said to a woman next to me, "You know what? As we walk in that deep snow, we will pray with the rosary. The rosary will help us. Mother of God will not abandon us." The woman nodded and said, "Good," and so we both prayed each morning on our long walk to work. There was another woman who always watched and accompanied us. She asked what the two of us were always talking about. We did not want to tell her that we were doing our rosary because we were afraid someone might take it away from us. She did not see our rosary; we hid it.

After a few days, an officer, whose name was Barabansch, and the interpreter came looking for me. The officer ordered me to come forward and asked me what I was doing everyday. He said that I was talking constantly every day on the way to work with the other woman, and he demanded to know what I was talking about. I had to tell the translator that we prayed with the rosary because the Mother of God would help us and not abandon us. Then the officer said to me," Give me that rosary!" He took it and left. One woman among us asked me, "You brought a rosary with you?" I explained that it was from my mother and it helped me cope with my misery all that time since I was deported by force. I had bought that rosary during a pilgrimage. But now that even my rosary was taken away from me, I was so very sad and depressed, and my friend and I, we both cried so much, every day. We felt so forlorn and helpless. Somehow the rosary had given us hope and strength to endure. Now we had no hope, no hope at all, and it seemed as if all the strength was gone. How would we now be able to survive our miserable existence here in the Russian *Gulag* [forced labor camp]?

Ten days after we were deported to that labor camp, one woman among us died. The translator, Mrs. Reichmann, said, "Take the woman away." They took her just as she was, with whatever clothes she was wearing. They took the body of that poor young woman and threw it on a wagon. There was no prayer, no religious service, nothing. They just threw her on that wagon without any respect, without any regard for the person, for the life that that woman had lived. We cried and cried out very loud until the officer came inside and shouted angrily at us because we all had cried and made such a loud noise. He shouted that Hitler did all that and that we better build things up again. Oh, those were bitter hard times, so bitter hard.

Then one day we were taken out of that camp and were moved next to a railroad station. It was a long distance to walk to where we had to work. Officer Barabansch, who had taken away my rosary earlier, ordered me to come forward. I did, and he gave me back my rosary. But he told me to hide it right away in my pocket, to pray quietly, and to say nothing while I was praying. Eagerly I said, "No, I won't say anything, not a word." From then on, whenever we went to sleep at night, my friend and I took out the rosary and prayed, but very quietly so that nobody heard anything. When anyone came, we were quiet as mice because we were so afraid that they might put us in jail.

There was a boy, a young man who was working across from me. Very quietly he said to me, "May I come over to you and pray with the rosary too?" I replied, "Good, come over to us."

He risked coming over to us. Men and women were separated, but he stole over to our side when we prayed. We prayed ever so quietly together with that young boy. He was such a nice boy. He was so exhausted, so overworked, so thin and frail, so *kaputt* [broken]. He was starved, severely malnourished, and he was so very sick. It was no wonder! Every day, early in the morning, we had to get up and work very hard. We got some watery soup, but there was nothing in it but water, and now and then a piece of rotten turnip. We could all easily have died of starvation, and so many did. When we woke up early in the morning, we were never sure who would still be alive. Often, there would be a woman who would not get up any more, another one would not either, and yet another would not get up anymore. They could not get up and slave any more; they were all dead. Death was always lurking in that *Gulag*, taking so many young lives.

That gentle young German boy was deported from Poland. I asked him, "How did you get to land here? You are so young, too young to be transported to that Russian labor camp to do that hard physical labor." He said the Russians simply came and took him away from home. What a shame, what a nice boy, so kind and so well-mannered. Yes, the Russians had not only deported Germans from Romania but also Germans who lived in Poland.

Early one morning the cruel officer came. Desperately the boy called to me, "Mrs. Schauer, I can't any more. I can't, I really can't move any more!" Totally exhausted, he sat down at the staircase and cried bitterly. I felt so sorry and said, "Don't cry; it will be all right. You must tell the officer; surely he will understand." Well, he told him, but that mean officer screamed angrily and pushed the boy hard down the stairs with his booted foot. The boy lay there, motionless. He was dead. Oh, I cried so much; we all cried. Everyone liked that kind German boy from Poland. He, like us, was also an innocent victim, ripped away from home and transported into slavery for the Russians. He was a mere boy, about fourteen years old. That innocent child had to endure unbelievably hard physical labor under abominable conditions. He had to endure brutal beatings and starvation until his poor body finally could not take it any more and collapsed after the last beating. Yes, that boy was literally beaten to death in so many ways, until his exhausted and starved body could not move any more. "Mrs. Schauer, I can't any more. I can't; I really can't move any more," were his last words.

Those desperate cries of that gentle fourteen-year-old boy still ring in my ears even today, six decades later. Oh, we cried so much. With tears in my eyes, I asked that cruel officer, "Why did you have to kill him? Why do we have to endure this misery, these inhumane conditions? Why do we have to suffer so much? Why do we have to die here?" With rage the officer screamed, "Hitler destroyed everything, and you have to build things up again!" A wagon came. They threw the dead boy on the wagon as if he were any old object, and threw him in the mass grave, as they did with all of our people who died in that God-forsaken place. We watched and cried like little kids. We cried and cried. There was no end to our sorrow. My heart still hurts, just thinking of that young boy. Never will I forget him.

Another woman who was with us told us that her father was also transported to one of Russia's slave labor camps, and that he, too, died there. I don't know her name any more. Our dead were thrown in mass graves, and those of us who were still breathing had to get up every morning at the crack of dawn and slave until late at night while our poor bodies were aching from extreme labor, hunger and exhaustion. But that was not all. On top of our hard slavery, and after our hard day's labor, we had to endure the humiliation of the Russian children on the street on our long way back to the camp. Oh, what those kids did with us! They yelled, "Hitler, Hitler!" at us and threw stones at us, one stone after another. They even spit at us. That went on every day, every single day. I said, "We have nothing to do with Hitler." But Of course my words were in vain. Oh, what we had to endure: the humiliation and bullying, stone-throwing of the Russian kids, our aching bodies after long days of hard labor, and the ever-present hunger pains. The children's contemptuous screams, "Hitler, Hitler!" still ring in my ears. But I did have my rosary. I was so sure and hopeful that my rosary would help me.

One day Barabansch, the kind officer who gave me back my rosary, came to our camp. He was accompanied by a woman who had a two-year-old child. He called me and told me to come forward. I did. By that time I understood a little bit of Russian. The translator was with him and asked me if I would do Officer

Barabansch a favor. I was shocked. How could I, a German slave laborer who had no rights, do a favor for that Russian officer who had so much power over me? The translator said, "From now on, would you get up earlier every morning and walk to a woman, who lives further away, to get milk for this child?" I said, "I don't know how to get there; I don't know my way around here. I am not even allowed to leave here." I was afraid that once I got there, the woman might not ever let me leave. The Russians had so much hate toward us Germans. As a matter of fact, some of the Russian women were even crueler than the Russian men. But Officer Barabansch said he would come with me the next day and tell that woman to give me the milk and to let me leave right away to deliver that milk. Barabansch told me that it would be as follows: The woman would put a can of milk on the outer window sill of her house. I would pick it up, and next day I would leave the empty can on the window to pick up a full can of milk again. I would not even need to go inside the house. I understood the plan. From then on I had to get up even earlier than before, one hour earlier than the others. I had to quietly get dressed and walk for about a quarter of an hour to fetch the milk, bring it to the child's home and walk back again.

The next morning, Barabansch and I went to the house of the woman. She looked at me for a long while and asked me what my name was. I said "Anna." She replied, "Oh, Anja!" She was an elderly woman whose son was a Russian officer serving far away from our region. She had two cows and enough land to feed the cows. She handed me a container of milk to carry to the place where the child lived. Each day, I carried one can of milk and returned the next day with an empty can which she filled again.

After two days or So the translator came with me and told that elderly woman that I also had a small child at home and aging parents. The woman felt so sorry for me. The next day when I arrived, she came out of her house with a cup of milk in her hand and said quietly in German, "Anna. Come inside." She gave me that milk to drink and whispered quietly, "Yes, I too can speak German." From then on, whenever I came, she said quietly in German, "Anna, come in," and she gave me a glass of milk to drink every morning. Secretly she showed me evangelical books. But she had hidden them so that no one could see them. You see, the Russian Communists would not tolerate religion, and certainly not protestant literature. I think that woman was German, but she would not say so. She only said, very quietly when we were alone, "I, too, can speak German." Yes, every morning, as soon as she saw me coming, she would say, "Anna, come in," and she gave me that precious cup of milk to drink.

That little bit of milk helped me a lot. It might have even kept me alive because many of us were dying of starvation. I went back to the camp and told fellow captives, "See, Maria, Mother of God, always helps." They laughed at me. That little boy for whom I brought the milk, as soon as he saw me coming, he joyously ran toward me. Yes, that little one was so happy to see me every morning, and I was happy too. He reminded me of my own little child at home, whom I missed so very much.

As time went on, I was allowed to go into town. But we still got no food, except for that watery soup. We were so desperate and starved that we went begging. But they caught us and locked us up. Then we got absolutely nothing to eat, not even that watery soup. After that, I did not go anywhere searching for food. I said, "Even if I starve to death, I will not go anywhere any more." There, in this God-forsaken place, we had to endure our miserable conditions for five long years. Yes, those were five long, horrible and painful years. Even thinking about it brings back the pain.

There were Germans from Poland among us as well. One of them said, "You know, Anna, I will end this misery. I give up. I will go home. I will get me some . . . (I did not know what it was that he was trying to get). I will warm it up with water, and, I will go home." Well, that is exactly what he did. He drank some liquid that night. Early in the morning his head was very swollen, and by noon he was dead. Now he was "home." He did not have to endure that misery in Russia any more.

One day Officer Barabansch came and asked me if I wanted to work in a factory. I said, "I don't know how to work in a factory." At that time, when we grew up in Romania, we did not know of any factories. We knew farm work. Barabansch said he would speak with the other officer about my working in the factory. He brought me to him, and the officer said in

Russian, "*Charascho, charascho* [alright, alright]". The next day, they came and picked me up and brought me to an aluminum factory. Barabansch told me that nobody from my camp was allowed to enter that factory but that I would be allowed to work there. He looked around, and someone asked me from where I came. Barabansch answered for me. Yes, it was he who answered. He said that I was from Romania and that I was transported to this place to work. Then the man who asked the question shook his head quietly. Oh, that loud noise from those machines in the factory! I had to work there with all that noise. I was not at all familiar with what to do. I had never been in a factory before. I was from the farm and knew how to do farm work. I could not even stand that noise all around me in this factory.

One of the workers in this factory was a German man from Poland, who was also forcibly deported there. He told me that he would teach me how to operate the machines, and he did so for eight days. On the ninth day I could already work the machines by myself. It was loud there, but it was physically lighter work than the earlier hard labor. The factory was also closer to our camp. Now I did not have to walk such a long way to work. I worked with another woman there who was Russian, and she cried all the time. She was so sad and depressed. She often said, "We, too, don't have much to eat." She had so much empathy for me and was such a good-hearted woman. At mid day we got lunch, and what did we get for lunch? We got watery soup with something slimy swimming inside. But we closed our eyes and ate it. It was at least something. If one is hungry, one eats everything in order to survive.

After five long years, which seemed like an eternity, officer Barabansch came one night and said to us, "Tomorrow you will not walk to work; tomorrow you will be on your way home." I did not believe him because a few days ago, they had taken twenty people from our group and transported them to another forced labor camp. So why should we believe them now? We thought Barabansch was lying and that he only wanted us to slave at another place. The next morning, the cook said we should come and get something to eat. Of course it was watery soup. Then a little man came to count us. We had to laugh a little because he pointed at us with his finger as he was counting us. Then he said, "Now you go home." We could hardly believe it. Many of our fellow captives had already died there of starvation and exhaustion. But I was always lucky. I don't know why. Perhaps it was because of my rosary.

Now, we got new clothes from top to toe so that we looked presentable. Everybody could see how well off we were in Russia and how well we were treated. Officer Barabansch and the translator brought us all the way to Dnepopetrovsk, the border between Russia and Romania. We got out of the train and he said, "Well, Anna, now I will give you up." Then he brought us to a Romanian government office for paper work. When we were finished, he came toward me and thanked me for always coming every morning and bringing milk for his little child.

Then, after finishing the paper work, something unexpected happened that I will never forget. Barabansch, the Russian officer who was in charge of holding us captive in the camp, began to cry. Yes, he cried. With tears in his eyes he said, "Anna, we made a terrible mistake. We humiliated you because of Hitler, and we ourselves are not worth much more. Look what we did to you. Now when I go back, I have no work any more, and I don't know how things will go." Yes, that is what that Russian officer who was in charge of our forced labor camp said with tears in his eyes and a broken voice. It was translated from Russian to German by Mrs. Reichmann, the translator. However, his tears and broken voice did not need any translation. I lifted my rosary high in the air and said, "Look, my rosary!" Then he began to laugh.

He was a kind man, that Barabansch. He did his job. He had his orders and had to do his duty. He said that it was not his fault that we had to endure so much. I only have good things to say about that Russian officer. He was one in a million; he was nice to us compared to the other one who bullied us and shoved us around. Officer Barabansch had lived all the years while we were there near our labor camp with his wife and that little boy for whom I brought the milk. They were poor themselves and didn't have much either. They lived in two rooms with a wooden stove to cook and keep warm. She was a nice woman, but we couldn't speak with her. We hardly knew any Russian, and she did not speak German. I think it was rather big of that Russian officer to apologize at the end and tell us that they had done us wrong all those years. He did not have to do that, but he did. Yes, that was my Officer Barabansch, one in a million.

While we were on the train to Dnepopetrovsk, the conductor pointed at my rosary and asked me, "What is that?" I said, "That is a rosary to pray, and this rosary kept me alive in the Russian forced labor camp." He shook his head back and forth and said disbelievingly, "Really?" In Dnepopetrovsk we changed to the train that brought us all the way home to Arat in the Banat in Romania. It was on a Saturday evening.

Skinny to the bones, I finally arrived home. I weighed eighty pounds. When we drove into our yard, my father stood there with my aunt, his sister. I jumped out with joy to see them and asked, "Where is *Mutti* [mother]?" Dad answered quietly, "She is no longer with us. She is not alive any more." I said, "Of course *Mutti* is alive; she is inside the house." I could not believe that my dear mother was no longer with us. I had not heard from her for all those years. We were only allowed to write twice during these five long years, and we were only allowed to write, "I am healthy. I am doing well." Yes, two times in five years we were allowed to write those two sentences. Our captives took our cards, read them, and if our two positive sentences met with their approval, they mailed the cards out. That was all that my mother heard from me during all those five long years. Oh, what a painful shock it was to have lost my beloved mother. It was unthinkable not to see her dear face any more. She had kept the one card that she received from me from Russia. I still have it today.

Now I was home, but I had no job. So early Monday morning, six of us who had returned from Russia's labor camps drove to the employment office in Arat. We said, "Good morning," and looked around. The man behind the desk said, "Good morning. Are you deportees from Russia?" One of us who always spoke up fast said, "You already know who we are!" I said to her, "Be quiet." I was afraid. The man asked us where we worked and what kind of work we had to do in Russia. I did not tell him that I worked in a factory. But, pointing at me, one of the women said that I was working in a factory. Well, when the man heard that I had worked in a factory, he sent me to work at a glass factory in Arat. In the beginning it was not easy because I had to learn new things. Nothing in that glass factory was anything like that aluminum factory in Russia. But I learned quickly, and I worked there for twenty-eight years.

Then we left Romania for Germany. Of course I took my rosary with me everywhere I went. I have other rosaries, but this particular rosary means everything to me. It is my absolute favorite. When I die, my daughter will have to give it to me to take along so that we are always close together, my rosary and I.

Eva Doggendorf, née Geiring
Born January 7, 1921, near Schebel, Banat, Romania

"We were all starved and had not eaten an apple for years. So one after the other, we ran
under the apple trees and fetched . . . apples that had fallen under the trees. All of a sudden
"the bad wolf" [the watch man] came . . . .
Frightened, all of us threw the apples away. They fell like cannon . . . .
Our punishment: . . . Hard labor, night and day, for 36 hours straight,
Without a moment of rest or sleep."

EVA DOGGENDORF

Written personal narrative presented to me in July 2009 in Ingolstadt, Germany.

It was in the autumn of 1944 when a great danger loomed over us Germans living in the Banat region of Romania. Our men had to serve in the German military, and the war seemed lost. We heard that all the Germans living in Yugoslavia were being deported to Russia and that we too might be deported. Every day the Romanian police came to write our names, dates of birth and addresses on a list. When we asked them why they needed that information, they simply said that they did not know. Since I had two little children (one was two and a half and the other five years old), I thought that surely I would not be torn away from my family.

However, then came the fifteenth of January 1945, which changed our lives forever. It was a Sunday. Early in the morning, two men came, one in civilian clothes and one in a Romanian police uniform. They ordered me to get dressed and to go with them. They said that I only needed to show up and then I could go back home right away. My two little children remained with my mother—in—law. When I reached the street, I saw a group of our neighbors whom they had also gathered. They had gone from house to house, gathering all German women from age eighteen to thirty two.

They took us to a large hall and locked us up. Our loved ones followed us and were standing outside, but we were no longer allowed to talk with them. My mother came with my two children to the window. However, I could only wink at them. They told our parents that they should bring us warm clothes and enough food for three days.

At 8:00 pm, we were taken away from our village and had to march in rows, accompanied by armed officers to our right and our left. We marched into our neighboring village, Schebel [Jebel]. Our luggage was in a wagon. In Schebel we remained for three days, and our personal information was documented daily. We were told to gather in groups of thirty five people. On Thursday they brought us to Giulwes, at the Serbian border. There they again wrote down our personal information and put us into wagons. Our dear relatives and loved ones still followed us constantly, but we were not allowed to talk with them. We saw them only through the window. We were by now already carefully watched by Russians, not only Romanians.

Early Friday morning the dreadful moment arrived when we were put in cattle-train cars, and the train left the station. There was screaming, outcries, wailing and lamentations from the many relatives at the railroad station. My father had arrived with our horse and wagon after the train had already left. He was told he should drive all the way to Ulmbach [Neuputsch] where the train would stop again so that we could get wood to heat our train compartments. Hearing that, many wagons crossed the fields in the direction of Ulmbach. When they arrived, the train was about to depart. However, because of the desperate outcry of the people, the parents were allowed to deliver the packages they had brought for their children. From outside, the Russian officer unlocked the cattle-train compartments only slightly as our names were called. Everyone was allowed to take her or his package through that little slit of opening. Again, the train departed and brought us all the way to Freidorf where it stopped. There patrolmen came and ordered us to give up all knives and scissors. Whoever did not comply with that order would be shot right away. Of course we obeyed. Only one small knife was allowed for all thirty five of us in the over-crowded compartment.

There were wooden planks, two rows high, in our compartment. In the upper row were the younger people and in the lower row the older ones. In my row were all those who were gathered from various neighboring villages and regions. My sister, who was ill, should not have been deported. However, they took her anyway. My mother begged them to please place her with me in my compartment. However, they did just the opposite. I had to go to her compartment. Both of us were lying on the upper wooden planks.

Whenever the train stopped, the men were allowed to hurry up and get water. But it was very cold, and most of the time the train only stopped for a very short time. When we had to go to the bathroom, we had to climb down the cattle-train and do our business right in front of the Russian officer. When we had absolutely no time to fetch any water, we melted the snow with the help of the little belly stove that was in the middle of the compartment.

Our train ran continuously, night and day, toward the East with a few very short stops. One night we could not sleep. It was so cold that the ice inside glistened like diamonds. The ice on the train tracks rocked our train. Our wooden planks were swinging back and forth, and suddenly our little belly stove fell down. The bed linens of the lower planks caught fire. People were frantic and screaming. The men tried to put the fire down by covering it with blankets and stomping on it with their feet. But now everything was full of smoke. It was hard to breath, and there was no way out, we were all locked up. When the train finally stopped, we all drummed hard and loud with our fists on the locked door, so that they would hear it and let us out to get some fresh air. We were all smelled like smoked herrings.

On the second of February 1945, the train stopped again. We were again counted, and it was written down on a list how many men and how many women we were. Then we were split into two parts. They unloaded half of our group in Kramatorsk and the other in Tschasoviar.

There we were placed *po tshetiri* [into rows of four], and we had to walk with our luggage in our hands and on our backs until we came to the barracks. Inside the barracks were iron beds without any bed covering or pillow and an oven, but no wood. They put twelve women in each of those rooms. The

extremely high iron beds were on the left and right side of the
room leaving only a meter of space in the middle.

For two long weeks we had to lie on these ice cold iron beds.
We covered the iron with all the clothes we had, so that we would
not freeze to death. Early every morning we had to assemble in
a row for roll call and were assigned to do hard work.

During one early roll call we were told that we should
get up very early the next morning to fetch straw from the
Kolchos [large government owned land which the communist
government had taken from individual farmers], so that we
could sleep on it. We started already before dawn. It was a long
way to the *Kolchos*. It was already afternoon when we began
our walk back to our barracks. It was such a long walk and our
straw sacks felt heavier and heavier. The snow was knee high,
and it was very difficult to step ahead. Everybody wanted to be
the last one to walk in the steps of someone before them. To
make our heavy load lighter, we threw more and more straw
out of our sacks. It was two o'clock at night when we finally
arrived at our barracks, totally exhausted and with only a small
amount of straw. But we were young, and life had to continue.
In the evening we sat together and talked about home, how it
was and how it might be.

Early in the morning, marching all in a row, we had to go
to work in a big iron complex which was a huge heap of ruins
and soot. It had to be cleaned and built up again, and for that
purpose they needed cheap labor. It did not come any cheaper
than us German slave laborers. We had to pay for that which the
war had destroyed. Every evening we had to stand in a row for
roll call and had to listen that we were to blame for everything
and that we had better not complain.

As time went on, our situation got worse and worse. We
already had traded all of our clothes, bed linen, everything
we had for a little bit of food. That's how starved we were. We
were always hungry. Next to our barracks, Russian women
brought potatoes and turnips and offered to sell them to
us. We traded all our measly little possessions which we had
brought from home for food until we had nothing left any
more. Now we only had the food from the barracks. Twice

a day we got slimy watery soup with a spoonful of *Kascha* [unpeeled millet gruel] and a little piece of fish. Day in and day out, every morning and every evening, it was the same thing. At times we had to steal in order to survive. Whoever could not steal some additional food would get weaker and weaker and die.

When the war was over, we hoped that we would be allowed to go home. Even the Russians believed that to be true. In the middle of the night they knocked on our door and called out loud, "*Voina kaputt, Hitler kaputt!* [War over, Hitler ruined!]" We believed we could go home now. But unfortunately, going home was only a dream. We had to continue our slavery.

The winter was freezing cold, and we were not used to those deep freeze conditions. Whenever we wanted to warm ourselves in a room in the factory where we worked, an officer came in swearing and threw us out. In the evening, before leaving the factory and returning to our barracks, we had to stay in line and were searched to see if we had taken anything with us. We had no heating material in the barracks and had to steal a few pieces of coal from the factory. We hid those pieces of coal in our pants between our legs and that's how we walked in a row through the gate, alongside our guards, into our barracks.

Oh, there were many accidents. After unloading the coal and iron, the women had to clean the train wagons on which the ores were carried. One woman, Anna Bruck from Johannisfeld, fell out of the wagon, and the train rolled over her. She lost both legs. Her fellow laborers covered her in her coat. Later, she was brought to a hospital. She still lives today with prosthesis. Accidents happened also at the train tracks. Six girls had to push a train that had stopped on its track. When the train began to take off, one of the girls was so severely injured that she had to be brought to the hospital. Since she could not work any more, she was permitted to take a train home.

In the third year, they brought Dr. Schütz, a German prisoner of war, out of prison and into our barracks. He saved many of our lives. Often they brought severely malnourished people that looked like skeletons to him. Those poor souls were so weak and cold that they fell down in a corner of the factory and almost froze to death. Dr. Schütz literally breathed life into them and woke them up from death that was hanging over them. Liesl Kühn and I often helped Dr. Schütz with the frozen half-dead people. That good doctor gave us a lot of courage and important suggestions on how to survive. He even helped the families of the Russian officers who lived in town by making house calls.

Our barracks was encircled by three layers of barbed wire, each layer three meters apart. In between each row of barbed wire were very thin rolls of wire. Once, the three Birkeneuer brothers managed to escape somehow. However, the Russian village children recognized the strangers and reported them at once. The brothers were brought back to the barracks, and they were lined up to be shot in front of our eyes. We begged for their lives and promised that none of us would ever even consider or try to escape. Thank goodness the guards listened to us and put their guns down.

In the summer we were brought to a *Kolchos*. We had to work there in the fields from dawn to dusk. We were wearing shoes with only wooden soles. When we walked to work, they made a loud rattling sound as if a battalion of horseback riders were riding by. We were so tired even early in the morning that none of us spoke a word. When we had to plant the potatoes, we tried to do it very fast so that we would have a minute to lie down flat on the ground between two rows of potatoes for a moment of desperately needed rest.

I remember clearly one day when we passed by an apple orchard. One of us called out, "Look how beautiful those apples are! They are already ripe. I don't think there is anyone here. I'm going to get one of those apples." And into the orchard she went. The others could not resist. We were all starved and had not eaten an apple for years. So one after the other we ran under the apple trees and fetched not only one apple, but every one of us filled our pockets with apples that had fallen under the tree. All of a sudden "the bad wolf" (the watchman) came and chased us out while swearing and insulting us with great contempt: "*Nemetschi-Parazit* [German parasites]!" It still rings in my ear. Frightened, all of us threw the apples away. They fell like cannons.

Now we were all wet up to our knees from that high wet grass in the apple orchard. Our guard brought us back to the barracks and reported us to the lieutenant, his superior officer. That officer was very angry with us and sent us back to work. We feared that this incident would have its dire consequences. At roll call in the evening, we were threatened again that we would be punished. However, since a few days passed and nothing happened, we thought that we were forgiven.

Then the harvest time came. Early at dawn, we had to work with the *Dreschmaschine* [threshing machine which separates the straw from the wheat] or we had to cut and bind the straw. It was most difficult to work on the windmill where the wheat had to be cleaned. We had to pour the wheat with a bucket into the high container. Two of us had to pour the wheat from the left and the right side, and one of us had to turn the machine. I had to turn and turn the machine until I was dizzy. I thought the evening would never come. However, when it was finally evening, we were not allowed to quit working. The brigadier told us that it was the order from the barracks for us to work all night long. We said, "That cannot be. We worked all day long and are exhausted. We just can't go on any more. It's not possible." The brigadier said, "Oh, yes, it is possible." We had to continue. We were forced to gather the bundles from the field and bring them to the threshing machine. We did that all night long and longed for dawn to come so that we would be able to rest our weary bones and get some sleep.

In the morning we got breakfast: watery soup and 500 grams of bread. That was the usual *Kolchos* ration. The threshing machine began to thresh, and we were ordered to get back to work. We were beside ourselves. How could it be that we were forced to do such hard labor for 36 hours straight, without a moment of rest or sleep? We were by now quite awake and angry. In the evening, at roll call, we complained. The commander of our barracks simply asked us whether we had forgotten about our time in the apple orchard. This was our punishment. Our actions were not forgotten.

Our camp in the *Kolchos* was a long former sheep stall with a low ceiling. That was our "home." We lay on the straw covered floor with one blanket, one next to the other. Nearby was a valley with a little spring of water. That is where we went to cook something when we came home late at night. Our pots were soldier helmets which we found in the fields. The whole field was a cemetery. What did we cook? We gathered grass from the field and sometimes our extreme hunger pains even dared us to steal a potato or two. We rubbed stones together to make a fire (we had no matches) and cooked ourselves a soup. We had no salt, and many suffered from diarrhea. Later on we stole some salt when we had to unload it. We crumbled the few grams of bread into our soup. We were able to stay alive because we were young and could endure it.

In the autumn we had to work in a factory in town, or we had to lay railroad tracks. Whenever there was the slightest complaint about any of us in the factory, that person was arrested and got only two hundred grams of bread. They may have been arrested, but they still had to work hard in the factory. Whenever we were sick, we still had to work unless we had high fever. When we were sick but did not have high fever, we were accused of pretending to be sick and had to continue working.

There was a never—ending fight with the bugs that almost ate us up. The whole barracks was infested with bugs. Bugs were crawling everywhere. Once every week we heated our iron beds with petroleum to keep the bugs out. However, that did not deter them. They climbed up the wall and fell down on us from the ceiling. We were literally food for the bugs.

My sister was so ill that she was allowed to go home in the autumn of 1945. The very seriously ill who could not work were deported back home. I wrote home constantly. Most people said," Why should I write? No mail ever arrives home." But I did not give up hope. One of my cards did indeed arrive home, and I even received a card back from my loved ones. That was a big celebration with my fellow captives and motivated them to write too.

In the autumn of the third year, there were only a few of us left. Many had died, and the seriously ill and those too weak to work any more were sent home. Since there were no longer enough left of us, the camp was closed. We were brought to two different camps. I was brought to Stalino. That was a huge camp where each room had about two hundred beds. It was again a new beginning. Everything was unfamiliar, and there were even more strict and harsh rules than in our previous camp. For example, on Sundays, instead of resting, we had to get up early and work in the *Kolchos*. It was very hard to work from dawn to dusk seven days a week. But we had to endure. They tried sometimes to console us and said that we shall go home soon. However, four years had already passed since our deportation from home, and we had lost hope of ever seeing our loved ones and home again.

In the autumn of 1949 one heard constantly about the closing of labor camps and that the forced laborers were to be released. But we never really could believe that anymore. They had promised us for almost five years that we would be allowed to go home.

Then one day, at roll call, our camp commander told us that we didn't have to go to work anymore but, instead, were allowed to go to town and buy new clothes so that we would be presentable when we return home. Hearing this, everybody was all of a sudden dead quiet. Nobody rejoiced; nobody could be joyful any more. We could not believe their words anymore.

I don't remember how many days we waited with our packed bags and our depressed mood. There was no roll call and no order to work. We were very frightened and asked ourselves what they wanted to do with us now. Where would they take us next?

Then, on November 6, 1949, it happened! Our camp commander came and asked, "Are you all ready?" Nobody answered. Then he asked, "Don't you want to go home?" Only then everybody began to scream, "Yes, yes, yes!" He told us to take our bags and we would be brought to the railroad station, but it should all happen very quietly we should not make any noise. We didn't know why, but we obeyed his command.

In the early evening of November 7, at about five o'clock, we were transported again in cattle-trains. It was snowing. The train took off, and we were all very sad, not knowing where they would take us now and what would happen to us next. However, the train was indeed rolling on westwards. It was rolling in the direction of Romania, our home land.

Late at night we arrived in Temeswar. The first people who were able to leave the labor camps had already arrived on November 13. They did not waste any time telling our families the good news that we would be coming.

From Temeswar we drove on until we arrived in Tschakova, near my home, where almost the whole community was eagerly waiting at the railroad station. My mother and my family were there too. My children looked at me shyly. They did not recognize me any more. I was foreign to them. Oh, that hurt! Overwhelmed by emotions, I could not speak a word. How much my children had grown during those horrible five years of my enslavement.

Our reunion was overwhelming. What those moments of reunion meant for us all can only be imagined by a person who has not experienced it. With thankful hearts we tried to forget what had happened, if that only would be possible. It was like a nightmare that should never, ever repeat itself.

Anna Frombach, née Bleche
Born October 16, 1923, in Jahrmarkt, Banat, Romania

"Who never had to eat imaginary bread
And never cried while working in the camp,
Toiling at forced labor night and day
Whether storm, rain, snow or sand,
Does not know what bitter hours are."

ANNA FROMBACH

Interviewed in July 2009 in Ingolstadt, Germany

There was a Jewish restaurant owner from Temeswar who was a regular customer of my father. He bought meat and wine for many years. He, like many Jewish businessmen in our area, often brought the news about current events and political happenings into our town, Jahrmarkt. Our townspeople were eager to hear the news. Sometimes the businessmen only made slight remarks; however, these remarks were often important to us, and we looked forward to them.

I remember, as if it were yesterday, how shortly before Christmas that restaurant owner from Temeswar came to pick up the pigs that we had raised for him and the freshly cooled wine. He made a remark that we hardly noticed at that time, but later in hindsight, I remembered it clearly. "Oh! Poor Anni, poor Anni! What a pity, and so young!" he said He must have already known at that time something about the intentions of the powerful politicians in Bucharest. Already a month later, I found out exactly what the empathic remarks of my father's customer meant. Rumors that the Germans in our Banat region of Romania would be deported began to rise right after the Christmas holidays.

On Saturday afternoon, the fourteenth of January1945 it was very quiet in our village. Berns *Oma* [grandmother Berns], who lived across the alley, brought the news that the next day all German people who were able to work would be gathered together. She said that Mari Reise had told the Berns family that the neighboring Romanian police hinted that the young

97

people should hide. I put on layers of warm clothes, took a blanket with me and went over to the Berns' house. Mari Reise, Lis Bindersch, Lis Berns and Hans Klessche were already waiting for me. All of us went through the garden to Anna Schmidt, the sister of Lis Berns, because Jakob, Anna's husband, also had to hide. All of us went to hide in the nearby barn of the Hansjerre farm. We thought we would be safe there because they had no family members who were of the age to be deported. We spent the whole night in that freezing cold barn. Nobody could sleep. I was twenty one years old and the youngest of us five.

Early next morning at seven o'clock, Anna Schmidt came and informed us that all was quiet and that no one saw nor heard anything. Hearing that good news, we left our hiding place and each of us walked back home.

At home, my dear mother had already heated water to warm my ice cold feet. Oh, that felt so good. It was Sunday; and I was looking forward to the early church mass because it was not just any Sunday, it was a special day. It was the Day of Prayer, January 15, 1945. All of a sudden there was a knock on the window. We saw *Oma* Berns, who put her face close to the window shield outside. She called very nervously, "Come quickly. Mari and Hans have come back. Down at the Neugasse [name of the street] people are already taken away from home."

I had never dried my feet so quickly. With my socks and my towel in my hands, I ran as quickly as I could through the snow to the Berns' home. Then, together with all the others, we ran again through the garden to hide in the Hansjerre barn. Frightened, we were hiding there until about 11:00 am. Then came our fathers and brought the terrible news from the Romanian and Russian police: "If the young ones are not there, the old ones would have to be taken away." That meant that our parents would have to be taken away instead of us. Well, we could not let that happen.

Frightened again, we left our hiding place and went home. It did not take long until a Romanian sergeant came to our home with a list in his hand calling out loud my name in Romanian, "Aniut(z)a, Aniut(z)a!." I was already standing in the room with my bag over my shoulder and two apples and two pieces of cake in the pockets of my jacket. When the uniformed man saw how frightened I was, he told me that I had the right to take along 70 kilogram of luggage. He said that he was not in a hurry. He encouraged me to pack underwear, clothes, and food. "No, I have enough," I said to his astonishment. Little did I know how absolutely necessary those clothes and those provisions would have been.

I was 21 years old. All German young girls and women from seventeen to thirty two years of age and all German men from seventeen to forty five years of age were taken away from their homes and transported to Russia as forced laborers. From our village alone they took 834 Germans: 453 women and 381 men. Out of these, twenty nine women and one hundred and two men died in Russia.

They brought us to a building next to the railroad station where they had collected many Germans from our village and surrounding areas. Not only did we, so frightened, have to spend the Day of Prayer there, but we had to stay there for three days.

On the seventeenth of January they forced us into cattle-trains, slammed the door and locking it from outside so that we could not get out. We were literally imprisoned in these dark cattle-trains. German men, women, young boys, and young girls, we were all together, all locked up in that cattle-train compartment. That was how we had to spend many days in that crowded dark cattle-train, until we arrived in Iase. Now they unlocked the door and put us onto another cattle-train. Again, we were locked up for many days. Finally, on February 2nd, the train stopped. Just as we feared, they had indeed transported us to Russia. It was bitter cold, and there was high snow everywhere. Deep snow or not, we had to walk for a long time in that knee high snow and freezing cold until we came to a camp.

When we finally arrived at that camp, there was a Russian translator who said, "We did not expect you until three weeks from now." The camp was not even finished yet, but they could not wait to fetch us away from our homes. During the next three days in the camp, they counted us and divided us according to what hard labor they ordered us to do. I was to work in a ditch where I had to carry heavy sacks of sand. I had to do that for a whole year. It was hard physical man's labor, and I was just a young girl. I carried those heavy sacks of sand every day, all day long, for a whole year. Then they ordered me to work in construction. We all were forced to do dangerously hard work. What was even worse, we hardly got anything to eat. Hunger ruled there. Hunger was the king. Severe starvation on top of extremely hard physical labor took many lives. Whenever someone died, we all cried.

We had to build a housing unit and had to work every day for ten hours, seven days a week. Those men who were masons did get a little money, hardly much, but at least something. But to us women they said that we were eight hundred and eighty rubles [Russian currency] in debt because of the transportation costs to bring us to Russia. In addition, the rent for living in the camp was eight hundred and eighty rubles every month. That's what they told us. Imagine that! Yes, on top of being taken away from home by force, being deported like cattle in the overcrowded cattle-train for weeks and brought there to slave in the Russian death and hunger camps, they told us that we owed them eight hundred and eighty rubles per month for rent and food. It was unbelievable! What food? We hardly got anything to eat; but we always thought of food. Hunger hurts. Oh, it hurt so much. But we were constantly warned by our Russian guard that we were in debt of eight hundred and eighty rubles per month. It is impossible to believe, but it is true that we were told to pay all that money. For what did they expect us to pay, for our back breaking labor, starvation and sub-human conditions in this hunger and death camp? However, we had nothing; we could not pay anything and did not want to hear any more about our debt.

One day we warned the guard that we would not work in construction anymore; we would go and work in the coal mines where the miners got a little bit of money. Well, he did not want that. So he told us, "Stay here; I will write you a good report so that this month you have no debt." And so he did. He wrote that we had no debt that month. But next moth we had again debt of eight hundred and eighty rubles. Actually, we really did not want to work in those coal mines because the labor there was intolerably hard, and people who worked in those mines died daily.

One day our officer was so smart that he took three men from our construction team and sent them to work in the coal mines. He said that one woman works as hard in construction as three men. So we were only women now, working in construction. We were always afraid of that officer. Whenever we saw him coming, we worked as hard as we possibly could. Our fear gave us strength. That Russian officer was very tall, strong and cruel. We had good reason to be afraid of him. Many a times he beat us; and he beat us hard when something did not go the way he wanted it to be or when he thought we did not work fast enough. Fear, starvation, over-exertion ruled in that place. Our situation was so unbearable that many people died.

Whenever one of us died, we all cried. We worked and cried. Almost every day we worked and cried. The Russian civilians who worked near us asked, "Why do you cry so much whenever someone dies? You should cry when someone is born. That is when all the suffering starts." Yes, that's what the Russian civilians always told us. They were themselves suffering. Yes, those poor Russian people had a very hard time too.

We German forced laborers worked together as a team of four to pour plates of concrete. We called our cruel officer "Schwarz." Whenever he came, we said, "Schwarz." Well, he soon figured that out. So we called him in Romanian "that father". Oh, it was such a hard time there. I labored three and a half long years under those conditions.

One of our officers was a Russian brigadier. He was always drunk and always carried a bottle. Full of despair, homesick, and suffering from immense hunger pains, I wrote a poem one day. We had no paper. We had no pencil or pen. So I began to write with a white stone on a piece of tin. One line followed another, followed another, and followed yet another until I completed the following poem: [translated from German into English below, followed in the original German]

Who never had to eat imaginary bread
And cried while laboring in the camp,
Toiling at forced labor night and day
Whether storm, rain, snow or sand,
Does not know what bitter hours are.

Wer noch nie Kommisbrot aß
Und weinend in dem Lager schafft,
Bei Tag und Nacht auf Arbeit stand,
Bei Sturm und Regen, Schnee und Sand
Weiss nicht was bittre Stunden sind.

Our officer came and said, "Anna, what is written there?" He did not know any German. I answered him in German, "I will not tell you what is written there." He seemed to be satisfied. He never really listened to my answer. He was always drunk. It was not at all bad for us that he drank so much. Whatever we did, how much we worked, it was always all right with him. He was not a bad person. He believed what we told him and always told us to continue doing our work. He was basically a good man who dealt with a bad situation by drinking. I always said it was like everywhere. Everywhere in the world there are good people and bad people. And so it was also among Russians. Most Russians themselves did not have anything either. At that time, there was hardly anything in Germany or in Romania, but in Russia there was absolutely nothing. The poor Russians suffered too. At any rate, that particular officer was a good person who had to do his duty, and the way he could cope was to drink. He was satisfied with everything we did. He never hit us, never raised his voice, and never ridiculed us. He simply wrote down whatever work we told him we had done that day.

Later, six of us worked near a street where water pipes were being laid. One day an old *Oma* came. She stopped quite a few feet from us and began motioning with her fingers back and forth. We thought she wanted to tell us something. Then she pointed with her finger at us. The others said, "What does that woman have in her hand?" I went forward. That old lady opened her hand. She was hiding little broken pieces of bread in her fist and had come to give them to us. Gratefully I took that handful of bread and divided it among the six of us. All six of us happily devoured those crumbs of bread. That elderly lady was, I am quite sure, poor herself and could have very well eaten those bread crumbs herself. However, she came all the way, carefully covering the little bread pieces in her fist, and risked being punished for giving us the bread.

The next day that wonderful woman, like a Good Samaritan, came again when the officer was not around and carefully motioned with her fingers the same way as the day before. The others were even happier than I that she came because now we had something to eat. Even though they actually were crumbs or very tiny pieces of bread, it was glorious food, and we were all so starved. We were all so happy to have that little bit to eat. One day she came with a piece of cake in her hand. Oh, what a feast that was! But, we all had to be very careful that the officer did not see that.

For a while, another fellow woman laborer and I were assigned to carry a heavy load of construction material near a house. One day, a woman who lived in that house asked us to come inside. We went inside. The woman had just cooked Borscht (a traditional Russian soup). She placed a huge bowl of Borscht in front of us and whispered in German, "Eat, children, eat." We devoured that Borscht in no time at all, the whole big bowl full of it. Oh, it was such a delicious soup, such a feast! For the first time, we had eaten so much that when we came back to the camp, we did not even look at the watery soup with the rotten slimy mushrooms swimming in it, which was what we got every day at that camp. The woman in that house who was so good and generous to us was German, but she was not allowed to speak German, and most likely, the Russians did not know that she was German. If they would have known, they would have taken her to a Siberian forced labor camp the next day. She took her life in her hands to help us and only whispered very little German when nobody was around. She told us that her relatives in Germany were also forcibly deported. Everywhere in Germany was hunger and destruction after the war.

I worked in that camp until May 1948. One day in May, a large commission came, including a Russian and a German physician and many officers. The physicians told all of us to get totally undressed. We were not allowed to wear anything, not even shoes. Imagine! We were all young women, but we had to totally get undressed and stand and turn around in front of all those men who were sitting there looking at us. It was horrible.

Actually, that turned out to be lucky for me. When I was dressed, I looked pretty healthy. And those people who looked healthy were brought to other slave labor camps. Now that I had to stand there totally naked, the Russian physician asked me what part of my body hurt. I answered, "Nothing hurts me." I was telling the truth. I really was not sick. Then the physician urged me to tell them what pain I had. I told him again that I had no pain. Then the German physician said in German, "Now, Anna, do tell us where it hurts." Then I finally said, "Well, alright, my back hurts after the heavy work." Of course it was no surprise that all of our backs hurt from all the hard physical labor we had to do from dawn to dusk. I did not say that our backs hurt because we were overworked, weak and severely malnourished. Well my luck was that I told the truth that nothing hurt me other than the back from that heavy load we had to do.

In front of me was a young girl who said that her stomach hurt her a lot. The physician examined her and found nothing wrong with her. Then the girl said it must be her gall bladder. They found nothing wrong. Then she said, "It must be my appendix". Well, the physicians found nothing wrong with her, and she was brought to another forced labor camp for another five years. I was so lucky that nothing was wrong with me, and that I told the truth. The Russian physician wanted to force me to tell her that something was wrong with me. I did not lie. I said several times, "Nothing really is wrong with me. Nothing really hurts me." Then the Russian doctor and the German doctor wrote something on a piece of paper. That was on a Thursday.

On Sunday, the Russian doctor came and we all had to stand in a row. Then he called out loud, "Gromback!" The Russians couldn't pronounce my name, "Frombach," correctly, and always called me "Gromback." Well, the doctor called out loud, "Gromback!" I was startled and scared. We did not want to go into another camp. We had gotten used to our camp now, and our lieutenant was not a bad guy. Our lieutenant came, and the Russian doctor told him to pick one out among us. There was another woman among us whose name was also Anna, like mine. She worked in the kitchen. When the physician asked which one of those women the lieutenant would pick, he pointed at me and said, "That one!" Then he said to the Russian physician, "She worked long enough and so very hard in construction." From then on, the other Anna, who worked in the kitchen, had to work in my place in construction. Because I told the truth, I did not have to endure hard construction labor any more.

Then we came to the *Kolchos* [large communist government owned land which the Soviet government took from individual farmers] where we were to work for three weeks. There we had to sleep on top of hay. Yes, hay was our luxury mattress. One evening a truck came. I could not sleep and was outside while the others were still asleep. I ran to the truck and was told that the truck came to take us away. The driver talked with the officer who asked that they should keep us one more day so that we could hoe the turnips. The men in the truck went inside while I woke up my fellow captives and told them what I had heard. One of them responded, "Are you dreaming?" She did not believe me.

Early next morning the officer who always ordered us to work placed us in rows, one after another. And then he said, "You are going home." We laughed. We did not really believe it. Then he asked us if we did not want to go home. "Oh, we would love to go home, but . . . ." Immediately he replied, "All right then. Now you hoe the turnips and then the potatoes. After you have done all that, sit down there, and at six o'clock they will come to get you." That's what he said.

Well, we worked in the turnip field. Then we worked in the potato field. When we were finished, we sat in the spot he told us to sit, and exactly at six o'clock came the truck he told us about. Then the officer told us that the cook had prepared something for us. We should go and eat, and then the truck would bring us to another camp. When we all got into the truck, people were asking, "Where are we going?" We were driven to another camp. Well, when we arrived at that camp, nobody knew about it, including me, until the lieutenant read it out loud: "Anna, Anna, you are going home." I did not believe it. It was too good to be true.

Well, it was true, indeed. On June 21, the transport left the camp, and on July 2, at 8:30 in the morning, I arrived home. I have to thank the dear Lord for that good luck. In spite of all the hardships, I can truly say that I was lucky as compared to so many others. It was my luck to come home and to come home alive. I thought about the many unfortunate people who were never able to return home, who had died in Russia under those miserable and inhumane conditions.

However, finally arriving home, after all those hard years, there was yet another bitter pill for me to swallow: we were dispossessed. Everything had been taken away from us because we were German. We had nothing and had to start all over again. We were allowed to live in our own home but we had to pay high rent. Yes, we had to pay a high sum of money as rent to live in our very own home. But, how were we to get money to pay that rent? We had to find a job and work very hard to pay the rent in order to stay in our very own home. Oh, those were hard and terrible times, too terrible to ever forget. I am old now. But I can never forget it.

Anna Riedl, née Weber
Born April 1, 1926, in Rekas, Banat, Romania

"We were literally in a Russian hunger and death camp forced to starve while doing extremely hard physical labor. Surrounded by death, I was right in the middle of it, exhausted and starving."

ANNA RIEDL

Interviewed in July 2009 in Ingolstadt, Germany

On the fourteenth of January, 1944, early in the morning, at seven o'clock, we were woken up. Six to seven armed policemen came and ordered us to pack the most important things, warm clothes and something to eat. They took us with them to the school house, and when we arrived there we found many Germans— women from the ages of seventeen to thirty-two and men from seventeen to forty-five years of age. The floor was covered with straw. We had to spend eight nights and eight days on that straw. Of course we were not allowed to leave. The Germans from neighboring villages, from Weltschek, from Janubar, and from Rekas were all brought there. Eight days later, a row of trucks arrived. I believe there were eleven or so trucks. Under the watchful eyes of the armed policemen, these trucks brought us to the railroad station. Trains were already waiting for us.

The armed policemen ordered us to get into those trains. These were not passenger trains; they were cattle-trains. The conditions in that cattle-train were unimaginably gruesome. They shoved us in like cattle and locked us up. There was no way to get out. We only had a little hole in the bottom of our compartment for our human waste. It did not matter whether we were women or men; we were all thrown together. It was dark in that cattle-train compartment, and it was freezing cold. We could not look outside. We could not see where they were taking us. When I was taken away from home, my parents had given me a little bit of ham, bread and some potatoes. Well, that did not last very long, and it was all frozen after a few days. Who on earth would have thought it would be such a long, torturous ride? We had hoped that they would just bring us to the border of Romania and Russia. However, our miserable ride continued for about fourteen to sixteen days and nights, long after we crossed the border.

When the train finally stopped, we found ourselves in Siberia, right in the middle of the infamous ice-cold Siberian winters. We could hardly get out; we were stiff and frozen, dirty, smelly, starved, weak, and forlorn after weeks of enduring that abominable cattle-train ride. We had hardly seen any light and had a hard time stepping down from that train. To make matters worse, there were Russian civilians lined up at the train station. They yelled at us, spit at us, called us names. At that time, we could not understand any Russian, but we knew what it meant to be spit at and face raised fists and angry faces shouting at us, "Hitler, Hitler!!" It is impossible for me to forget that horrible scene. To add insult to injury, we even had to clean up that awful cattle-train. Oh, it was so disgusting that many people vomited and got sick.

Waiting for us at the railroad station was, once again, a whole row of trucks. Armed with guns, the Russians ordered us to get into those trucks, after which they brought us to a place with nine rows of large barracks. We were in a forced labor camp. Oh, it was unimaginably freezing cold. It was minus thirty to forty degrees. How we shivered! Then they put us into various rooms in the camp. I don't remember any more how many people were to be in one room, but it was at least four people to a room.

Soon afterwards there was a roll call to make sure we were all there. After all the paper work was done, which took about eight to ten days, we were assigned our labor. I was forced to do physically hard labor in the coal mine. Initially, I did not have to work deep in the mine. I had to push the wagons full of coal that came up from deep down the mine shaft. It was extremely hard work. After two years, I had to work deep down in the mine and was given a lamp and a number. Now I had to push the heavy coal wagons down there. I don't remember any more how many meters deep it was, but it was very deep down under the earth. Oh, what hard, back-breaking work it was, even harder than before. It was even extremely hard for men, let alone for women.

That hard work in the coal mines went on for years. Every morning was roll call to make sure everyone was present. Then we had to walk with the watchman and his gun to the mine, which was about one kilometer away. It was bitter-cold winter and very high snow. We were not prepared for the brutally cold Siberian winter, and we were freezing, however, there was one small consolation. In that deep freeze, it was not so bad to work deep down underground in the mine. It was not that cold down there. Many also worked inside the mine when it rained. When they came out and walked back to the camp, all their clothes were frozen stiff. Even their eye lashes, their hair, everything was frozen. For those poor people, it was horrible!

Whenever we had to work the night shift, after working all night and walking back in the morning to the camp, we had to continue working the whole next day. Instead of being able to sleep after working so hard all night long, we had to clean the rooms in the camp, wash the floors and so on. The Russians always found something to keep us working, to not let us even rest for a moment. Let me repeat: all night long we worked deep inside the coal mine and then walked to the camp for a mile in that knee-deep snow and storms during the brutally cold winter. When we finally arrived in the camp, exhausted, we were not allowed to rest. Instead, we were ordered to work all day in the camp under the ever-watchful eyes of our armed guards. Then again, after that day's work, we had to walk once more in the bitter cold one kilometer to the mine for another night's back breaking labor. Then the process started all over again. It literally was endless work night and day without any rest. That's right: we were not allowed to sleep or even rest a moment, night and day. How long can a body endure that kind of brutal treatment? We were exhausted and starved. Many people died. We were truly in a hunger and death camp in Russia.

Many people died soon after we arrived in the camp. Three or four days after our cattle-train transport, the first person died. She was a young beautiful girl. Oh, it was so sad. I remember it as if it were yesterday. So many people died. During the first winter of February 1945, three people died. There was very high snow, and it was so bitter cold. The Russians just threw the naked bodies out at the edge of the village, without any clothing, without any covering. They just threw them out there on that ice-cold ground. Those poor, dead people didn't have any name plates, no identification, nothing. They lay there naked on the ground in Siberia.

My best friend in the camp was a woman of my age. One day I came back from work and she was dead. That young beautiful woman, my best friend there, was dead. She died of typhus. It was no wonder that typhus broke out under those abominable conditions. Many men, who were in their best years, between thirty-five and forty-five years of age, all fell down and died like flies, one after the other. Adding insult to death, the Russian guards would simply say, "The old ones, the old ones." The younger ones, like my brother, somehow endured. Those men were as skinny as bones. They looked like skeletons. That is what starvation and over-exertion had done to them. Yes, we were literally in a Russian hunger and death camp, forced to starve while doing extremely hard physical labor. Surrounded by death, I was right in the middle of it, exhausted and starving. I really don't know how I was able to survive it all. Somehow I endured. I was young.

If we had anything to eat, it was watery soup with fish heads and fish tails swimming in it. There were also plenty of worms swimming in it. Oh, it was simply awful. We were so painfully hungry. There was hardly ever any bread, and whenever we did get a little piece of bread, it was old, green, and slimy. It was not palatable. Yet, we did not want to die of hunger. So we closed our eyes and swallowed that rotten stuff.

On our way back to camp after work, we used to pass by a few gardens. In our desperate need for some food, we sometimes entered and stole a potato or two. However, when we arrived at the camp, we always were searched by the guards who took it all away from us. Every once in a while we were lucky: the guards did not find it. Once in a while there was a Russian guard who was compassionate and let us alone. Actually, those poor Russians did not have anything themselves; they were also in need of food. They were really poor, those Russians who lived there in Siberia.

Cruel as our Russian captors were, I will not forget a good Russian woman. When I was working deep down in the mine, there was an older Russian woman who was truly good to us. Well, it goes to show that there were also good people among the Russians. Others despised us even though none of us had ever met them before or done anything to them to make them hate us.

After a while the creepy situation with the lice and bugs started in the camp. That was terrible. The whole camp was infested. My goodness! Those head and body lice and the lice on the blankets, they were intolerable. One could not get rid of them. We had no peaceful moment. Every one of us had to have her head shaved. Now we were all bald. Oh, that beautiful, thick, long hair of the women and those beautiful, long pigtails of the young girls; they were all gone, all cut off. Not only did the Russians cut the hair on our heads, but young Russian men shaved off the hair on our genitals and underarms. Imagine that! We were all young girls and young women. Oh, that was unthinkably awful. They had no shame, those Russians, no shame at all. That awful situation continued until 1947.

The first transports carrying the very sick left the camp in 1945 and brought them back to Romania. The two transports in 1946 and 1947, who carried very sick people, also returned them to their homes in Romania. But after that, the people who were very sick were no longer given transport home. They were brought to the Russian occupied East Germany. Some of those severely sick deportees who were transported to East Germany recovered a little and tried to escape from East Germany in order to get back to Romania. It was, Of course against the law, but they longed to be home and tried their luck to cross the border somehow.

I was working in the labor camp in Russia until the very end, until 1949. My sister and my brother were there too. Once a year we were allowed to write a Red Cross card home. Only one card per year was allowed, and all the cards were carefully read and examined. We were only allowed to write, "I am doing fine." After 1948, we were allowed to write just a little bit more. We also had a little bit more freedom then. For the first time we were allowed to leave the camp and go into town. We even began to get paid a little. Now we were able to buy a little bit of food at the market. That helped somewhat. We were always hungry, always starved, and always exhausted from hard physical labor.

In 1949, two months before we were released, the word got around that we were to leave soon. When it really happened, our joy was tremendous. We were transported in open wagons and sang our folk songs. At home they had heard that another transport was coming from Russia. Our mother happened to be at that time in Temeswar, and exactly at that time we arrived at the railroad station. My father was also there with a horse and buggy, which he had borrowed from a Romanian neighbor. Oh, what joy it was to see my dear parents again! We all hugged and hugged each other so much and drove home to Rekas. When we arrived, there were already many people gathered to welcome us, eager to see who was coming home, hoping their loved ones would be among the returnees.

Thank God my parents were still there and the house still remained. But I learned that even though we were in our own home, we were totally dispossessed by Romania and had actually to pay rent now to continue to live in our own home. All our possessions, our house, our land, our farm were taken away from us, and we had such a beautiful farm. The horse and buggy in which my father picked us up from the railroad station belonged to our Romanian neighbors. They were good people. When they heard that a transport was coming from Russia, they loaned my Dad their horse and buggy so that he could pick us up from the railroad station, in case we were among those returning home.

We had lost all our possessions, but we had each other, and that was worth more than anything. And so we had to start all over again. It was hard, but we survived. I got married, had kids, and life went on.

My brother risked escaping from Romania to West Germany with his wife and his son. They took only a handbag, so that nobody would suspect anything. They had to walk through deep waters; my brother carried his wife on his back through the water. After many dangerous trials and tribulations, they finally reached West Germany. They had a long story to tell about their dangerous escape.

It was our luck that my brother was now in West Germany and my mother-in-law too. Before you were allowed to leave the country, you had to have a close first-line family member in Germany fill out forms and give a lot of money to the government to be able to leave Romania. Since the Germans in Romania had been dispossessed and had nothing, the relatives in Germany had to pay the Romanian government handsomely to get their loved ones out of there. Finally, we got our papers and received the long-sought permission to leave Romania. In 1987 we left to live in Germany and be free. It hurts to think about what happened to us before we came here, but that is how life was. I am free now, but not free of my painful memory.

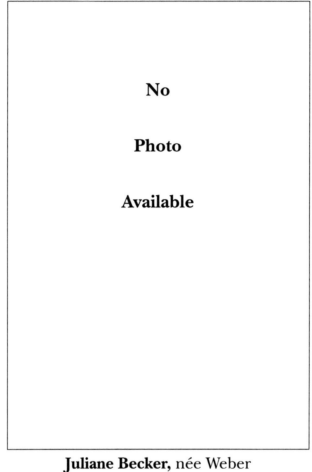

Juliane Becker, née Weber
Born May 21, 1916, in Sankt-Andreas, Banat, Romania.

"My sister's poor body did not survive all that cruelty. She was one of the first ones who died in that labor camp in Russia. I raised her four children, together with my own four children."

JULIANE BECKER

Interviewed in July 2007 in Ingolstadt, Germany

M y husband and I will celebrate our 75th anniversary on the 23rd of August 2007. Yes, we are still together, and we live here in this wonderful Josef Nischbach Senior Home. We married when we were 21 because we were both teachers and would not get teaching positions together unless we were married. We wanted to stay in the same village at home. So we hurried up and got married, but we didn't get to be in the same village anyway. Far too much happened to us, and it is far too much to tell. It is a wonder that we survived all that horror of World War II and the years that followed.

On the morning of January 15, 1944, on her thirty-first birthday, my sister was taken away. The Russians came, stole her from her four children and home, and deported her to Russia as a forced laborer. Her youngest child was five, and the oldest was ten years old. For about four years my sister gave birth to a child almost every year. It was my luck not to be deported because I was the mother of a very small infant. Those women who had a tiny infant were allowed to stay home. Unlike my dear sister, I was the lucky one.

My sister and I were very close. As they took her away in their truck, I tried to follow with my sleigh. It was such high snow that extremely cold winter. So as long as I could, I sledded alongside that open truck, as they drove her away. I called out, "I will come with you! When we two are together, it is easier." She gave me such a big hug from afar and called out loud again and again, "Sister, I know that as long as you are home, my children will have a mother." I still hear those words, even today. I could not disappoint her. I had to do all I could to be a good mother to her four children.

We were living in the city in Romania. My sister's older children were already in a private German middle school. But then all boarding schools were closed; all convents were closed; and the German nuns had to leave. Now what to do? Not only did the Romanians close all our schools, but they dispossessed all Germans in Romania. Our home and all our possessions were taken away from us. How were we now to live? How were we to survive? How were we to take care of all of our children?

After a while, I was lucky to get a position in the city. So we took my sister's four children to the city with us. Now we had seven children all together (four of my sisters and three of mine) but no home to live in. That was in 1945. Then in 1953, the eighth child arrived. I gave birth to another daughter. Today she is our sunshine. She is a musician

Let's come back to January 15, 1945, when my sister was taken away from home. A truck took my dear sister to the railroad station where she was transported in a cattle-train, under sub-human conditions, to Russia. There, in a Russian labor camp, hungry and freezing during the bitter cold winter, she was forced to do hard physical labor, day in and day out, under abominable conditions and under starvation. Her poor body did not survive all that cruelty. She was one of the first ones who died in that labor camp in Russia. She was so courageous. People who were with her told me later that even while they were transported in that horrid cattle-train, she tried to console others, "Don't cry; don't cry; we'll be able to make it," she would say. Yes, that was my sister. She was so positive. She didn't want tears; she didn't want people to despair and give up. Instead, she encouraged all to sing. Before she died, she was not able to breathe because she had a severe throat infection. But she didn't get any medical care, no medicine at all. My cousin, whom they also had taken away, was with my sister when she died. My cousin said that my sister asked to use a little petroleum cooker to boil some water that she could inhale to soothe her aching throat. The Russian guard, a woman who used such a petroleum cooker regularly, said to my sister, "No, absolutely not! "

My sister and the other forced laborers had to do extremely hard labor in the coal mines. Every day they had to walk a long way in the bitter cold to get to the mines. About ten o'clock at night, after slaving all day in the mines, they had to walk back to the camp in the dark, bitter-cold night, making their way through knee-high snow. Their feet were frozen. Even the boots were frozen. When they returned to the camp, exhausted and starved, they even had to cook dinner on that petroleum cooker for that beast of a guard who was in command over them. I am sorry to use such harsh words, but that woman was beastly. She would let the laborers use the cooker to cook her dinner but not to boil some little water to soothe my sister's infected throat so that she could ease her breathing.

Before my sister died, she could not speak any more; her vocal cords were so severely swollen that her throat was now all closed. So she wrote the following: "I have a good husband who will take care of our children." Her husband said something similar before he was killed in Berlin just before the war was over. A man who was with him when he died, visited us later and told us that a grenade hit my brother-in-law and tore an arm and a leg off him. That man wanted to carry him on his shoulders. Unfortunately, all the soldiers were so weak and could not lift or carry him. My wounded brother-in-law said to him, "Bring me to that tree, put me under that tree, and let me sit there. I have a courageous wife who will take care of my four children." Yes, that good man, that good buddy of my brother-in-law, came back and told us what had happened to my sister's husband. We did not know that he was dead and were all waiting for his return. Yes, that is how it was. Both, my sister and her husband, died in the same year, and each trusted the other to take care of their four children. I raised her four children, together with my own. We did everything possible for my sister's children to continue their education. There were no private German schools any more. So they went to Romanian public schools.

My sister did not survive even one whole year in that terrible labor camp. She was taken away from home on January 15, and she died on August 20. At home, on the same day when she died, August 20th, her beloved dog died. Imagine that coincidence! That story almost borders on the unreal. It is not explainable, but it is true.

Let me tell you a little bit about that dog and my sister. Since I was a teacher in a German school in the city and lost my job because all German schools were closed, I moved with my children to our village and lived at my sister's place. She had a dog that she had found as a puppy lying in a field with a broken leg. She took that puppy home and brought him to a veterinarian. The puppy got well, she raised him, and he was such a good, faithful dog. He was a German shepherd who was truly watching over her and had a special connection with her. What a coincidence that he died on the same day as my sister. That dog loved my sister who had saved his life when a Russian was about to shoot him.

Here is how she saved his life: There were Russians everywhere in our community. One day, a Russian officer came and wanted to come inside our house, which was located in the middle of the village. Those Russians came to make their usual tour of observation and inspection. Our dog ran toward the officer and bit his boot. My sister heard the barking of the dog and ran out. At that moment, the officer drew his gun and wanted to shoot the dog. The dog's name was Bendel. She threw herself over the dog and saved him. The officer was standing there and looked at that scene where a woman would risk her own life to save a dog. In the meantime I came out too, because I heard it all. I saw the officer standing there and looking at my sister, who was lying on the ground protecting the dog. He was astonished that my sister was willing to risk her own life in such a manner. Whatever he said, I didn't understand. I did not speak Russian at that time. Later on I learned Russian, and I can speak it now. At any rate, that Russian did not come into the house any more that day to make his inspection. The children came out of the house also and looked at that amazing scene. The Russian looked at all the children. My sister said, "Yes, those are all my children." He looked at them all, said something and left. After that he came every day and brought the children something: sometimes candy, sometimes cookies, sometimes German butter from the Alps.

That dog was somehow connected with my sister and her sorrow. One can't explain it, but in the middle of August of 1945, shortly before my sister died, he just stopped eating. He stayed in his little dog house and did not come out anymore. I went to him and brought him a little milk and food, but he did not touch any of it. He did drink some water, though. On the 19th we called the veterinarian. He examined him and said that he did not know what was wrong with the dog. He only knew that the dog did not have any illness. His physical exam showed that the dog was physically well. Later he did not even drink water anymore. On the 20th of August, I remember it well, I went to feed him, but he was lying in front of his dog house, dead. It was the exact day when my sister died. I don't know how to explain it.

A deportee to Russia, who was in the same labor camp as my sister, was sent home to give birth to her baby and told me why and how my sister died. I had a piece of paper on my nightstand on which I had written down all the special things and moments about each of my sister's four children that occurred while she was gone. I wanted to share these special moments of the growth of each of her children with her when she returned. Never had the thought occurred to me that she would never come home again. That forced labor camp in Russia had killed her. She was such a young, vibrant, and positive woman. Yes, that hurt, and then to tell all her four children that their sweet mother was no more; it was very painful for all, very painful indeed.

Both my husband and I were all of a sudden fired from our teaching positions in our school because my husband had to serve in the German military. My father was a wealthy farmer, and any one who owned some property was called an exploiter by the Communists. Thus, we lost everything and had to work all kinds of odd jobs to survive. We were still on school vacation when on the 31st we got the letter which said, "*Betreten Sie nicht mehr die Schwelle der Schule.*" [Don't set foot in this school any more]. The exact same thing happened to a relative who was the principal in another school. My husband, who was an excellent athlete, got a position later.

Since we were thrown out of our jobs and our home, we needed to rent a place to live. There were plenty of empty houses. They were empty because the German families who owned them were chased out and Romanians either moved in or became the landlords of those German homes. Those dispossessed German buildings needed to be managed. So I worked for the city administration. But, since I was a German, I did not get a job in the office; I had to walk from house to house. But, at least it got us something to eat. After three years I got the courage and went to the capital city, to the Ministry of Education, and asked to be placed back in my teaching position in my former school. The ministry in the capital city had no idea that we were fired. Imagine that! We were still registered there as teachers. Yes, it was the local secret police who took away our jobs. The city official could not believe what had happened to me, that I lost the job.

I was lucky that I spoke perfect Romanian. I tell you, learn another language; it may save your life! Of course the Romanians were pleased to have me work for them because most of the Germans did not speak any Romanian. My mother spoke hardly any Romanian. Again, I was lucky. All of our school children were German. In our trilingual region lived Romanians, Hungarians and Germans. Our school was German. My last four years there a German teacher was about to lose her position because we did not have enough German children attending the school. In order to help her stay, I took over the Romanian section. I taught Romanian so that other German teacher could teach German, and thus, she did not have to lose her job.

Communism came to Romania as soon as the Russians marched in. The first years after the war I taught 7th and 8th grade students. At that time I was principal of a school as well. During communism, the dominant word was "meetings," and there were more meetings all the time. There were countless meetings every day. I had no time for my children. I always had to go to those procedural meetings. One evening my youngest son wanted to go skiing with a friend of ours who had come to visit us. I was again at a school meeting. My two girls were out participating in their sports activities, and my two boys were alone at home. Siegfried, our older boy, fried liver for supper. The little boy, Peter, who was in second grade, did the ironing. My friend said, "What? Peter, do you have to iron?" He said, "Who else should do it?" That was how we organized things. Everybody had their daily duties. Otherwise our household would not function with eight children. Well, at least the children had the benefit of being raised to be self-sufficient even though it was not out of free will but out of necessity. In spite of it all, we were together, and we enjoyed each other. We did not let the unfortunate circumstances get the best of us. We did not let the Russians or Romanians take our positive spirits, our hope away. We sang a lot to keep our spirits up. It kept us going.

Unfortunately, my husband could not spend much time with us. He was a coach and always active with sports from early in the morning until late at night. From seven o'clock in the morning until ten o'clock at night, he was on duty with sports-related activities, even on Sundays. Most games took place on Sundays. So every Sunday he had to be at the sports field by 8:30 AM.

When Romania was under Communist rule, there was much misery and distress. There was a great need for many things, just about everything. Whenever people saw someone coming from the West, and they saw all the things that person brought, all the many things that were not available in Romania, they were amazed. Many German people tried to escape to Germany. Some Germans who were trusted by the Communist party got permission to leave, but they never came back to live in Romania; they left to live in Germany and stayed there. That was how it was with us, too. We also left for the West as soon as we had a chance.

My husband went to West Germany in 1972. My daughter-in-law was a champion athlete and lived near Speer. My husband was able to go with my son and daughter-in-law as athletes to the Olympic Games in Munich in 1972, receiving special permission from the police of our city to leave Romania for a short time. After they were in Munich and experienced the freedom and life in West Germany, my son and daughter-in-law did not come back to Romania. They also talked my husband into staying in West Germany. He was lucky to immediately get a teaching position. At that time, there was a shortage of teachers here in Bavaria. So in 1977 I joined them in Munich. My husband's sister-in-law got permission from Bucharest through the Olympic Committee to go to Munich. They, too, never returned to Romania. Now, we are all free in the West.

Anna Nover, née Loris
Born February 24, 1905, in Jahrmarkt, Banat, Romania.

"We had to pay for that which the war had destroyed."

ANNA NOVER

Personal written narrative presented to me in July 2007 in Ingolstadt, Germany.

A rumor was floating that the Germans would be deported to Russia but nobody wanted to believe it. Then it happened. January 14, 1945, is the terrible date burned in our memories. My father was in the alley. All of a sudden he hurried into the house and called, "They already are coming in the alley with a few women."

My sister Elisabeth was only sixteen years old. What to do? Shall we hide? But where can we hide? We ran through the garden and hid in the vineyard. On the street nearby, we saw gunned patrolmen go up and down the street. They encircled the community, so that no one could escape. Soon after my father came and said that the patrolmen had lists of young German people. If the people on the list were not there, they would take their parents. Of course we did not want that to happen. Therefore, we decided to go back into the house. As we reached our garden, we already saw patrolmen at our fourth neighbor with a list in their hands. They saw us and shot into the air. We stopped at once. The men in uniform came toward us and scolded us with great anger. I only understood the word "Hitler."

After we changed our clothes, we were forced to go with them. My sister Elisabeth wasn't even on the list because she was born in November 1928, and too young. However, because we were hiding, she had to go too. They took us to a large room full of German people and kept us there for two nights and

days. My husband was serving in the Romanian Air Force. I had
to leave my two-, six-, and eight-year-old daughters behind with
my parents, and I felt as if my heart would rip apart.

On the 16th of January, they brought us to the main railroad
station in Temeswar and forced us into cattle-trains that were
already waiting for us. And so began the endless treacherous
journey "East." It took sixteen days. On the second of February,
1945, we arrived at Nowotroizk in Russia. There our forced labor
began. I had to work with a woman named Kathi Seibert (her
maiden name was Linz) in construction. Kathi also was not on
the list, since she was born in 1912, one year older than the age
limit of 32 for women to be deported. She was taken in place of
her sister who was very ill.

As forced laborers in Russia, we worked with masons and
carpenters from Jahrmarkt to build a new kitchen. After work
the men would take some wooden planks and go into the village
to exchange the pieces of wood for some food. On the first of
August the men gave us a few nails and leftover glass. We, too,
wanted to try our luck exchanging those for food. We were
always so very hungry.

We did go into the village and soon found an interested
person who would exchange our "goods" for food. We first got
a half liter of milk; another half liter we were to pick up the next
day. But that never happened. We were also able to get a few
potatoes, some garlic and a few cucumbers from three other
houses.

On the way back to our camp, a huge truck passed by and
blew the horn. We moved over to the side of the road. The truck
stopped. A foreign officer and two soldiers with guns jumped
out of the truck. The officer pointed to the truck and shouted,
Dawaj [Come here]! Very scared we replied in Russian that we
had to go to the barracks. It did not matter; we had to get on the
truck. The truck took off, and when we past by our camp, two
girls were just coming out. At once the truck stopped, and the
foreign officer quickly jumped out and wanted to force those
two girls to get into the truck. However, one of the officers of
our camp, who was standing nearby, saw that and called out
loud, "*Frauen weg* [Women, go away]," and ran toward the truck.
The foreign officer jumped immediately into the truck, and the

truck took off very fast. Now we knew that something was not right and waved to the others.

When we came to a big building, the truck stopped. Our abductor went inside the building. I said to Kathi, "Come, let's jump out." But the man who sat next to us did not let us. Now we began to cry. After a short while the foreign officer came back with two men in uniform. They asked us in Russian if he was our officer. We said, "No!" They laughed out loud, and the truck slowly continued to drive on. We passed by a colony of our fellow forced laborers from home who were on their way back to their barracks from work. They asked us why we cried and where we are going. I shouted out loud that we didn't know where they were taking us and asked them to please write down the number of the truck and report that to our camp officers.

It was five o'clock in the afternoon when we were taken from Novotroizk. Six hours later, at 11:00 pm, we arrived at the place where the abductors took us. A gate opened and the truck drove into the court yard. The soldiers bought a ladder so that we could climb down the truck. They brought a bench. The officer told us to sit down and left. We cried bitterly. A man came and asked in German, "Children, why do you cry?" I replied," Is there still someone here who speaks German? Where are we, and why were we brought here? We have to report to work early in the morning tomorrow." The man introduced himself and told us that he was the translator, a German *Siebenbürger* [Transylvanian Saxon] from Romania. He told us that we were in Stalino and that we had to work there from now on. To console us, he said that we were not the only ones there. Then he brought us to a cellar and lit a candle. There were indeed our people from Bruckenau, Orzydorf, Knees, Neubeschenowa, Kleinsanktpeter and a couple from Panjowa. They were all brought there by the same method as we had been.

Now we were prisoners in this place. During the day, we had to work at a construction site where we had to clean the rubbish and work on renovations. We had to pay for that which the war had destroyed. Since our clothes were in Novotroizk, they gave us working clothes. We were not allowed to have any contact with the other people in the camp and were strictly separated from them in the dining hall. Apparently nobody was to find out how they brought us here. We did our daily labor and slowly had to accept our plight. Most of the forced laborers there were *Siebenbürger Sachsen* [Transylvanian Saxon Germans].

It was not until June 1948 that we were finally released from our forced labor and I was able to see my husband, my children, my parents and siblings again. Life continued. My husband died in 1984. Since 1990, I have lived with my children and grandchildren in Germany and thank the dear Lord that I was able to survive all that.

Katherina Valentin
Born Nov. 6, 1918, in Neu-Arad, Banat, Romania

"We had to load rubbish on a wagon, and we were the horses that had to pull the wagon."

KATHARINA VALENTIN

Interviewed in July 2007, in Ingolstadt, Germany

I was twenty seven years old when I was taken away from home and deported to forced labor camps in Russia. There I was to do hard forced labor in three cities: Marganetz, Netopetrovsc, and Usla. Every day I had to slave outside for eight hours. We German forced laborers had to clean the rubbish from the bombing of those cities. Then we had to load that rubbish on a wagon, and we were the horses that had to pull the wagon. It was so cold our eye balls felt like they were freezing. Not only did we have to do incredibly heavy labor, but we had to freeze at night. There was no heat.

Later I worked in a saw mill. It was ten kilometers away from our labor camp and a very long distance to walk. Early in the morning we had to walk ten kilometers to our work place, work hard all day, and then, exhausted, we had to walk the ten kilometers back again to the camp.

After that I had to do heavy labor on railroad tracks. One can hardly believe how we were able to survive all that hard work with the kind of food that we got. It was watery turnip leaf soup, and if one was extremely diligent, one got a spoonful of rice in that soup.

In Usla, the last labor camp where I was, there were no houses, only sand, just like in a desert. Our barracks were under ground. Our beds were wooden planks. The place was so infested with so many flies, lice and bugs that it was impossible to sleep. I got malaria there and was so dangerously ill that they had to send me back home. Years later, I still suffered from it and could not work.

Magdalena Kasznel, née Kilzer
Born February 20, 1920, in Jahrmarkt, Banat, Romania

"When I was finally set free from my slave labor in Russia and returned home to Romania, my little child had already died, and I could see him no more . . . My older son did not recognize me any more."

MAGDALENA KASZNEL

Interviewed in July 2007 in Ingolstadt, Germany

Oh, it was horrible when the officers came to take me away from home. My little baby was one year old, and my other little son was three years old. But they ripped me away from those small helpless children. My children cried, my mother cried, and I cried. It was terrible. But the officers tore me away from my little children and transported me on a cattle-train to Russia. It was horrible. I was actually not on their list to be transported to Russia. However, their quota for the number of Germans to be transported was not quite full. Some people were missing; so they took me. My father was there, and they took him away too. He was one of the oldest men, but he was also transported to Russia to slave under forced labor. Now my mother was all alone with my two little children.

They transported us to Russia on a cattle-train. We were over-crowded with no heat, no hygiene, no bathroom, no light, no heat, and no food. We were freezing and hungry and locked up in that dark train wagon, and had to endure all that for weeks before we got to Russia.

In the labor camp in Russia, I had to do extremely hard work, as did all of us forced laborers there. I was exhausted and always hungry. We hardly got anything to eat and were all malnourished. I was in Russia for four long years under Russian slave labor.

In 1949, when I was finally set free from my slave labor in Russia and returned home in Romania, my little child had already died at the age of four, and I could see him no more. Oh, that hurt so very much!

When I arrived home, my older son was already seven years old. He had cried so much when I was taken away. Now, when my mother and son picked me up at the railroad station in Romania, my son did not recognize me any more after all those years. We all cried at that railroad station. We had cried bitterly when I was forced to leave four years ago, and we cried again at the same railroad station. My little boy had grown up without me, and he did not know me any more. He was now seven years old. It all hurt so much. It still hurts today, many decades later [tears were rolling down her cheeks].

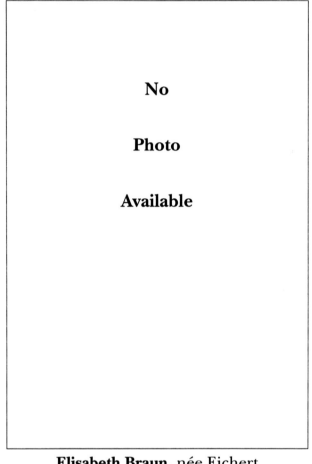

Elisabeth Braun, née Eichert
Born November 27, 1919, in Billed, Banat, Romania

"They tore me away from my two little children, who cried when I left . . . They took me away from them and deported me to Russia."

ELISABETH BRAUN

Interviewed in July 2007 in Ingolstadt, Germany

It is very hard to talk about all that happened to us. I was 25 years old when the Russians came and took me away on January 15, 1945. They tore me away from my two little children, who cried bitterly. I was forced to leave them behind when they deported me to Russia. The Russians could care less whether the little ones cried for their mother or who would take care of them. They took me away from them and deported me to Russia.

There, in a labor camp in Russia, I was forced to work extremely hard under the worst conditions. In the rain and in the snow, we had to be outside without any protective clothing, always outside. There was a railroad track which was broken, and we German slave laborers had to fix it. It was such heavy work. We had to lift up those heavy iron rails and fix them. Whether rain, snow, or blizzard, we always had to labor every single day outside without any protection. When I was not working on the train tracks, I had to cut trees and carry bundles of wood and do all kinds of heavy work. Exhausted, my fellow German forced laborers and I would come back to the camp wet, cold, shivering, and oh, so hungry.

Every day I suffered from severe hunger pain and exhaustion from that hard labor. After slaving there for two years, I got too sick to work. Because I was not of any use to them any more, the Russians transported me to the Russian-occupied zone of East Germany. Unfortunately I was not allowed to go back home to Romania where my children were.

Under Russian communist rule, it was illegal to leave East Germany. I learned that my husband was in Austria where he had been a prisoner of war. What to do now? My husband was in Austria, my children in Romania, and I was stuck in East Germany. It was another kind of prison. No matter what, I just had to risk getting out and join my husband in Austria. After much careful planning, I took my life in my hands on one fateful night, managed to cross the dangerous communist guarded bobbed wire fence, and escaped to the free West Germany. It's a long story. But I tell you, what a glorious feeling it was to be finally free of communist rule.

Now I was free to go and join my dear husband in Austria. When I arrived in Austria, I had no good clothes to wear; I arrived there just as I had left the labor camp in Russia. I was wearing those old trousers, a jacket and a Russian hat. My husband came to pick me up in Klagenfurt. I looked so miserable that he did not recognize me at first. You can imagine how our tears were flowing when we saw each other again after all those horrible years.

We were so happy to be together again, but what about our two children from whom I was torn away in Romania? How much we longed to be reunited with them. It was too risky to cross the multiple borders to go to Romania. Many who tried to do so had lost their lives. It was too dangerous. We could not risk for our children to become orphans. They had gone already through too much hardship. After I was deported in 1945, my grandparents took care of them. In 1951, our two children were force deported, together with my parents, to the Bărăgan for five miserable years. My husband and I would have to try some other means to bring our children to the free West.

However, where shall we live in the meantime? Since our ancestors migrated in the 18th century from Elsass Lorraine (which was Germany then) to the Banat in Romania, we decided to move to Elsass Lorraine which is now a part of France. Later we moved to Ingolstadt, Germany and tried very hard to bring our children to Germany. The Romanian government would not let them out without getting a great sum of money from us which we did not have. We worked hard and saved every penny to buy our children out of Romania.

At last, in 1960, we had all the money demanded by the Romanian government to buy our children out of Romania and bring them to Germany. That was fifteen years after the war was over. We had missed all those years of our children's childhood. No one could give that back to us. They were grown up now. With eyes full of tears, we fell into each other's arms and would not let go. Never will I forget that moment. However, no matter where I am, no matter how much I try, I cannot shake off all the hardships we had to endure. It is too painful to talk about that bitter destiny of ours. So let's not talk about it any more.

Franz Engel
Born June 12, 1927, in Bethausen, Banat, Romania

"The women, they worked and they cried bitter tears. They did not only suffer from extreme exhaustion but also from starvation. They did not at all resemble the beautiful women they were when they were snatched away from home. Now they all looked like skin and bones, a mere shadow of the women they were when taken away from home."

FRANZ ENGEL

Interviewed in July 2007 in Ingolstadt, Germany

By telling you my story, I want the world to know what I saw with my own eyes, what we had to endure, and especially what young German girls and women who were forcibly deported to Russia had to suffer.

I was at home in Bethausen on January 14, 1945. Bethausen is about 20 km from Lugow, the state capital. I had heard that Romanian soldiers were occupying the region where I lived. I heard them say that they would go to the German Embassy and "have some fun" with those Germans. Hearing that, I left on that Sunday. On Monday I was hiding in a Romanian village where my father was very well known. He knew many people there, and some of them hid me from the Romanian soldiers. Early next morning at 5:00 AM, I wanted to leave that village to go home, but it was already encircled by Russian and Romanian soldiers who had arrived at night. I thought nobody would know that I was home so I could hide there. However, it was too late. I could not leave any more. The Russian and Romanian officers seeking Germans had already arrived.

Early in the morning they gathered all the German women from eighteen to thirty-two years of age and men from seventeen to forty-five years of age. By noon, they had already gathered all the Germans and brought them to Lugow, the capital city. There, we were shoved into cattle-trains and locked up. There was no toilet, no water, and no heat. Desperately, they dug holes through the bottom of their train compartment to use as toilets, and the poor women and young girls tried to cover themselves with blankets whenever they needed to use these holes.

My father was serving in the war; my mother was alone with my little brother. There was nobody else at home when the Russians came and searched for us all. They searched in every corner of our home and property, in the barn, in every building, and in the yard. With pitchforks they pricked deep into our stacks of hey hoping to find someone hiding there. Finally they saw that no one was hiding there and left.

However, my luck did not last. Uniformed officers caught me in that village where those acquaintances tried to hide me and forced me along with many other Germans from our area into a cattle-train. It was freezing cold. We had a little oven in the overcrowded box car, but no means to heat it. After many days, when we were in the midst of Romania, the train stopped. We were in the first box car, right behind the locomotive. As soon as we stopped, an officer came and opened the door. I jumped quickly down to gather wood, so that we could warm ourselves. All of a sudden, the officer closed the door, and I could not get on to the train any more. I was standing there, shivering. I wore a coat, but I did not have a hat or gloves. I ran as fast as I could alongside the train. Finally the Romanian officer did open that door, and I was back on the train again. At that time I was about seventeen years old. When one is young, one thinks one can do anything.

The train went on until Iase. In Iase, we got off the train to fetch some water and some bread. I was always the first one to get out and fetch things. There was always a whole brigade of guards to watch us while we were fetching that little bit of bread and water. Not a minute was wasted; we were immediately off again onto the train. After crossing the border into Russia in that train, we came to a place where the Russian soldiers went to the West, and we were to go the East. We already met other Germans who were deported there, too. More than two weeks had passed since we had been taken away from home, and it was already February.

We were now in Russia, in the region's capitol city of Kapitalnia. There was a big Russian movie house, like a big ballroom, and all of us were ordered inside. It was crowded, with one thousand and seven hundred people in that room.

The Russians started to divide us according to what they needed us to do. One Russian was standing at the door, and another was counting, "One, two, and three, 'raus' [out]" As soon as he called, "*raus,*" we were ordered to go outside. Many mothers and children, and entire families were ruthlessly separated. They could not even make a case to be together. They also could not exchange their assigned post with anyone else in order to remain together. Those Russians did not have an ounce of mercy or pity. There was a mother who desperately wanted to be with her teenage daughter to protect her. However, the Russians would not have it. That mother could not be with her daughter; she could not protect her. Oh, how she cried!

Next, we were out in the open air. Huge piles of snow were everywhere. It was bitter cold and windy. I had a little suitcase, which I dragged like a sleigh in the deep snow. We had to walk in that deep snow during that ice-cold winter for about five kilometers until we reached a camp in Stalino [now called Donetzk]. That camp had wooden barracks, which were totally infested with bugs. The bugs were everywhere. There were bunks—mere wooden planks, one on top of the other, in three layers. That is where we had to sleep. We were cramped like sardines. There were forty people in one such little barracks, one on top of the other. The place was freezing cold, the bunks were hard, and the bugs fell from the ceilings. To make things worse, we even brought the lice with us, courtesy of the long ride in that awful cattle-train. Oh, there is so much to tell!

In Stalino (now called Donetzk) we were forced to labor in coal mines. The Russians had also brought Germans there from Hungary. Men, women, and their grown young children were all forced to slave in that coal mine. There were seventeen-year-old girls who had to do unspeakably hard labor in those mines. It didn't matter whether they were girls or not, it didn't matter whether they were teenagers or not, they had to do heavy physical labor, which was even extremely hard for men to do. Women had to push heavy wagons of coal. The mine was about eight hundred meters deep. Whenever the belt sprang out of the tract, the Russian guard got very mad. He yelled at us, kicked us, poked at us, and called us all kinds of nasty names. The entrance to the coal mine was only one meter high. So we had to crawl on our hands and feet. We could not even stand up. The air was so dry. It was so hard to breathe; but we had to endure it all day long. I felt so sorry for the young girls and women. I wished I could have helped them.

Those who were not working in the mines had to work with lumber. The wooden logs were ice cold in the winter. We had to make one meter high piles of those wooden logs, one next to the other. The women had to hand those ice cold logs of wood from one to the other before piling them up in stacks. It was very hard labor. Many people did not survive that hell.

Oh, what we Germans had to endure! It's too gruesome to talk about. There were also some Russians among the forced laborers. Even they were not allowed to go home to their families. Russia needed them in the coal mines, and they had to continue their hard labor there in those coal mines under abominable conditions, just like we did. The Russian regime knew that if these Russian laborers would have any contact with the West, which had a better life and a much higher standard of living, they might defect. So they did not allow their own countrymen to leave and go home to their families. They did not want them to cause any unrest or trouble or even talk about the abominable and inhumane conditions of those forced labor camps. So those poor Russians, too, had to remain working hard in those coal mines.

Many people died in that camp in Stalino. There was one older man with us in the brick factory. He was utterly exhausted and could not do that heavy labor any more; but he was pushed and pushed by the Russian guards. One day his starved and severely overworked body just could not take it any more and he died. There were so many who died of sheer exhaustion and starvation, especially the older ones. Now, after the first people died, the question was where to bury them. They had to be buried, but where? The Russians found a place where many German prisoners of war were buried. That was where they made us bury the first German victims of this labor camp. We had to take the bodies to that place, and if we somehow still had a blanket, we would place the blanket over the bodies and put them in the ground. That was their funeral, their reward for their slave labor and starvation in that Russian death camp.

Oh, how the young girls cried! Each of those deaths affected the young girls and women very much, but they had to continue working like slaves, carrying heavy loads day in and day out, regardless of weather conditions. They worked and they cried bitter tears. They did not only suffer from extreme exhaustion but also from starvation. They did not at all resemble the beautiful women they were when they were snitched away from home. Now they all looked like skin and bones, a mere shadow of the women they were when they had left home. Oh, how those poor women, those innocent young girls, had to suffer. One could cry to heaven!

Those of us who survived in Stalino until October 25, 1949, were released that day. The Russians handed us over to the Romanians. We got a train ticket and were transported back home to the Banat in Romania. We all looked like skin and bones; we all had suffered so much. There are no words to describe the torturous conditions that the poor women and young girls had to endure at the Russian Death and Hunger camps. I still can't bear to think of it. It was the darkest time in our lives.

Helmut Graf
Born February 28,1929, in Sackelhausen, Banat, Romania

"It was a catastrophe, an unspeakable heinous crime that cried to heaven, what the Russians,
an entire Russian battalion, had done to those two young German girls."

HELMUT GRAF

Interviewed in July 2009 in Ingolstadt, Germany

Even as a man, there are times when you can hardly bear thinking of all of the tragedy that happened to us, but you can't forget it. The unspeakable brutalities that the Russians did to German women and young girls and other terrifying experiences come back again and again in your mind. They are impossible to forget.

I was born in the Banat in Romania and fled in October 1944 with my parents from Romania to Silesia, Germany [the eastern part of Germany that had become Poland after WWII]. My father was a teacher and was offcred a teaching position in Silesia because at that time there were hardly any teachers left in Germany. Most of them had lost their lives in the war. We were in Silesia for about four months, from October until February 13. That's when my father got a notice to join the military. I was fifteen years old and thus required to join the German *Volkssturm* (Folk Storm, a mandatory youth organization at that time). Our work in the *Volkssturm* was to make sure that the Russians didn't get there so quickly. We dug ditches so that the Russians could not go through so easily with their tanks. Such nonsense! My father said to me, "We have to get away from here." With his help we left Silesia on February 13, 1945. It was just in the nick of time. I heard later that Russian partisans, who were not a military unit, came there two days later and shot everybody.

My dad had to go to Prague to register in the Union, and we fled to lower Austria where my dad's sister and mother lived. Unfortunately, that region also fell into Russian hands.

So we left from there with horse and wagon all the way back to Romania. As soon as we arrived in Romania, they took our horse and wagon away from us and put me into prison for six months.

In prison I was treated abominably. The Russian leader of that prison camp was a scoundrel, a hateful man who delighted in torturing us. I am sorry to use these words, but it is true. After our hard labor during the day, he would constantly wake us up in the middle of the night and force us into the courtyard where he ordered us to do pushups for an endless amount of time. The ground was so dusty. There had not been any rain for a long time, and we were so dirty, dusty, and exhausted, but we had to do those push ups in the middle of the night. We also had no opportunity to wash up; there was not a drop of water for us. The food was unspeakably bad. I was lucky; my mother brought me every week a package of food.

In the prison camp, the Russians came and counted every one of us. I was the youngest. They pointed their guns at us and dragged all of us through the entire city. I was so ashamed. I had been a student there in the *Gymnasium* [German high school]. Now the people saw me being dragged through the streets with the gun pointed at me as if I were a criminal. Later on, that kind of thing became routine. For six long months, we had to endure that humiliation in addition to forced hard labor. We had to take apart canons, which were left behind by the German military. The Russians also took pianos, furniture, everything they could get their hands on from the German homes. Under armed supervision, we had to package all those stolen items and get them ready to be transported to Russia. Those Russians couldn't play piano, but they stole the pianos anyway, together with just about everything that was German. Those Russians stole anything and everything that seemed to have any value. Everything that belonged to Germans was gone. The Russians took it all, and we had to pack it up for them. What terrible times! The Russians looked especially for watches. They were crazy about watches. They wore the stolen German watches all over their bodies. Some covered their whole arms with watches, and they even hung watches around their necks. Most of those

Russians were poor peasants. A watch was an important status symbol for them.

Now let me tell you how the Russians treated the German girls and women. I can hardly bear to talk about it. It makes you sick. In 1945, right at the end of the war, we left for Austria. We were then in a region where there were many fellow Germans. Among them was a woman with two daughters. One was seventeen, and the other was nineteen years old. When the Russians came, they ran after women like crazy. The Austrians nearby snitched on the Germans and told the Russians, "Go there; there are two German girls." An entire battalion of Russians raped those poor two young girls all night long. Yes, an entire battalion of Russians was there, all night long raping those two poor young girls. The girls cried and screamed out loud. I can still hear their screams. When that entire battalion of Russians was done with them, the girls were half dead. It was a catastrophe, an unspeakable heinous crime that cried to heaven, what the Russians, that entire Russian battalion, had done to those two poor German girls. They were two such beautiful girls, especially the younger, seventeen year old one; and we could do nothing, nothing at all. That was in1945, right at the end of the war, when the Russian Red Army marched in. I shall never ever forget that unspeakable tragedy, that abominable, unthinkable, beastly crime!

I will also never forget the date of the thirteenth of February 1945. My father had to go toward the direction of Prague and landed in Dresden. Exactly on that night, the entire city of Dresden was bombed and totally flattened and wiped out. My father was in a train very close to Dresden. They pulled the train out and re-routed it. He wrote us later that what he saw of the entire beautiful city, which was called the Venice of the East, was only fire and flames. The multitude of phosphorus bombs totally destroyed and wiped out that entire beautiful city and everyone in it.

It was my father's great luck that at the very last minute his train was rerouted about three kilometers away from the city of Dresden. That saved his life. He wrote us later, "There were 150,000 people in Dresden when the bombs fell and wiped out the entire city." But today, nobody writes at all about 150,000 people who were killed by the bombs that were thrown over Dresden. They say that about 30,000 or 50,000 died. You have to know that the entire city of Dresden was full of refugees from Silesia and all the other far-Eastern provinces of Germany as well as German refugees from Poland. All had fled to Dresden, away from the far Eastern regions, away from the Russians that were marching in. They all fled westward, trying to escape the Red Army. All those refugees were in Dresden when the deadly bombs fell and totally wiped out the entire city, killing everyone in it, the natives of Dresden as well as that large swarm of refugees. There were 150,000 people or more, all dead, not 30,000 or 50,000 as reported in the media of the victors.

Personal Narratives of Ethnic Germans Deported to the Bărăgan Romania

Magdalena Reb, née Berger
Born February 12, 1929, in Jahrmarkt, Temeswar in Banat,
Romania.

"All the tears of the unfortunate people who were captured and who lost their lives under forced labor in the wasteland of the Bărăgan will be forever burned in the memories of the survivors who had to endure all that agony and who are not able to forget it."

MAGDALENA REB

Interviewed in July 2009 in Ingolstadt, Germany

I had been a teacher in Warjasch for about a year. I was married and had a baby that was exactly five weeks old, and we were happy. It all changed in June 1951. In the middle of the night, from Sunday to Monday, we knew something was not right, but nobody knew what it was. In the middle of the night, I heard boot steps of about five or six persons. I woke my husband up, and we were very quiet. After about half an hour, there was a knock on the window. My husband got up and opened the door. A man was standing in front of him with a gun. He was Romanian, and he demanded the key to the gate of our driveway. We lived in a house with a long driveway that had a gate which was always locked. Then more men, all carrying guns, came into the house and told us that we would be transported to another region within a fifty kilometers diameter, and that we could choose where we wanted to go. However, we knew that was not true. One of the men said, "We brought a horse and a wagon. Take with you whatever you want, whatever you need, and then we will transport you to the railroad station."

Well, I had that little five week old baby who was still sleeping peacefully in his bed. After all, it was three o'clock at night. I did not need to take a bottle of milk since I nursed the child [tears were running down her cheek].

We gathered the most important things. By now it was about two o'clock in the afternoon. I looked outside. The street was totally empty. There was not a single person walking in the street. Then it started. One wagon after another rolled by, all in a long row, all in the direction of the railroad station. We were ordered to get on the wagon. I could not climb up on the wagon with that baby, because the wagon was piled up with furniture, chairs, and stuff. "All right, then you are allowed to walk with the baby carriage alongside the wagon," said one of the men with a gun in his hand. So I walked on the footpath with the baby carriage but always feeling the gun on my back. My husband was walking in the middle of the street, in front of the wagon, while the Romanian police held a gun to his back.

When we arrived at the railroad station, there were many people lying in the dirt and dust on the floor outside the station. They were all Germans. We had to stay at the station for three days. There were about seventy cattle-train box cars waiting for us, and after three days we were forced to get on those cattle-trains. We had no idea where we were going. In our group was a physician of our town, Dr. Reich, and his wife. We stayed together with them in the same box car.

Before the train left, we were locked up like cattle in that cattle-train under the most despicable conditions for about a week. Then, on the 18th of June, the train stopped. Since I had this little baby, I was hoping we would arrive soon, wherever they were going to take us. But what did they do? I had thought that we would be landing at a railroad station, a normal railroad station. But no, that did not happen at all. The train drove until the end of the railroad tracks, which ended in the middle of nowhere. We were in the middle of the fruitless, desert like Bărăgan of Romania. Long before the forced deportation started, they had laid railroad tracks into the Bărăgan wasteland and literally ended those railroad tracks in the middle of nowhere. There was only grass, no tree, no bush, no building. But there were plenty of thistles. Far, far away one could see a sliver of a body of water.

We were ordered to get off the train. Stiff from sitting for days in such cramped quarters in that cattle-train, we finally got out. I was so looking forward to getting out of that miserable cattle-train and into a camp of some sort or to land somewhere

where I could find some shade and nurse my baby. I had hoped that someone would somehow greet us and show us around. Well, none of that happened. Instead, we were all transported with a wagon about ten kilometers from the place where the train tracks ended. There was no camp. There was no house, no shade, nothing—literally nothing but a wasteland in the intense heat of this desert. On purpose, the train tracks were planned and laid so far away from any other place, any community. The tracks ended where no one could be in touch or get together with any civilians who were not transported there into the open grassland.

Well, there we were in the scorching sun and blistering heat and no shelter in sight. We asked the Romanian officer, "Where shall we live?" The armed officer replied, "You build yourself a hut." We asked, "But with what and where?" He replied. "A wagon will come and pick you up and bring you somewhere." My husband said to me, "Look over there. Do you see? There is a thick dust cloud. I bet they will bring us there."

Well, they did not bring us anywhere. A truck that had made that dust cloud came. A Romanian policeman stepped out of the truck and placed a stick in the ground with the number 311. He said, "Here is your place to live." It was a little marker for our family in the middle of absolutely nowhere. Forty meters away, they placed another family. It was evening. Every forty meters, there was a family lying on the ground. The Romanians had deported entire German families into this wasteland on cattle-trains and dumped them there in this intense heat. We heard many bitter cries, swearing, and much more. We were dumbfounded and forlorn and waited for what would happen next, what was to come.

Well, night fell upon us. What to do? We took the wooden wardrobe, the movable closet that we had brought with us from home and placed the closet of Dr. and Mrs. Reich back to back with ours, a few feet apart. So on one side was the closet of Dr. Reich and on the other side was ours. Dr. Reich had been a physician in our town. We put the bedding on top of the closets and covered them with a big cloth. Then we crawled under it, and that's how we survived the first night. Early in the morning, when we crawled out of that makeshift "tent," we looked around to see where on earth we were. Wide and far, there was nothing, no tree, no bush, but further away we saw a little body of water. It was a pond which was covered with reeds. We stood there, wondering what would happen next.

Romanian police and soldiers came and told us that we had to make our own brick out of mud. There would be enough water which we could fetch from the pond. They told us exactly what the size of the bricks was to be and how many for each hut. I still remember it: two thousand seven hundred bricks were to be used for one hut or one dwelling hole, as I called it. That was to be big enough for four people to live in. Now we had to make bricks out of nothing if we wanted to be somewhat protected from the environment and not be under the open sky night and day, come rain or shine.

Well, what were we to do? We had no choice but to busy ourselves to fetch water from the pond and try to make mud bricks. We all tried to do that the best way we could. Each family was to be about fifteen meters apart. The water we fetched from the pond was needed to cement the mud. My husband and I put dirt and water together, smoothed it out, and when it was dry, knocked the excess parts off. Since it was extremely hot (an unbearable, scorching fifty degrees or so Celsius), the mud bricks dried within one day. And that's how we went on, day in and day out.

We also had to do one day a week of what they called "volunteer community service," labor for the schools, the police, and the military buildings far away. I wanted to excuse myself because I had the little baby. Then (please excuse my next words) the illiterate Romanian communist from Bucharest said to me, "Comrade, whoever does not know how to work, him we will teach; and whoever does not want to work, him we will force!" [Big tears were flowing from her cheek as she tells this; there was a long moment of silence before she could speak again]. On our passports we were stamped and identified as "D.O" [*Domizil Obligatore*], which meant "obligatory workers." We were only allowed to move and work in a space no further than fifteen kilometers around in a circle.

It was so hard to endure our harsh conditions with my little baby. Our Dr. Reich said, "Frau Reb, nurse that child. Don't give him anything else to eat, even if he is hungry. Mother's milk is pure and clean. He will have less of a chance to get sick." That was good advice. That was what I did, and that child did not get sick. He grew up like a gypsy in that wasteland.

One day, I brought my little son to a neighbor. She was a ninety-year-old woman. You know, the Romanians had forced entire German families out of their homes: the elderly, children and all. They spared nobody. Well, that ninety-year-old woman promised to take care of my little child for a while. She gave him a little melon to eat, and he had the worst case of diarrhea. It was so bad that Dr. Reich said, "Frau Reb, I don't think he will be able to make it through the night." But luckily, that little child did not die. He was plenty hungry, but from then on he got nothing else but mother's milk.

On the 23rd of August the following happened: On that day, a huge thunderstorm came. That was such a violent thunder storm, unlike we had ever seen. The pond was overflowing. What to do now? We shoveled a hole in the earth, crawled into it, and covered it up with reeds. What happened next? The water came into that hole and everything was under water. I put my little child on a box inside the hole and covered him with some tin. the next day, everything was deep in water, and the bricks which we so laboriously managed to make were now mere mud.

Then we had to start all over again. We needed again 2,700 bricks for each little dwelling. But then they allowed us to get together with another family and build a hut together for two families. Two families could share a brick wall and build their huts on each side of that wall. We lived on the left side of the hut, and on the right side of the shared wall was the Burger family from Warjasch. Mr. Burger was eighty years old, and his wife was seventy. Yes, even at that old age, they were forced from their home and brought by cattle-trains to this God forsaken place. Now homeless, they had to work hard, hunger, and try to survive.

One day, after that heavy rain storm, inspectors came and asked, "How far are you with your brick making?" It was an impossible situation. We could not make 2,700 bricks because the heavy downpour of rain had destroyed everything. I said to one of the Romanians, a Communist from the Bucharest region, "I can no longer go on like that with my little baby." He yelled and called me swear words in Romanian that were so bad I won't even translate them. Then he repeated the warning he gave me earlier: "Comrade, he who does not know how to work, him we will teach, and who does not want to work, him we will force!" Dr. Reich, who heard his curses and threats came to my defense and said, "That woman cannot continue like that; she is on her last rope." The Romanian shouted angrily, "You cannot tell us what to do. You have nothing to say here." Dr. Reich had to be quiet and his wife too.

And so our miserable existence continued. We worked together with the Burger family and managed to build that hut [see photo below]. With my bare hands, I smeared the dirt and water to make walls for our hut and then let it dry. My husband cut reeds to cover our poor dirt hut so that we would have some sort of roof. He had to go into the pond to get those reeds, but he did not have any special clothing. He went into the water with the regular clothing he had. When he came out of the lake, he was full of blood sucking leeches. I was stunned. I don't know how he managed to keep on cutting reeds for three days. It was a good thing that he went in the pond with his shoes and clothes on. Therefore, thank goodness, there were no leeches on his body. Well, leeches or not, now we did have some sort of roof over our hut.

And then the winter came. Christmas in that hole—I really cannot say hut, was green. The wheat and the kernels, which were in the dirt, grew out of the wall. Now we lived in a green hole until it dried up. It was a long and cold winter. And our little child survived it all. He was sleeping between the two of us, my husband and me so that he would be warmer. That was how the first year passed. We had to build that hut before the bitter cold winter came with two meter high snow, just about as high as our hut.

In the spring of 1952, my husband had to work in a pig stall. That was very hard work for him. He was a lawyer and not used to physical labor. The farmers among us had it much easier because they were used to physical labor. They helped him and picked him up when he could no longer stand. At that time, I remained in the hut with our child.

There is one experience I would like to share. There was an old couple, about eighty or ninety years of age. They were taken away from home and transported into the Bărăgan because they were quite wealthy and had owned a lot of land. In other words, they were quite wealthy. What I want to tell you is that those two old people could not build a complete hut for their shelter. They were too weak to do that, but they were held captive in that Bărăgan and not allowed to leave. Many of us helped to make a hole of a hut for them, and in that miserable hole that poor old couple had to exist for five years.

In 1953 our child got violently ill. Dr. Reich said to me, "If the child does not get any change of air, he will not survive. He just has to get out of here." That was when I made a plan to take that little child away from that wasteland and bring him back home into the Banat. Somehow, I got on a train, and bribed every train controller (Schaffner) to not give me away in case the police would come and inspect the train. We were only allowed to move in a fifteen kilometer radius, no more. As mentioned earlier, we Germans all had to wear the letters "D.O." which identified us as forced laborers, and so that we could not run away. However, I simply had to get my little child out of there. I had to take that chance to bring my child out of the Bărăgan. Come what may, I needed to bring my little child home to Jahrmarkt, an area where there was no deportation of Germans into the Bărăgan.

It was in autumn 1953. I got out of the train and left the railroad station holding my child in my arms. It was dark. That was important because I had to make sure that nobody saw me. An aunt of mine saw me, and she took our child and ran quickly in front of me in the direction of home. All at once she asked my little boy, "Why did your daddy not come with you?" The child answered, "Stalin does not let him." He said that really loud. I thought I would fall down, my knees shook so badly. Then I told my aunt to please not ask the boy any questions. I left him there with my aunt. Of course I could not linger; I had to hurry back to that Bărăgan wasteland, hoping that I would not be found missing. It was with a heavy heart that I kissed my little boy good-bye. He was there for half a year, and he got well again. After that, my mother succeeded in bringing him back to us. She did it the same way as I did: very carefully planned, illegally across Siebenbürgen. When he returned, he did not recognize me anymore. At that age, a six-month absence makes a big difference. However, as soon as I put my red scarf on, he said, "Mama." I always wore a red scarf in the summer because of the intense heat.

We were young, and in 1954 a second child, a son, was born in that hut, that hole of our existence. Dr. Reich helped with the birthing. I was so lucky to have him there. He helped me a lot. Then the bitter-cold winter and high snow came. We tried to survive on potatoes and wild clover. It was very poor nourishment, all right. During the winter, I did not have to physically work so hard, and in my pregnant state, that was definitely a good thing. There were a few potatoes to eat, and beans and black bread and a few onions. I tried to nourish the little one with wild clover leaves, which I picked from the grassland. I used those clover leaves as spinach. One tried whatever one could to stay alive.

One day a woman among us said to me, "Mrs. Reb, we got a letter from our daughter." I could not believe my ears. It was inconceivable to us that anyone would ever get a letter there in that wasteland. Nobody ever got any letter. There was no mail anywhere. Heck, there was not even an address. I went to that couple, and I read the letter myself. The letter reached them not directly, but through the region of Siebenbürgen. The letter read, "Dear parents, you don't need to write to me where you are and how it is with you. I saw you on television in the *Weekly News*." Yes, imagine, and that was in the United States of America where they saw us. Wow! Therefore, first, there must have been a spy somewhere at some time to report our inhumane conditions. Secondly, somehow people got word to higher circles about our miserable slave-labor conditions and published it in the press. That is why I am convinced that far too little was done to help us although those gross human rights violations against us were known to the outside world. That was about 1953. By then, I had already been there for three years.

Five years after our deportation, on the third of January in 1956, a date I will never forget, my husband, the children and I were brought to the police station. The Romanian police told us that we were free. Oh, what wonderful news! It was the first good news we got since they brought us to that awful place. Indeed, they told us that a wagon would soon come and we could go home. What joy, what anticipation, what hope we had now!! But we had nothing to put in the wagon except our broken old furniture which we had brought there five years ago. We got into the wagon, and on January 15 we arrived in Jahrmarkt, Romania, where we stayed with my mother. My father was already in Germany. So finally, in 1956 we were given our freedom from five years of slavery in the Bărăgan.

Life in Romania was very difficult. We Germans had already been dispossessed in1945. We had nothing, and it was a time where you could not get ahead even when you were lucky to find a job. That was when we decided to write an application to the Romanian government for permission to leave Romania and move to Germany. Our application was denied. We wrote another one; again it was denied. We wrote yet a third one; again it was denied. That went on and on for many years. With each application, we had to pay a handsome amount of money to the Romanian government, just to leave the country. My mother was already in Germany with my father. My dad had three brothers, and all four of them got together and settled in the Bodensee region in Germany. Even our *Oma* [grandmother] was already in Germany. Only we were still in Romania, starving and fighting for our existence. The Romanian government would not let us go without demanding more and more sums of German money (much higher currency than the Romanian currency at that time) per person. However, the paradox was that we were not allowed to have any foreign currency and could not pay for our release.

One day a man came to my parents in Germany and asked if they would not want us to come to Germany too. Eagerly my parents said, "Yes, of course. How can that be done?" My father's youngest brother, who is now 86 years old and still alive today, flew from Germany to London, England to a certain Dr. Jakober. Here is how it happened that we got to be free:

After staying eight years at home in Romania, we arrived in Singen in Germany in 1964. Twenty five thousand American dollars brought us there. Yes, we got literally out of Romania and into Germany because of twenty-five thousand American dollars, which was demanded for our release. My father and his four brothers were already there. One day, a man came to my mother and said, "Whenever you want to, I have a possibility for you to buy the freedom of your children." He gave her the address of a certain Dr. Jakober in London. That Dr. Jakober was a Jewish person and a former wheat merchant in the German region of Siebenbürgen, Romania. He had a list of Germans who might be able to leave for a price. Right away, my uncle, the youngest brother of my father, flew to London and visited that Dr. Jakober. This Dr. Jakober only said, "Place $ 25,000 in a particular account in Switzerland, and in six months, the children shall be with you." But how should my family communicate that information to us? We were living under a strict communist regime behind the Iron Curtain where leaving was strictly forbidden, and all mail was opened. My mother was very smart and far ahead in her thinking. She wrote us the following coded message: "Dear children! In September of 1963, we bought a house for you in Switzerland. It was extremely expensive. It cost $25,000, but you cannot move in yet because other people are still living in it. It will take six more months." I knew right away, that no house was bought. She was talking about the money that they had to pay to Romania so that we were allowed to leave. It was the price for freedom. That is how we were finally able to be allowed to leave Romania.

Believe it or not, exactly six months later, on the 6th of April 1964, the mail man was standing there at the door of our home with our passports. We were the very first of our group to leave. At that time hardly anyone was able to leave, and over time the Romanian government demanded more and more money per German head in order to leave Romania. Of course some people were also a little envious of us because they had to stay behind. But I had always said to my husband, "We have paid with starvation, sweat and tears all those long five years in the Bărăgan; our leaving is more than paid for."

So in 1964, eight years after being released from our forced deportation and labor in the Bărăgan, my husband, my two sons and I were able to finally leave Romania for good and move to Singen, West Germany. I was so glad that my two boys were healthy. By then one was ten, and the other was 13 years old.

By then they spoke perfect Bavarian. On the passport of the boy who was born in that "hole" of the forced labor camp in Bărăgan, it reads that he was born in the Bărăgan. Our first boy was born at home in the Banat.

See, here is the photo of the little hut for two families that we built out of mud with our own bare hands, without any idea how to do it.

The hut built by the Reb's (Photo taken in 2001)

My husband died in 1995, and I got married again to another Banat Swabian German who was lucky that he did not have to endure the hardship of the forced labor as we did.

My second husband has a nephew who one Sunday in 2001 read in the newspaper that a memorial was being built in Perieti Noi in memory of the Germans who were deported to the Bărăgan to do forced labor. Periti Noi was not far away from the place in Bărăgan where we were transported and slaved for five years. That memorial was financed by former forced laborers,

Banat Swabians who were deported there and are now living in Germany.

My nephew wanted to go there and see that memorial. At that time, a few trees were already growing there. I told him how to get there and just about where we built our dirt hut. I asked him to drive to Fundata, the place where my husband and I had to slave and exist for five years. Lo and behold, he found our hut. It was still standing. You know, all huts, when we built them, looked alike. But he did find our hut. I told him the exact location in relation to the pond. The number was no longer there because later during our stay there, the numbers were taken away. In the picture, he was standing there in the middle of that memorial. It is amazing that that old hut still looks so good after all those decades. As seen from the photograph, we lived on one side of the hut, and the Burger family lived on the other side. We shared the wall. After we left, Macedonian Romanians moved into our hut.

At the inauguration of the memorial, many former Bărăgan deportees who now lived in Germany and built and funded that memorial had come from Germany for the opening ceremony. They looked once more at the site that had been the most painful and miserable part of their lives. They are people whom I don't know. So the nephew of my second husband sent me that picture, which I treasure very much. He wrote on the back of the photograph, "June 2001—Bărăgan, Romania." That memorial is about thirty kilometers from Funtada, where we were forced to labor. As soon as I got the photograph, I had it enlarged. Yes, indeed, it is amazing that the hut, which we built with our bare hands out of mud, still stands.

I know a landsman, Peter Burger, and his daughter. He comes quite often for a visit. He had also been deported and was in a hut next to us in Funtada. He wanted to show his daughter where he was enslaved in the Bărăgan. He drove with his daughter to the Bărăgan. His hut was no longer there, but our hut was still standing there. So he stood for a while in front of our hut. An old Romanian woman came out of the hut, and said, "What do you want? Who are you?" Peter said, "The hut in which you live, I know the woman who built it." Yes, he drove there with his daughter, Gundi, and showed her how we had to live there at a most traumatic and painful time of our lives.

My husband and I said, "Never again do we want to go to that place. Never again do we want to go to Romania. Do you know what I thought, just before this interview with you? I thought, "I hope I don't start crying or swearing when I tell you what happened to us." I was 21 years old when they took me away from my home and brought me to that God-forsaken place to build it up with bare hands. Never, never again do I want to go there.

Many decades have come and gone. But all the tears of the unfortunate people who were captured and who lost their lives under forced labor in the wasteland of the Bărăgan will be forever burned in the memories of us survivors who had to endure all that agony and who are not able to forget it. Honestly, I tell you, I need another sixty years to forget the trauma of those miserable years. But even then, I think I will still not be able to forget that horrible nightmare. I don't really talk about it; it is too difficult and too hard to understand. I want to forget it. I am telling you, there are things that happened I would rather forget but can't.

Anna Dewald, née Kori
Born July 8, 1934, in Morawitza, Banat, Romania

"When we were finally set free from five hard years of forced labor in the Bărăgan, we were
shocked to find that our home was occupied by Romanians."

ANNA DEWALD

Interviewed in July 2009 in Ingolstadt, Germany

In June of 1951, those Germans and others who lived near the border of Yugoslavia and Romania were deported by force in cattle-trains to the Bărăgan, the Romanian desert-like region. After five years of forced labor, most of them were allowed to return home to the Banat.

Even before the deportations of German people to the Bărăgan started, Germans in Romania were not allowed to freely travel beyond certain limits imposed by the Romanian government, which highly influenced by the Soviet Union, had turned Communist.

I was very young, 17 years old, and in trade school in Temeswar. My older brother was there too. One day my father said we should come home to Morawitza from school. We carried with us only the train ticket with our passports. Those Germans who were home had their passports taken away from them to restrict the distance of their movements. At that time Germans in Romania were only allowed to go a certain distance and no more. Well, when my brother and I boarded the train in Temeswar to go home to Morawitza, and we did have our passports.

Now we were in our village in Morawitza, but we did not know that some people had snitched and given our name to the Romanian authorities. When we returned to school in Temeswar, I was told to come to the principal's office. "Why?" I asked. "I didn't do anything." As soon as I entered the principal's office, they told me, "You are under arrest." I was arrested because my brother and I rode thirty kilometers further in the train than we were allowed to. While I was being arrested, I said, "I have a brother; please, I have a brother. Where is my brother?" They answered, "We have him already." Then they took me away. I thought they would take me to see my brother. But unfortunately, that was not going to happen. I was not to see him. They locked me up in a cellar in Temeswar with eleven other people but not with my brother. After they brought us out of the cellar, they transported us to Bucharest. There they put us into a prison, my brother separate from me; all men and women were separated. They convicted my brother, who was one year older than I. However, because I was not yet eighteen years old, I was there only one month for the hearing. Then they had to let me go because they could not convict me. I was too young.

A policeman came to my prison and said, "Let's go." But where was I to go? He took me through the capital city, Bucharest. Then he said, "I know where I shall bring you." Well, he brought me to the police station. From there he brought me to Calarasi. There I spent one night. There were two rooms, and the policeman was with me in one of those rooms. I was seventeen years old and it was night. I was afraid. But nothing happened; nobody came. No harm was done to me. Early in the morning I asked, "What now?" The policeman said, "At two o'clock we will take the train." And so we did. When we got off the train, he said, "To whom do you belong? Who are you? Are you a Kori?" Kori was my maiden name. "Yes," I said, "I am a Kori." He spoke a little German and said in German, "Now we will go to my house. Your parents don't live far away from us, and then you will disappear 'into the blue,' and I want you to know that I have absolutely no idea where 'the blue' is, no idea at all." He was an older man, a kind and good-natured man. He closed an eye and let me go "into the blue." He let me go home. And that is how I got home. When I opened the door, my mother asked, "Where is your brother?" Well, I didn't know where he was. We did not know for a long time where he was until a man who had also been imprisoned came and told us. We were imprisoned because after school we went thirty kilometers further in the train than we were allowed to. The Romanians did that.

There was a time when the Yugoslavians and the Romanians at the border did not get along. Sometimes in history they were friends and allies, while at other times they were enemies. At that time in history, they were enemies. The Romanians took all families who were born on the border of Yugoslavia and Romania and transported them to the wasteland, the desert called the Bărăgan, in Romania. At that time they transported not only Germans but also those Serbian families whom they suspected to be followers of Tito. That forced transportation of people into the Romanian Bărăgan went on from 1951 until 1956. It was a forced deportation, and nobody was allowed to leave. In our passports we all had the stamp "D.O.," meaning forced laborers, so that we could not escape. If we would try, we would be easily identified and severely punished.

During the five years that we were captured there as forced laborers, we had to work very hard in construction. The Romanian government wanted us Germans to build up that barren land in the Bărăgan. Of course we were not allowed to leave the Bărăgan. Our situation there was so bad that in spite of the danger of being caught, my father risked his life so that our family could escape our miserable existence there and go back home.

Somehow we made it home and my brother and I went back to school. However, after a short while we were arrested and transported again to the Bărăgan where we had to labor for five long years. During our five years of forced labor in that deserted wasteland of the Bărăgan, we German laborers managed to build eighteen villages for Romania, practically out of nothing, with our bare hands and bitter tears.

When we were finally set free from five hard years of forced labor and transported back home to the Banat, we were shocked to find that our home was occupied by Romanians. We had to start all over again.

Elisabeth Mann, née Lenhardt
Born December 16, 1917, in Knees, Banat, Romania

"After five bitter hard years, we Banat Germans had built eighteen villages in the barren grassland of the Bărăgan, all for the Romanians whose forced laborers we were. It cost us not only five years of our stolen lives but much hunger, blood, sweat and tears."

ELISABETH MANN

Interviewed in July 2007 in Ingolstadt, Germany

On a hot day in June 1951, Romanian officials took me away from my home and deported me with many other Germans to the Bărăgan grassland of Romania in a cattle-train. We had to spend several miserable weeks in that cattle-train under conditions too gross to talk about. Then the train stopped. The Romanian officers opened the train doors and let us out. We were in the middle of nowhere. Indeed, the train tracks had literally ended in the middle of nowhere. There was not a tree, not a house, not a building in sight. There was no place to hide from the hot summer's scorching sun. There was no housing for us, no roof over our heads, nothing.

We were left there in this grassland without any shelter. Quickly we had to do whatever we could to protect ourselves from the harsh environment. So we had to start building some sort of shelter with our bare hands out of whatever we could find in that barren land. These very primitive make-shift shelters were our protection from the scorching heat of the summer and the storms, snow and ice of the ice-cold winters. Not allowed to leave, we were literally prisoners, forced to do hard physical labor, day in and day out. Overworked, hungry and starving, and unprotected from the severe climate, many of us died.

We were brought there to build up that barren grassland out of nothing. There, in the middle of absolutely nowhere, we German force laborers had to construct buildings under the free sky. Whoever was too weak to work hard was simply locked up.

I was slaving away there for five long years that seemed to never end. One year there was such incredible heat in the summer, and there was no water. Oh, how we suffered and yearned for a drop of water! And one year in the winter, it snowed so much that we could not look out of the little primitive dirt hut we had built for our protection from the severe cold. It was not really much of a protection.

After five bitter, hard years, we Banat Germans had managed to build not only buildings but eighteen villages in that barren grassland of the Bărăgan, all for the Romanians whose forced laborers we were. It cost us not only five years of our stolen lives but much hunger, blood, sweat and tears, and most painful of all, the lives of many of our loved ones. Our destiny was a painful one, and it still lingers on in memory and sleepless nights.

Franziska Graf, née Krems
Born December 18, 1933, in Schag, Banat, Romania

"Freedom is not that everyone can do what he wants, but that he is not forced to do that which he does not want to do."

LIFE OF ETHNIC GERMANS IN COMMUNIST ROMANIA

FRANZISKA GRAF

Interviewed in July 2009 in Ingolstadt, Germany

We lived in the Banat, the German region of Romania. Under the Russian-style communist rule, there was no freedom in Romania. Everybody in Romania was under constant observation. There was absolutely no freedom of speech or conduct. The Secret Police were always watching us. They were everywhere. And every one of us was ordered to observe our neighbors, our co-workers, even our own family members. We were to report to the Romanian authorities whenever we saw or heard anything that was not allowed. We had to be always careful what we said or did. We could not trust anyone. That was such a terrible thing: being constantly watched, having to be constantly careful, not being able to speak without fear, and not being able to trust anyone. You know, whenever someone lives in a jungle, instinct teaches them to protect themselves from danger. That was exactly what we had to do. We had to sharpen our instincts in that dangerous jungle in order to survive. Our instincts helped us survive under the oppressive communist regime. We had a feeling that whenever there was a meeting, there were most likely two or three spies among us, like the

Secret Police, who were there to listen to every word we said and report back to government officials. We were always afraid to speak our minds, always afraid of the powerful and watchful eyes of the Secret Police.

Now we are here in the West, in Germany, and we can say and do what we please. We are free to speak whatever is on our minds. Those people who have never experienced what it is like when one has to be always very careful and trust absolutely nobody for fear of being watched, listened to, misinterpreted or reported, they do not fully appreciate or know what freedom really means. Here in the West, in Germany, you can do what you want; no one forces you to do what you do not want to do. I have always said,

"Freiheit ist nicht
Dass jeder das tun kann was er will,
Sondern dass er nicht das tun muss
Was er nicht will."

Freedom is not
That everyone can do what he wants to do
But that he is not forced to do that
What he does not want to do.

Yes, that is freedom!

Long after the war was over, German people in Romania were sold like slaves. The dictator, Ceausescu, said once in his most intimate friendship circle that his "best export is the Germans" because officially, Germany paid Romania eight thousand DM for every German person who left Romania. Unofficially they paid much more. That was still when Helmut Schmidt was Chancellor of Germany. That payment was the only way that the Romanian government would allow up to eleven thousand of us Germans in Romania to leave Romania per year. Over a period of twenty years, we tried tirelessly, again and again, to leave Romania. Finally, after twenty long years, we were able to get out. It was thanks to the official German government, which paid 8,000 DM for each of our family members, that we were able to finally leave Romania. For many people, that official process took too long, and they privately found some way to pay the Romanian government the money to leave the country. As time went on, the Romanian dictator Ceausescu and his Secret Police began to ask for additional money from the German people. He did not want us to leave Romania that easily, without squeezing as much money out of us as possible. Yes, one could indeed say that German people in Romania were sold and were in the Romanian dictator Ceausescu's own words, his "best exports."

At that time, Romanian citizens, including all of us, were not allowed to have any foreign currency, no foreign money, not even a single dollar or a single German Mark. Any foreign currency would have been taken away. In addition, I would have needed to report to the Romanian authorities and explain how, where and from whom I got that money .The paradox was that even though we were not allowed to have any foreign currency at all, the only way for us to get out of the country was to pay for our freedom in a foreign Western currency. Let me repeat, in order to buy our path out of Romania, the Romanian government demanded foreign Western currency; however, they made it unlawful for us to have any foreign currency. That was the paradox.

How were we finally able to leave Romania? There was a so-called "gardener" in the district of Temeswar who became famous with the Germans eager to leave Romania. He was not really a gardener, but a sort of middle man who, after receiving a handsome sum of money from Germans, would make arrangements for them to leave Romania. So our relatives had to come from Germany, go to that so called "gardener" and give him their hard earned German Marks because if that money would have gotten into our hands, it would have been a reason to put us in jail. As time went on, the services of that "gardener" became more and more popular, and he became increasingly more greedy and sophisticated in asking for more and more money. For example, he had many catalogues from the West, and the merchandise in those catalogues whet his appetite. So in addition to the money demands from the German government, he also asked individuals who wanted to leave Romania for money in order to purchase expensive items in those catalogues. He simply said that he needed those items to get us out of Romania. For example, he wanted an especially expensive fishing rod which cost 800.00 DM, or some other really expensive luxury items. Starting from that "gardener" up to high government officials, there were many Romanians who wanted something and asked for it. However, there was absolutely no receipt or proof that they got the money. Whenever there was a denial that the money or goods were given, the relatives from West Germany needed to again bring money and items that were requested in order for their loved ones to be released. Yes, that is what was going on in Romania and the Romanian government at that time.

As time went on, the official price for Germans to get out of Romania went up to 20,000 DM per person. But again, that was only the official price. Many people came from West Germany with 60,000 to 80,000 DM per person to desperately buy the freedom of their loved ones. There were families who had to pay up to 100,000 DM to buy their freedom, to be able to leave Romania. And how were the Germans able to accumulate all that money? They went to work in households, did all kinds of hard labor anywhere they could, seven days a week. They saved every penny for many years in order to give their hard earned money over to the Romanian government to buy their freedom.

That is why it took such a long, long time for us to be able to leave the country. The permission for us to leave Romania was dragged out so extremely long, until at last sufficient ransom to satisfy the greedy Romanian government and other Romanians was paid. After twenty long years of endless requests, we were, at last, allowed to leave Romania in 1982. We went to Austria where I had relatives. My mother was eighty one years old at that time

In Germany we visited my cousins, the children of my favorite uncle, after he died. That favorite uncle of mine was forced to go to war when the war started. From the first day until the end of the war, he was always at the front. He was able to come home only once a year and only for a very short time. And then when he returned next year, another baby of his was born. I liked that uncle very much, and I always liked to listen to him. He had a gift of speech. He told us about the horrors of war, what he had experienced and what hell it was at the front. Later, he lived near Dachau in Bavaria, Germany. He had two children.

I shared with my two cousins my vivid and fond memories of their father. They were surprised to hear my account of what he had told us about his experiences in the war. They said, "Our father never told us anything about the war, not a single word, no matter how much we asked him." They also told me that he never celebrated his birthday on the day he was born. However, he did celebrate it on a particular day in February. And here is the reason why: when he was fighting at the front somewhere near Stalingrad, the German soldiers had by then no longer any proper protective warm clothing for that brutally cold winter in Russia. The German soldiers were not prepared for that bitter cold; they had to sleep outside in Russia's deep freeze without a roof over their heads. One morning, out of the hundreds or thousands of the German soldiers, only very few woke up after a bitter cold night. With the exception of a few, they all froze to death. When my uncle woke up that morning and found all the stiff bodies of his friends and buddies who froze to death over-night, he considered that day his second birth. From then on, he celebrated his birthday not on the original day of his birth but on that particular day in February when he woke up alive while almost all of his comrades froze to death over-night. Every year, on that particular day in February, one could not talk with him. On that day he would not utter a word. Hc was so much living in his memory of all his friends and buddies whom he had lost that horrible night near Stalingrad. He would never talk about it either. It must have been so immensely traumatic for him, such a painful, living nightmare.

YUGOSLAVIA

Brief History of Yugoslavia and Ethnic Germans in Yugoslavia

At the end of World War I, the Habsburg ruled Austro-Hungarian Empire collapsed. The South Slav regions of the Austro-Hungarian Empire joined with Serbs and Montenegro and founded the sovereign Kingdom of the Serbs, Croats and Slovenes in 1921. Immediately after the adoption of the new constitution, serious political problems developed. Trying to get rid of national and ethnic rivalries, King Alexander renamed the Kingdom of the Serbs, Croats and Slovenes in 1928. The new name was Yugoslavia. For the first time in their history, all the South Slavs, except the Bulgarians, were united under a single government of self-determination in the newly named Yugoslavia.

Yugoslavia and World War II

At the beginning of World War II, a coup broke out in Yugoslavia which made Adolf Hitler very angry. On April 6, the German air force attacked Belgrade, the capital of Yugoslavia, and on April 17, the Yugoslav Army surrendered to the Germans. The German minority in Yugoslavia was granted preferential treatment over the ethnic Yugoslav people. The independent state of Croatia, which was created 1941-1945 within the Nazi occupied Yugoslavia, was home to approximately 200,000 ethnic Germans (Wildmann et.al. 1998). Croatia remained allied with the Third Reich until the last weeks of the war (Schmider, 2002). The ethnic German minority in the Banat region of Yugoslavia was about twenty percent of the population (Annabring, 1955).

In 1941, a resistance movement developed under the direction of the Croat illegal Communist Party. This partisan party was lead by Josip Broz, who was nicknamed Tito. While Germany was crumbling, Tito's communist political and military rule was established in 1944. On November 29, 1946 Yugoslavia was proclaimed a federal peoples' republic. On January 31, a new constitution modeled after Soviet Communism was adopted and a one party communist dictatorship was established. Following the example of the Soviet Union, the communist Yugoslavian government confiscated large estates, nationalized industry, banking, and transportation (Pridonoff, 1955; Hoffman and Neil, 1962).

Germans in Yugoslavia

Ethnic Germans lived in what is known as Yugoslavia when that area was part of the Kingdom of Hungary. At the invitation of the Hungarian monarchy, German settlements began in the 12th century. After Maria Theresia of Austria became Queen of Hungary in 1740, the recruitment of German settlers was intensified. Between 1740 and 1790, more than 100,000 Germans immigrated to the Kingdom of Hungary (Annabring, 1955). The Germans were permitted to retain their German language, schools, culture and religion (predominantly Roman Catholic). They developed fruitful farmland, drained marshes near the Danube and Theiss rivers, built canals, roads and cities. They transformed the grassland in Batschka and the Banat (now Vojvodina) into a fruitful agricultural wheat chamber (Meyer, 2005). The collective term to describe the German-speaking population who lived in the former Kingdom of Hungary is *Donau Schwaben* [Danube Swabians] because many of them settled along the Danube river valley. According to the 1931 census (asking individuals which mother tongue they spoke and which religion they practiced), there lived 499,969 ethnic Germans in Yugoslavia (Schieder, 2004, p.4E).

The Treatment of Germans

During the final months of World War II and the years that followed, the treatment of civilian ethnic Germans in Yugoslavia may be regarded as a classic case of "ethnic cleansing" on a grand scale (Barwich, Binder, et. al, 1992). At the end of the war, more than 200, 000 Yugoslav German civilians (mainly women, children and the elderly) had remained in Yugoslavia. More than 63,635 of them perished under the communist rule (Wildmann, 2001).

After the founding of a second Yugoslavia, headed by Marshal Josip Broz Tito, Yugoslavia was under communist rule. One of the first orders of Tito's business was the decree on November 21, 1944 that all Yugoslavian Germans were "enemies of the people" (Scherer, et. al., 1999, p.131). Consequently, a campaign to cleanse the country of ethnic Germans began. Ethnic Germans in Yugoslavia were completely stripped of all civic rights. The now communist Yugoslavian government confiscated all property of the country's ethnic Germans, without compensation, regardless of their citizenship or whether they have lived there for hundreds of years.

Houses were plundered, women were raped. Meyer (2005) reports the following: On November 23, 1944, the Krajiska partisan group in Hodschag (Vojvodina) forced 181 elderly German men and two women to get undressed and force marched them to a ditch on a street to Karavukova where they were shot to death. In the milk hall of Kikinda, 136 Germans were beaten before their noses, tongues, ears, and eyes, and men's penises were cut off, and they all bled to death. In a field near Brestowitz, Tito's partisans buried Germans up to their neck, and then cut their heads off as if they were cabbage. In Homolitz, the partisan Sremska-Brigade massacred 173 ethnic Germans, while in Semlin, near Belgrad, 241 German civilians were executed. In Pancevo, partisans massacred 222 German women and men, and the rest of the 5,000 Germans in that town were expelled; 1,200 brought to forced labor camps (Meyer 2005, p. 101).

Very old and very young ethnic Germans were imprisoned in Yugoslavian death and hunger camps in Gakovo, Rudolfsgnad, Krusevlje, Molin, Backi Jarak, Valpovo, Krndija, and Sremska Mitrovica (Sunic,1995). The ethnic Germans who were able to work were dispersed throughout the countryside and used as slave laborers. Out of the 350,000 ethnic Germans in the Vojvodina, only 32,000 remained according to the census of 1958 (Sunic, 1995). Reconstruction of the death camps revealed that out of the 170,000 ethnic Germans that were interned between 1944 and1948, more than 50,000 died of severe mistreatment. Many died as a result of exhaustion, severe malnutrition, or untreated disease. Very young children (less than three years of age) and very old people were interned and starved to death (Sunic, 1995).

The documents of the Danube Swabian Cultural Office, which contain the names of most victims and some of their perpetrators, reveal that between the autumn of 1944 and spring 1945, a total of 9,500 ethnic Germans were killed in Yugoslavia (Meyer, 2005, p.102).

Much of the credit of the economic miracle of Tito's Yugoslavia must go to the tens of thousands of German forced laborers who helped greatly to build up the impoverished country. In addition, to all the confiscated factories, businesses, and shops of ethnic Germans, confiscated real estate and farmland of Yugoslavia's ethnic Germans amounted to about one million acres. All that German property became state owned Yugoslavian property of about twelve billion US dollars in 2012, taking inflation into account (Sunic, 2002).

Personal Narrative of an Ethnic German Deported from Yugoslavia to Russia

Magdalena Kubrikov, née Volkner
Born May 29, 1926, in Topola, Banat, Yugoslavia

"A fourteen year old Russian boy believed that all Germans had horns. That is what he had been taught in school. One day he came and touched my head. He searched every inch of my head to feel my 'horns.' I wore a scarf. He took my scarf off and wanted to see if any horns were growing on my head. He carefully felt every part of my entire head again and said, 'What? Don't you have horns? We learned in school that all Germans have horns. Are you sure you are German?'"

MAGDALENA KUBRIKOV

Interviewed in July 2009 in Ingolstadt, Germany

I was born in 1926 and lived in the predominantly ethnic German-populated Banat region of Yugoslavia. At that time, Germany seemed far away to us Germans who lived in Yugoslavia. There was no communication technology, no telephone, no television, and certainly no internet like we have now. So, geographical distance was much greater. I remember my Papa delivering pigs to Germany before the war. As a child I remember saying, "Papa, may I put a ribbon on each pig with a piece of paper that reads 'Bogner' (our family name) with our address on it, so that the people in Germany know that it comes from our family?" I was only a child but I thought when our pigs got to Germany, our address had to go with them because the pigs were raised on our farm in Yugoslavia. I only wanted to show the people in Germany that we were Germans too. Those were my ideas as a child. We were Germans living in a neighboring country, but we retained our German language, our culture, our customs, our traditional clothing, and our folksongs. And yes, we did like to sing.

In late October 1944, we heard through the grapevine that the Russians would be coming to look for us Germans and take away our homes. We had a beautiful farm. We also knew that the Russians liked to drink, search for German girls and women and rape them. Therefore, one night we carried our entire supply of schnapps and dumped it on a manure pile, so that when the Russians would come, they would not get drunk on our liquor and do us any harm. My father said, "They shall not get drunk and harm my daughter." I was the only child. Our town was like a ghost town then. You saw no one on the streets, even during the day. Everyone was afraid to get out of the house.

We had some jewelry. My Dad put it in a tin can and hid it in the barn with the horse carriages. My father took me up high in the barn where the pigeons were, and we dropped the jewelry down the barn's chimney. Then my Dad said to me, "Remember, when we want to get the jewelry back, we have to make a hole in the floor of the barn." But we never got to do that, never got to see that jewelry ever again.

One night, a Serb came to our home (my mother spoke Serbian), and he said to my mother, "The children will be taken away to Russia." I remember saying, "Never!" He said, "Yes, they will come and take you away." My mother took his warning to heart. What could she do? She baked bread for me that night. I had a little tin box, and in that little tin box she put some jewelry. That was the jewelry that my father had brought for me when he was in Budapest at a congress in 1938. When he returned from Budapest, he had brought me a ruby ring, matching earrings, and a cross with a ruby in the middle. My mother said to me, "I will put this jewelry inside the bread, so that no one suspects it, and when you are in need, sell it." And indeed, later I was in great need in Russia's Death and Labor Camp. I sold my precious jewelry one piece after another for food, and that was how I was able to eat a little and not starve to death [she cried].

It was the second day of Christmas (December 26), when we were ordered to report early the next morning at five o'clock to the City Hall or we would be shot. It was repeated that whoever would not show up at the City Hall the next morning would be shot. Those were the orders. There were girls and women from eighteen to thirty years of age, all German, who were taken away from their homes, gathered in a big hall, and were deported to Russia for forced labor. That is what happened to me.

After they gathered all of us Germans together in the City Hall, we had to walk twenty—two kilometers. We spent the night in Kikiwa in a milk hall. Then we were brought to a camp near the Romanian border, the village of Nageldorf. There they brought more young German girls into the camp. Among them was a woman whom they had brought to that milk hall two days before us. Two young girls came and said to her, "Last night your mother died." Oh, Jesus, that woman had three children, and she frantically began to run out of that camp. However, the armed Serbs who were standing guard did not let her out. She went to the barbed wire fence and wept and begged, "Please, please let me out; I have three little children. My mother died last night, and there is no one to take care of my little kids." The guards would not let her go. She fell on her knees and begged again, "Please, please, I beg of you, please let me out!" Her desperate pleas could have moved a stone but not the Serbs. What did those Serbs do? They shot that poor woman in cold blood. Yes, they shot her right there. That was the first time I saw someone die, the first time I saw a body, the first time I saw someone fall down and die. I was only eighteen years old. I had never before seen that in my life.

Then the Serbs forced us into a cattle-train which deported us to Russia. All of us cried bitter tears. It was such a long, long way from home, and the conditions in the cattle-train were so unbelievably bad. It was not even fit for cattle. When we crossed the border into Russia, a Russian officer came and said, "You don't need to cry. The Yugoslavs wanted to kill all you Germans (he motioned with his hand to his neck, indicating that they wanted to cut our heads off). We saved you so that you can work for us." We thought that could not possibly be true; but it was indeed true.

The next day, we were again pushed into cattle-trains. There was no straw on the floors of those wagons, nothing, just the bare floor. We only had what we were wearing. When we were taken away from home, we were told that we would be working for two weeks on our own land, but those were lies, nothing but lies. We had to endure the indignities of that cattle-train for more than three weeks. On the Polish border, we had to change trains because the train tracks in Poland were wider than those in Yugoslavia. There were about fifty to sixty women packed tightly in one cattle-train compartment. The doors were only opened every two to three days. The situation was like this: whenever the door was opened, the box of our human waste was emptied. However, whenever we had to urinate, we had to do it as close to the door as possible. There, by the door, the urine was dripping down and froze. So whenever the locked door was opened from the outside, we had to walk over that frozen urine. It was a most bitter cold winter. It is a miracle we survived those horrible weeks in that miserable cattle-train without food, drink, seats, bed, toilet, or any basic necessities to survive. Quite a few did not survive that awful train ride. They died on the way.

Then we arrived at a labor camp in Russia. One Serb, who at home had delivered sand to our *Gymnasium* [German high school] had been in Russia during the First World War and spoke Russian. Well, that man snitched on us to the Russians. He told them who and how many of us went to high school because those who went to high School, or those who had any higher education were considered to be, in the eyes of the Russian communists, children of capitalists. Well, in our group I guess I was one of them, and so was an engineer, the wife of a protestant minister, two students and three *Abiturienten* [high school seniors preparing for the National Exam]. One of our teachers who had taught in our *Gymnasium* was with us too. In addition, there were some grade school teachers. All of us "capitalists" were given especially hard physical labor. We had to go to crack and crush stones for making bricks. That was even harder physical labor than the coal mining that the others had to do. And we were always afraid, always in fear. Punishment was lurking at every corner.

There was nothing in that camp to allow us to live even half way decently, to even clean ourselves after the hard day's dirty work. Everybody got a piece of rough soap and two liters of water. Since there was a shortage of water, three or four of us washed our faces together. Only if there was a little water left did we wash the rest of our bodies. Later, some men in our group put some bricks together in such a way that we could have some sort of a way to heat the water or snow in the winter. When we got back late at night from work, we gathered some snow, and after gathering a good amount, warmed it up over the brick. That is how we were able to have some water. But we had no matches, and it took a long time to create heat and get the bricks warm.

We were a total of 604 German forced laborers in that labor camp. More than one hundred died during the very first year. That's how unspeakably inhumane the conditions were. Let us not forget that those who died were young people because the German women they deported were between the ages of eighteen and thirty—two. It was so bitter cold, minus thirty degrees Centigrade, and the earth was frozen stiff. That was why whenever our people died, the Russians just scratched the surface of the earth a little bit and threw the bodies right there on the ground, no grave, nothing. In the spring, they had to dig deeper and put all the bodies under the ground, that is if the foxes and wild animals had not already ripped the bodies apart. Oh, it was horrible, too terrible for words to describe. Those beautiful young German girls and women, all dead lying there in the open, all winter long. Often their flesh was torn apart by wild animals, and we could do nothing about it. We had absolutely no rights, no rights at all. Oh, I have no words to describe those unbelievably abominable inhumane conditions. It was truly a living nightmare, which too often re-occurs in my dreams.

The Russians always said that we were uncultured, that we had no culture. In their eyes we were all Nazis. I rolled the "r" when I spoke. So one Russian guard always called me a Jew and bullied me to no end. One day I could not stand it any more and said, "If I were Jewish, I would not be here." That he did finally understand. The situation was such that our Russian guards always tried to find something about every single German person so that they could bully us, and they did plenty of bullying. Yes, indeed, there was no end to their bullying. Oh, how they bullied us! They called us uneducated and uncivilized.

There was a fourteen-year-old Russian boy who believed that all Germans had horns. That is what he had learned in school. One day he came and touched my head. He searched every inch of my head to feel my "horns." I wore a scarf. He took my scarf off and wanted to see if any horns were growing on my head. He carefully felt every part of my entire head again and said, "What, don't you have horns?" I stared at him in total disbelief. Then he said," We learned in school that all Germans have horns." Now he had seen firsthand that under my scarf, there were no horns growing on my head. Yes, imagine that. The Russians taught children in school that we Germans were wild beasts with horns. Unbelievable!

After we were there for a month, more Germans were brought in. They were deported from their homes in Hungary. These Hungarian Germans had it especially hard because they spoke German and Hungarian, neither a Slavic language. Therefore, they had a much harder time understanding Russian, a totally different Slavic language. We Germans from Yugoslavia were lucky as compared to the Germans from Hungary because we could learn Russian relatively fast. That is because the Yugoslavian language is closer to the Russian Slavic language but totally different from Hungarian. The Russian officers could not understand the Hungarians, and vice versa. They always screamed, "You don't understand because you don't want to!" The officers would yell and beat them. But we learned quickly what was going on and took the Hungarian Germans under our wings. We translated for them and taught them a little Russian until they learned the most important words and phrases which they needed to know in our everyday miserable existence.

There was no end to the hard work we were all forced to do. Every day we had to finish a certain amount of work. Whenever we were not able to finish all the work we were ordered to do, we had to work not eight, but ten or twelve hours continuously without a drop of water, without a piece of bread, without a break. That was so miserable one cannot imagine it. We had practically nothing to eat or drink. In the morning we would get 700 grams of bread and three times a day some sauerkraut floating in the water that was supposed to be soup. We divided those 700 grams of bread into three parts. We saved some crumbs, so we would have something to eat when we came back after the day's long labor. Sometimes, when we came back at night, our crumbs were no longer there. Starving comrades were so desperate, they had eaten our crumbs. So all day we got nothing to eat except that little bit in the morning before going to work. Somehow, we kept going. I could have easily died of starvation and hard labor. I really don't know where those of us who survived got the strength to do that hard labor with hardly any food to fuel our severely overworked bodies.

Yes, we starved, we froze, and we slaved for five long nightmarish years during which many died. Whenever someone died, my friend, Ms. Burg, and I tried to remember their names. Just in case someone was able to go back home, we wanted to let their relatives know what happened. That was why we kept trying to recite and remember the names of the dead.

As a result of working so brutally hard in the coal mines, my friend got a hernia. However, she did not get an operation because she was German, and Germans did not receive any operations, not even if their lives depended on it. However, the officer gave her a break and put her in the kitchen to work. It was lighter than her usual work in the coal mine and was a little help for her and for me also. We were always hungry, always starved. We were malnourished to the brink. So many people died of starvation. When my friend went to work in the kitchen, she managed to smuggle some crumbs of bread for her and me. Even if it was only a few tiny crumbs of bread, not even a handful, it kept us alive. She was such a poor girl; she had nothing. By selling my jewelry, I was able to help her a little bit, and me too. Little did my father know that his present from Budapest would keep me and my friend alive and save us from starvation.

When I worked in the coal mine, the tunnel was so low that we had to work on our knees. That was why I got severe medical condition where my knees got swollen as big as bowling balls and hurt very much. We had to wear a locksmith suit. That suit was stiff and did not allow us to really kneel. Our fake doctor, a Russian who never was a physician, was sent to the coal mine to work there as a physician. Well, that fake doctor simply took the water out of my knee with a big needle, and next morning I had to go back to the mine and work again on my knees. My knee is full of scars (which I still have), and many people's knees got badly infected and were full of pus. I had to have three to four operations on my knee after I was released from Russia and was in Germany.

On September 8, 1947, I had an accident. I was working in the mine when the fragile ceiling collapsed, and I was totally covered with coal stones. My right foot was stuck against my chest because the coal pit was only 90 centimeters high. I wanted to crawl out, but my right foot was stuck under my chest, my left foot was straight, and the stones kept falling on top of me. I screamed and screamed as loud as I could. Our German men had already run out of the mine. An old Russian man, who had been working in coal mines for thirty two-years, heard me, and he and another Russian who was with him dragged me out of the mine. That old kind man carried me over his shoulders all the way to the camp. There were no carriages in that camp in Russia. I was not able to move. I had to lie for three months on the straw covered floor. After three months I could walk with the help of crutches. Because I had no broken bones, only a severely squeezed chest, I had to go back to work in the coal mines. It is because of that accident that I was never able to have children. I had severe inner injuries which pressed at my uterus. Years later, after I came out of Russia, I had many lower abdomen operations. The doctor said to me, "It is a wonder that you are alive."

While working in the coal mines, I got pneumonia twice. Then I finally got an easier job and did not have to work in the coal mine any more. Once I worked as a nurse. In 1948, a baby was born in the camp. I had absolutely no idea what to do, but I had the job of a nurse. So I said to the pregnant woman, "You just have to wait until Katy comes out of the coal mine. She knows what to do." I was clueless, and I had never seen a baby being born. I thought the woman would die. I thought her uterus was coming out. Thank goodness Katy finally came. She was an older woman, and she cut the umbilical cord. The next day our officer came. He laughed and said, "Jena, I did not know that you had no idea how to help bring a baby into the world." How should I have known? I was only eighteen years old.

The child that was born was a boy. He was our David. His illiterate mother was a maid, and she got that baby from a Russian who had raped her. She thought that because the baby was half Russian she might be released earlier and be able to go home. But, that did not happen. When we were released after five years, she was afraid that the Russians would take her child away from her. To all our relief, that did not happen either. Yes, that was our child in the camp. He was our David.

During the last two days, some of us got mail from our families who were in Austria or even in Germany. That was always a ray of light. But my family was not in Germany or Austria. None of my family members wanted to flee Yugoslavia where we had lived for generations. My father was very religious and often said, "Nothing will happen to us; they know that we are not Nazis." But, in November of 1944 he was shot by Serbian partisans. Yes, he was shot by Serbs; there was no Russian among them. It was the Serbs who shot my dad. He was forty-eight years old. A friend of ours, who survived and was an eyewitness of my dad's shooting, told us that Dad knelt on his knees and prayed, and that was when the Serbs shot and killed him. Please, excuse me [her tears were running down her cheeks]. My mother was not even allowed to announce the death of my dad in Yugoslavia. She announced it later in Germany. She could not do so in Yugoslavia because the Serbs did not give out any documents whatsoever. They did not want any written evidence of the fact that they shot a multitude of German men. In April of 1945 my mother was dispossessed. Our home, our beautiful farm and all our land, everything was taken away from us by the Serbs, and there was nothing we Germans could do about it.

We forced laborers at the labor camp in Russia had a little relief during the last two years. Now we got paid a few rubels [Russian currency] for our labor. You know how the Swabian Germans are: the first thing we did was to buy ourselves some underwear and stockings. I also bought some fabric, grey fabric with stripes, like those of a man's suit. Out of that fabric, I managed to sew myself a dress, and that was the dress in which I came home. Yes, indeed, that was my homecoming dress.

After five, hard, slaving years in camp, the Germans from Hungary were allowed to leave for home earlier than we Germans from Yugoslavia. There was some unrest in the camp. One of our Russian officers was always fair to us. He said, "You also would be able to go home to Yugoslavia, but your Tito [the ruler of Yugoslavia at that time] does not want you. Tito does not want any Germans in his country." Indeed, in October the Germans from Hungary were released from their forced labor in Russia and brought home. We Germans from Yugoslavia could not return to our homes in Yugoslavia. We were transported to the Russian occupied sector of Germany (East Germany) at the end of November. We arrived in the now Russian-ruled communist East Germany on December 2, four days after leaving that Russian labor camp. Of course the Russians thought we would remain in East Germany because we were German and we could even speak Russian by now.

When we arrived in the city of Frankfurt an der Oder in East Germany and were sitting at the railroad station, there was a man whom I will never forget as long as I live. He was wearing an old and used black coat, a French beret and leather shoes with wooden soles. He was walking back and forth, hands on his back, and saying in a low voice, "Children, go to the West; children go to the West; children, go to the West." Then he vanished. He probably was afraid of the Secret Police that were watching and listening everywhere in Russian-occupied East Germany. After a while the man came back again, hands on his back, going back and forth and saying, "Children, go to the West; children, go to the West; children, go to the West." We thought that must mean something; he must be trying to tell us something. We had just arrived in East Germany from Russia and were waiting at the platform of the train station to transfer trains to Steingabel where my distant cousin lived. We were so uninformed about the political situation in East Germany that we couldn't quite grasp what this elderly gentleman was trying to tell us.

Many Germans who were transported to East Germany (which in 1949 became the GDR) from Russian labor camps escaped from East Germany. Only those few who had relatives in East Germany remained there. Honestly, we have to be very thankful to that elderly gentleman who risked his life, in his own way, to give us that good advice. I took his good advice, and it definitely changed my life forever. I had no relatives in the GDR except for a cousin of my father who lived in Steingabel. So I came to him with two others from the Russian camp, and we slept in the kitchen. We were five people all together. It was exceedingly crowded and uncomfortable, to say the least.

During our last days at the Russian camp, the Russians kept on saying, "There is no sugar in Germany "(they meant East Germany). So from that little money we had in Russia, we could have bought ourselves a pair of stockings. No, what did we do? Instead of buying a little something for ourselves, food or stockings, every one of us bought a pound of sugar with our last pennies so that we might be welcomed in East Germany. And when we arrived there and delivered our sugar, they laughed at us and said, "We have plenty of sugar here!" Once again we believed the Russians.

The worst was when, after five long years of slave labor, the women returned from Russia and never found their children. Unless the children had grandparents or a relative to take care of them, they were placed in orphanages. There were so many children who lost their parents. What a tragedy.

Here is a case in my own family: One of my cousins, the father of a little child, a little girl, was a prisoner of war in Yugoslavia; the mother was deported to Russia. The child remained with the *Oma* [grandmother]. But the *Oma* died. Now the child was brought to a kindergarten. Luckily the father was a prisoner of war in Yugoslavia. He was a butcher by profession. So he worked in a butcher shop for the Serbs and was able to smuggle some meat. He went from kindergarten to kindergarten, orphanage to orphanage, to find his child. But he did not find her. He searched and searched for his child. Finally, somehow, he found her in Old Serbia. He drove to Old Serbia, took some sausages with him and asked to see his child. However, he was told, "You can't see any children now; the children are all sleeping. But when they wake up and if the little girl recognizes you as her father, you may take her with you." He prayed very hard while he was waiting. The little girl's name was Erna. However, now her name was not Erna any more. She was given a Serbian name in the orphanage, so that she would be adopted by Serbs. When the children came out of their sleeping quarters, there was a dark haired child among them. That child stopped in front of him (he too had dark hair) and said in the Serbian language, "Are you my Daddy?"

They both had darker hair than the rest of the people there, and the child recognized him, although she did not respond to her original German name, "Erna." That father never lost sight of his child. That was just before Christmas. A short time later, both of them somehow managed to cross the Yugoslavian border to live freely together in Germany. At that time, his wife was still in the Russian labor camps. When she retuned from Russia, after slaving there for five years, all three were united in Munich, Germany. There are many, many German children who were adopted by Serbs in Yugoslavia. They have no idea that they are German. Imagine that!

We have been told that our house in Yugoslavia is no longer there. In the middle of our property, there is only a hut consisting of one room and one kitchen. Everything else is gone. We were told that the Serbs took the wooden planks out of the house because they had nothing else to burn to help them keep warm. It is no wonder that without the wooden beams to hold the house together the roof fell down. That's how our house, our beautiful home for generations, was destroyed. Well, what would you expect? They had Serbian illiterate people settle in those German homes. About 85 % of the people who moved into those German homes and farms were illiterate. They thought wheat and corn grew by itself, just like the plums on the plum trees in Serbia.

My mother was also transported to a labor camp in 1944 and was there until 1948. A former Hungarian farm worker who used to work at our farm was able to get my mother out of the camp in 1948. He took her to live with his family. There, my mother slept with his four children in one room. She had to report to the government every day that she was going to work; otherwise, she would not get any food.

For my family Christmas time is always the saddest time. It holds such tragic memories. Papa was shot shortly before Christmas. I was deported on the second Christmas day (Dec. 26), and our family was dispossessed on December 5, 1945. Everything terrible happened to our family around Christmas time. As long as my mother lived, Christmas was for us always a sad day, a day of mourning. It was the time when we could not help but think of those horrible times in all our lives.

Those who did not live through those experiences really can't imagine it. I often think, "How was it possible for us to be able to live through all that?" It took all our strength and tremendous will to stay alive. We had one thought: "I want to be home again, at least one more time." Those people who gave up their hope, they died in Russia, and there were so many of them [tears in her eyes]. They were carelessly thrown on the ground, like old useless objects. There was no grave for these unfortunate people, no funeral, no tombstone, nothing but the most horrid conditions of their far too early and unfortunate deaths.

No one talks about the German civilians who were forcibly deported to Russian slave labor camps. Yes, we were civilian deportees. That was the horrible thing, that they took civilians during the war and transported them for slave labor. Mothers were ripped away from their smallest babies and transported in cattle-trains to Russian death and hunger camps. I do not think such a thing happened before, in any war. But the Serbs, please excuse me, they have for a long time thought of taking over the farms and property of all us Swabian Germans in the Banat. That was their goal. My father already talked about it. He said that since the First World War the Serbs wanted the Germans out of Yugoslavia. At that time, after the First World War, the British said, "But where shall they (the Germans) go?" However, during the Second World War, the victors of the war agreed to the dispossessions of the Germans in many regions of Europe. The Serbs delivered us to the Russians as "volunteer laborers." We were mere slaves to the Russians, without any rights, any rights whatever. The Russians wanted us to build Russia up again. In their eyes, we were all Nazis. What did we Banat Swabians in Yugoslavia, who did not even live in Germany, know about the Nazis? We had nothing to do with them. At that time, it seemed to us in Yugoslavia that Germany was far away. Yet it was those German civilian women and children who lived in the far eastern regions of Germany as well as in Poland, Romania and Yugoslavia, who had nothing to do with Hitler but had to pay the highest price for the deeds of Hitler and his Nazis. That is not only my opinion. It is the experience of those who had to live through it all.

During the first years in the camp, the Russians always called us "uncivilized" and "uneducated." That fourteen-year-old Russian teenager who carefully examined my head was even taught that we have horns. Later, however, after the Russians got to know us, they did say, "We did not know that about you. We did not know any better." Oh, how deadly propaganda and lack of knowledge can be!

Oh, it was tragic, the situation we found ourselves in. What happened to us was unspeakably cruel and deadly. No one can even imagine it, even if I tell you, it's hard for you to imagine. I have never been in Yugoslavia again, never. I don't want to ever go or be there again either, never! That is something I could not muster. I think one of two things would happen: either I would immediately fall down and faint or I would get very depressed. It was cruel beyond words what had happened to us.

I must say, our good Lord must have loved us a lot; otherwise, we would have not been able to come back alive from Russia. I prayed every single morning when I went down into the coal mines at that forced labor camp, and I prayed very hard late at night.

I thank the dear Lord that I can live now, here in Germany, with my husband in this beautiful Nieschbach Home. The two of us pray each evening. My husband had to suffer ten years in Russia's hunger and death camps. We can never forget it and say, "Every day is a present for us." Those people who had to experience that hell and survived it, they appreciate every day being able to live a free life.

CZECHOSLOVAKIA

Brief History of Czechoslovakia and Ethnic Germans in Czechoslovakia

The Czechs and the Slovaks are closely related Slavic peoples who trace their origin from the early middle Ages. Their history shapes the background of Czechoslovakia.

The Czechs and the Slovaks were part of the multi-ethnic, multi-religious Austro-Hungarian Empire. The Czechs lived primarily in Austrian controlled regions of Bohemia and Moravia (see Map of Germany 1914), while the Slovaks were primarily ruled by the Hungarian controlled region of the empire. The Slovak resistance to Magyarization [Hungarianization] by their Hungarian rulers in the 19th century, together with tensions regarding their ethnic and religious policies, led to unrest within the empire.

Toward the end of the 19th century, the Czechs and Slovaks shared a common goal, despite their cultural differences. Both groups desired independence from the Austro-Hungarian Habsburg Empire and began thinking of a Czech-Slovak unity. In World War One they fought on the side of the Allies (France, Great Britain, Russia and the United States) and won their support for the independence of Czechoslovakia after the collapse of the

Austro-Hungarian Empire (Lukes, 2000; Hamberger, 1990). On October 28, 1918, the Czechoslovak National Council in Prague proclaimed the establishment of a free and united Republic of Czechoslovakia (Hughes, 1961 p. 108). The new formed nation had a population of over 13.5 million people and inherited 70 to 80 % of the industry of the Austro-Hungarian Empire. Most industry was located in the primarily German populated Sudetenland region and was developed, owned and controlled by ethnic Germans (Hughes, 1961).

The German population in Czechoslovakia insisted on their autonomy within Czechoslovakia. After President Beneš refused, the Sudeten Germans desired to merge the Sudetenland region with neighboring Germany or Austria (see maps of Germany in Appendix 2). President Beneš refused because losing the predominantly German Sudetenland would mean a big loss of a major industrial region of Czechoslovakia. To redistribute wealth, the Czechoslovak government confiscated some of the land owned by prosperous ethnic Germans and redistributed it to the Slovak majority.

Czechoslovakia and World War II

Threatening a war, Hitler demanded that the predominantly German borderland of the Sudetenland region be united with Germany. On September 29, 1938, the Munich agreement (signed by Germany, Great Britain, France and Italy) declared that Czechoslovakia cede this borderline Sudetenland region to Germany (see map of Germany 1914). In November 1938, Czechoslovakia was reconstituted in three autonomous parts: Czechia (Bohemia and Moravia), Slovakia, and Ruthenia. With its hostile German neighbors on three sides, bad relations with neighboring Poland, and the Munich agreement of France, Italy and Great Britain, Czechoslovakia was left without allies (Liddell,1973, p. 6). In complete violation of the Munich agreement, Hitler proceeded to not only annex the Sudetenland but also to occupy the entire country, sending President Beneš of Czechoslovakia into exile. On March 16, 1939, Hungary, a close ally of Nazi Germany, annexed Sub-Carpathian Ruthenia and southern portions of Slovakia. Hitler's fascist regime expelled more than a thousand Slavs who lived in the Sudetenland, took over almost the entire country of Czechoslovakia, and inflicted much terror on the Czech people (Liddel, 1973).

Underground resistance in Czechoslovakia against Hitler's Nazi Germany grew. By November 1939, a Czechoslovak National Committee, under the leadership of exiled Edvard Beneš in England, was organized and recognized by Great Britain and France. While in exile, Beneš negotiated with Great Britain, the Soviet Union and France for the nullification of the Munich Agreement. On December 12, 1943, a treaty of mutual assistance with the Soviet Union was signed. On May 8, 1944 (a year before the war ended), Beneš signed an agreement with Soviet leaders that the Czechoslovak territory, liberated by the Soviet army, would be placed under Czechoslovak civilian control (Glotz, 2003). In May 1945 Czechoslovakia was liberated by Soviet and American troops, together with Czechoslovakia's own resistance forces. The Czechoslovak government was headed by Beneš as president, and Zdenek Fierlinger, the former minister to the Soviet Union, as prime minister.

On June 29, 1945, Czechoslovakia signed an agreement that incorporated Ruthenia into the Ukrainian Soviet Socialist Republic. In February 1948, when the Communists took power, Czechoslovakia was declared a people's democracy. Its foreign policies were primarily based on its alliance with the Soviet Union even though President Beneš had hoped for an independent state which would continue to be associated with the United Kingdom and the United States (Davies, 2007). It soon became clear that Czechoslovakia would neither be independent nor reconstructed, as President Beneš, who refused to sign the Communist Constitution, had hoped. The Communist Party took control of the government, the judiciary, the police, and the army. On June 27, 1948 the Communist and Social Democratic parties were replaced by the Czechoslovak Communist Party modeled totally after Soviet style rule. Strict book and press censorship was established; land and industry were nationalized; and private ownership and capital were abolished (Glotz, 2003).

Germans in Czechoslovakia

Germans had settled in the Central European territories of Bohemia and Moravia (later Czechoslovakia) for over one thousand years. In the 14th century, under the German Emperor Karl IV, they established a new Habsburg capital in Prague, "which became one of the most majestic cultural centers of Europe. This legacy remains visible today" (Institute, 2012, p.1). As a result of close affiliation with Germany, Germans were recruited and encouraged by the Emperor to settle in that area. They built urban centers and cultivated rural land on the German border of Bohemia and rapidly formed the elite ethnic group over a vastly Slavic Czech majority (Institute, 2012, p.1.) Thanks to German architects, Bohemia had become a center of baroque architecture. In addition to architecture, Germans contributed greatly to rural development, politics and Catholicism of Bohemia and Moravia. Even though the Czechoslovakian influence grew after 1918, Prague retained a significant amount of German cultural life until 1945.

By the 16th century, Hungary and Croatia became part of the Habsburg Empire. After the Muslim Turks were defeated in 1526, Bohemia became a province of the German dominated Habsburg Empire for four hundred years. In the Habsburg era, people from Germany were actively recruited to settle in and develop various regions of the empire. The majority of Germans came from southern Germany and settled predominantly in the border area of Germany and Bohemia near the Sudeten and Erz Mountains. They developed fertile farmland in this unpopulated area and built a strong economy. This region became known as Sudetenland and its people as *Sudetendeutsche* [Sudeten Germans]. They retained their German language, south German culture, which were similar to that of Austrians, and their Catholic religion (Catholicism was compulsory under the Austrian Habsburg rule). They built German schools and churches and built a prosperous German enclave in a nation that had a Slavic majority. In the 19th century, the Sudetenland and Bohemia embraced industrialization and became one of the most significant industrial regions of the country, enjoying a booming economy. After 1918, all Germans living in

Czechoslovakia were known as Sudeten Germans, and the term *Sudetenland* began to assume a wider meaning.

Those Germans who moved to Slovakia, which was under Hungarian rule for about a thousand years, were invited by Hungarian kings after the 14th century. They settled predominantly in the Carpathian Mountain range of Hungarian Slovakia, where they enjoyed autonomy from 1370 to 1876. They retained their German language and culture, established German schools, worked hard and prospered. The Carpathian Germans, as they were called, made many significant contributions to their adopted country in such areas as urban development, the arts, agriculture, and politics (Kann, 2000). Their autonomy was reduced after the Hungarian Revolution and Magyarization [Hungarianization, the imposition of Hungarian culture].

The Expulsion of Germans

Toward the end of World War II, anti-German hysteria and revenge ruled in Czechoslovakia, due to the atrocities committed by the Nazis. Ethnic Germans in Czechoslovakia were forced to wear white or yellow arm bands with the letter "N" [*Nemee* for German], so that every German person could be instantly identified. Germans were not allowed to take public transportation, nor move beyond seven kilometers of their residence. They were only allowed to buy food within such an extremely short time span that all the women who were to do forced labor from dawn to dust were hardly able to buy food.

As retribution against the deeds of the Nazis, President Beneš started an ambitious national cleansing campaign (Frommer, 2004). On May 16, 1945, two or three days before the Russians arrived in Czechoslovakia, President Edvard Beneš called for the "liquidation without compromise" of all ethnic Germans and Hungarians in Czechoslovakia (Glassheim, 2000, p. 473). His speeches were not calling for those Germans who were guilty to be punished, but for expulsion of all ethnic Germans in Czechoslovakia. His solemn vow in a broadcast from Kaschau on May 16, 1945, at about 4:00 to 5:00 PM was, "Woe to the Germans, woe to the Germans, thrice woe to the Germans; we will liquidate them" (M.v.W., 1951, p. 1).

1951, p.1). Germans made up about 28 % of the total population of Czechoslovakia. The number of ethnic civilian Germans in Czechoslovakia at that time was 3,295,000 (Schieder, 2004, Vol. 2). In the spirit of ethnic cleansing and ethnic homogeneity, Edvard Beneš ordered the ethnic Germans and Hungarians to be expelled from the country.

Almost three and half million ethnic Germans, whose ancestors had built up and lived in various regions of Czechoslovakia for one thousand years, were totally dispossessed and expelled from the land they called home. German schools and churches were destroyed and the wealth of the German people and churches became that of Czechoslovakia (Institute, 2012). The Beneš Decrees allowed and encouraged private citizens and soldiers not only to expel ethnic Germans and confiscate all their property immediately without compensation but also to use any form of violence (Glotz, 2003).

The liquidation campaign of President Beneš led to gruesome and hateful excesses against Germans: Rapes, beatings, torture, starvation, and death. Many Germans became "human lanterns" which even Czech eyewitnesses confirm: They "were hanged, gasoline was poured over them while they were still alive, and set on fire" (Glotz, 2003, p. 204). In the words of Victor Gollancz, "the Germans were expelled, but not with a lack of exaggerated consideration, but with the most unthinkable highest form of brutality" (1946, p. 187). Ethnic German civilians, mostly women, children and the elderly, were taken away from their homes, including those Germans who were actively opposed to the Nazi regime. They were driven like cattle and interned in barracks, schools or theatres where they were subjected to gruesome acts of torture, bullying, starvation, and often beatings until death. In their despair, many committed suicide (F.B., 1947). The clothes of thousands of women, teenagers and even young girls in those internment buildings were often torn to pieces due to rape and mass rape. Since so many women had been raped in those camps, the Russians would later search for and take half grown girls, nuns, and old women to as their rape victims to avoid venereal disease (Glotz, 2003, p. 203).

To make room for the Soviet tanks, the barricades that had been built earlier, had to be removed, and the German women were forced to do that since most German men were by then prisoners of war or missing in the war. The Czech mob attacked and brutalized those German women. Some were so traumatized that they died on their way to work. The torture continued while the women were forced at gun point to remove those barricades.

The homes of the interned Germans were immediately confiscated and occupied by Czech families.

After the temporary internment of Germans in schools, barracks and movie houses, they were brought to large internment camps housing 10,000 to 15,000 Germans and held captive under miserable conditions. There they had to suffer not only brutalities and starvation but also night and day constant rapes of women and girls by groups of Russians who came in an out of the camps (Schmidt, K. 1957). Many children and teenagers who were brought to the former concentrations camp in Theresienstadt were constantly tortured and found their deaths in that concentration camp The rags which the people had to wear in that camp were smeared with swastikas (Schieder, 2004, Vol. IV/2, p. 81).

After the internment camps, surviving German women, children and the elderly were transported in cattle-trains to the German border and then left there to fetch for themselves. In those areas with limited public transportation, large groups of Germans were forced to march for many days at a fast paste, under gun point, constant ridicule and threat of execution, in the direction of the German or Austrian borders without any food or water. Those "misery marches" of mainly women carrying their infants, children and the elderly, were led by revolutionary guards or Czech soldiers who delighted in chasing the people, worse than cattle, beating and whipping them, often to death. The streets were filled with dying and dead German civilians (Glotz, 2003).

Most notorious among these misery marches is the well known Brünn Death March. Late in the night from May 29 to May 30, 1945, more than twenty thousand German women, children and the elderly, including mothers with babies in their arms, were gathered in Brünn, the capital city of the province Moravia (Neumeyer, 1981). After all their jewelry was taken or ripped from their bodies, they were force-marched at gunpoint more than fifty-six kilometers [thirty-five miles] south toward the Austrian border, without food or drink during those hot days. Those who slipped or were too exhausted, too weak or too old to go on under these torturous conditions were whipped, beaten or shot dead by Czech guards who were riding along on horseback. More than 1,700 people died during the first day (Knopp, 2004, p. 391). When the survivors reached the Austrian border, the Russians did not allow them to enter Austria. There the Czech guards forced them into barracks in nearby Pohrlitz, where they were kept for weeks under the most miserable and inhuman conditions. Countless women, even those over eighty years of age, teenagers and children were constantly raped by Russians (Neumeyer, 1981). Mothers who desperately tried to prevent the rape of their children were shot dead (Neumeyer, 1981). Between 8.000 to 13.000 human beings died during that death march. About 700 of them are confirmed of dying either by murder or disease (Rozumet and Zdenek, p. 209).

There were many such misery marches, including one of women and children from Jägerndorf, and that of the men from Komotau. All those marches were accompanied by torture, hunger, and death (Zatschek, 2004; Mükusch, 1947; Ehm, 2004). In August 1945, three months after the war had ended, came the Aussig Massacre. Ethnic German families, including small children, were brought to the river Elbe in Aussig, lined up at the bridge and all shot dead (Wheeler, 2000).

Most Germans living in the Slovakia region of Czechoslovakia (Carpathian Germans) were captured by the Red Army (Institute, 2012, p.13). The largest expulsion of Carpathian Germans took place at the end of September 1946. After the Germans were taken from their homes by Czechoslovakian volunteers and soldiers, they were interned and transported to the Soviet Union or Germany. More than 40,000 Carpathian German civilians were expelled and deported for forced labor to the Soviet Union. 13,000 of them died during the transit alone due to inhuman conditions (Zentrum, 2012). Later, many Germans were transported to the Soviet occupied zone of East Germany. Nearly three hundred imprisoned Carpathian German civilians were executed after they were forced to dig their own grave. The youngest of the victims was a seven month old baby (Carpathian German Home Page, p.13). To complete the ethnic cleansing in Czechoslovakia, Hungarians were also expelled from Slovakia to Hungary.

The ethnic German expulsion campaign in Czechoslovakia was so radical that by 1950, it completely destroyed nearly the entire thousand year old German minority population, regardless of the great contributions that ethnic group had made in developing fruitful farmland out of unpopulated regions, developing world class cities and cultural centers such as Prague, and developing industry where none existed before. The expulsion of the entire German ethnic group resulted in one of the largest forced refugee communities of the twentieth century (Institute, 2012, p.13).

PERSONAL NARRATIVES OF THE EXPULSION OF ETHNIC GERMANS FROM CZECHOSLOVAKIA

Josef Antoni
Born 1926 in Glaserhau, Slovakia (now Sklene, Slovakia)

"The partisans lined the German civilians up to stand next to the ditch. The machine guns were pointed at them. A partisan gave the command to fire. They started firing and shot them all in cold blood."

JOSEF ANTONI

Interviewed June 23, 2008, in Michigan, USA

In the early fourteenth century, my ancestors used to live in an ancient German community in what was then Hungary. It included a circle of twenty-five German towns. Our town, Glaserhau, was established by Germans in 1327. That's how ancient it was. At that time, Slovakia was part of Hungary. When the Hungarian king (in the early 1300s) visited the region, he requested the landowners there to bring in German settlers to develop the area. The Germans came, settled there and built schools, churches, entire communities, a total of twenty-five towns in that region alone. Our education was in German because when Czechoslovakia was born after the First World War, there were three-and-a-half million Germans living in what had become Czechoslovakia. And because of a large German population in our area, we could maintain our German schools. It's absolutely amazing that throughout all those years, since the thirteen hundreds, the Germans kept their German traditions and language, and basically remained German. Throughout the centuries, we had no problem with the Slovak people; we lived alongside each other in peace. I don't remember any ethnic frictions or ethnic problems in our region. However, unfortunately, the war changed that forever.

In the summer of 1944, our peaceful situation changed drastically. There was a Communist uprising. I was working in Bratislava, the capitol of Slovakia, but went home on vacation to our farm to help my parents bring in the harvest. Rumors were spreading that rebels, Communist partisans, were taking over German towns and terrorizing German people. It was not possible for me to go back to Bratislava because the partisans had dynamited a railroad tunnel that connected our town to the other towns. We were stuck and could not go anywhere. There were no trains and no busses. There was no transportation whatsoever. So I stayed home.

One day, around the beginning of September 1944, while we were having lunch, I looked out of our window and saw a group of those rebels, those partisans, coming down the hillside. They were wearing those recognizable scarves around their necks; you could tell they were rebels. They were not far away from us. So I grabbed whatever I could and ran out into the woods and hid there overnight. The next day, everything seemed quiet, so I came back home. It remained relatively quiet for a while. Then those rebels, those partisans, returned, occupied our town and gave all kinds of orders to all the Germans living there. If you did not do what they wanted you to do, you got shot. Oh, yes, they really did mean business. Those rebels were not only Slovaks; there were also Russians and Communists from other countries among them. Even some units of the Slovak Army joined what was called the "Communist uprising." Around September 20th or 21st, the partisans went from house to house and ordered the men to get dressed right away. They demanded, "Take a shovel with you if you have one. If you don't have one, go without it." They took them to a nearby school, presumably to work.

I was eighteen years old at that time and extremely lucky that I was not one of those men that were taken away. I was working in a neighboring town. A few days before the 20th of September, about thirty young men were needed in the neighboring town to dig fox holes, and I was one of those thirty young men. That was my luck. I was away digging those fox holes when the partisans went from house to house in my hometown to take the German men away.

After the heavily armed partisans had gathered all the German men in the school building, they walked with them to the railroad station where a cattle-train was already waiting for them. They loaded them into that cattle-train, about forty to forty five men in each box car of the train. As soon as all the men were in those cattle-train box cars, the train took off. Two miles away from town, the train stopped. The partisans ordered twenty men with their shovels out of the first box car, locked the box car and asked the men to use their shovels to dig a ditch. It was actually to be their mass grave. It took all the men over an hour to dig that ditch. When the men finished digging, the partisans opened the first two box cars and ordered the men to get off the train. Then they lined the German civilians up to stand next to the ditch. The machine guns were pointed at them. A partisan gave the command to fire. They started firing and shot all the German civilians in cold blood.

My Dad was in the first box car and among those twenty men whom they ordered out of the box car to dig the mass grave. He was standing more or less in the first row at the edge of the ditch. As soon as they started shooting, he quickly made himself fall into that ditch. There was blood all over. When the first shooting was done, the partisans opened the other two box cars, but this time they did not line the men up any more. So now the men ran all over the field, and the partisans were shooting and gunning them down. A few men were able to get away. However, from almost one hundred men in the first two box cars, only three remained alive: my dad, the priest from our town, and a school friend of mine. When the shooting stopped, the train took off. There were still some men in the remaining box cars that were not opened. My brother was in one of them. For some reason they did not open his box car. That was his incredible luck.

My father was still in the mass grave down there. After the train left, my dad said that he heard some voices above speaking German and saying, "If anyone down there is still alive, get out and disappear in the nearby woods." My dad managed to crawl out of the bloody mass grave, which was covered with dead bodies and blood, and ran into the woods. Whoever was able to still run ran to those woods, ran as fast as he could away from that mass grave. My dad was slightly wounded, just a scratch. He said, "Maybe God saved me because I have ten children to take care of." He was so very smart and fast thinking to jump in the grave before they shot him.

In the meantime, rumors got around that there were survivors out there in the woods. Someone came into our house and said that he wanted to talk with my mother. He told her that my father was alive, that he was out there in the woods, and that he needed some clothes and food. So my younger brother, who was fourteen years old then, took food and clothes out there into the woods. He knew the area very well where he was to meet my dad. Indeed, he found him there in the woods and brought him those clothes and food. He hid in those woods for about two weeks with the other survivors. After the German Army came through our area, the men left their hiding place and returned home.

Oh, and the priest who survived, that is a story in itself. Oh, what that priest went through! He got out of the grave the same way as a friend of ours, but he was captured by the rebels. They brutally beat him and threw him back in the grave, alive. Oh, what he had to endure; but he survived and eventually worked himself out of the grave. He made it! He is in Southern Germany now and told us about it when we saw him there.

But let me tell you what happened to the poor German women after all the men were shot. The day after the shooting, we were still working in the neighboring town, digging those fox holes, as mentioned earlier. Well, we saw from far afield a lot of women and children and heard them scream. They were bending down, getting up, bending down, getting up and screaming. Oh, were they screaming! We didn't know what was going on. It just so happened that a young kid, maybe he was eight or nine years old, was passing by the area where we were digging those fox holes. He was carrying a container of food and told us, "Yesterday all the men got shot in our hometown." And then he said, "There was an announcement made on the loud speaker, 'Anybody who wants to bring food to the men we took to work yesterday may do so.'" Can you imagine that ultimate cruelty to ask the women to bring food to their husbands when the rebels knew very well that they had shot all their husbands dead? Eager to bring food to their husbands and sons, the women and their children walked to where they were told to go with their food. Then the armed guards walked them to the sight of the massacre and the mass grave. That was when we saw all those women and kids running around, frantically screaming, and desperately searching for their loved ones among the dead bodies. They could not find my brother. He was the lucky one.

One hundred and eighty seven civilians were shot on that day at that Massacre of Glaserhau. They were killed because they were German. They were poor farmers and had nothing to do with Hitler or any politics. They were busy growing crops and making a living. Every one of their wives was now a widow, and one hundred and eighty-seven mothers lost their sons. The women of our entire hometown were now alone. Their husbands and sons were shot dead in cold blood. For example, the mother-in-law of my brother Willi was now left all alone with four daughters because her husband was killed on that day. Glaserhau was not the only town that was tragically hit at the hands of the Communist partisans; there were many such tragedies in many German towns in Slovakia.

Among all the horror of that massacre, there was still a glimpse of humanity. Let me tell you about one humane story. At the railroad station, when the train was already loaded with Germans to be killed, one of the partisans went along the train, stopped at every box car and asked, "Is there anybody in here under fourteen?" My brother-in-law, Erwin is his name, was sixteen. His neighbor said, "Oh, this kid over here, he is not fourteen yet." Erwin said later, "I will never forget that good neighbor and that partisan man. The partisan quickly grabbed my hand and pulled me out of the box car." That partisan, in spite of what terrible deeds he was doing, still had a heart and saved that young boy from the deadly firing squad. Instead of facing that firing squad to be shot, Erwin walked home. A few years later he married my sister and came to the United States. He had a full life and died many years later in Philadelphia.

I was working in the neighboring town to dig those fox holes for about two weeks or so. The thirty of us worked during the day, and at night we slept in box cars. We had seen American and Russian planes drop supplies for those rebels who did that massacre. Early one morning we got a surprise. We didn't have to work there any more. An officer showed up and said, "You are free. You are free to go home." But he told us, "Stay together because there are partisan rebels scattered in the woods. So stay together; don't go alone." We followed his good advice and stayed together. Unfortunately, one person in our group got shot and killed because he went alone somewhere. But we were able to walk home. It was when I got home that I learned about the whole awful story of the massacre and all the dead men in our village.

My dad was too old to serve in World War II. He served in the First World War. I got drafted during the last few months of WW II in January 1945. Then I was a prisoner of war for a year in Austria under the Americans. It was my great fortune not to be imprisoned by the Russians.

When the war ended, the German people had to leave their homes and all their property behind in Czechoslovakia. At first, there was not a forced evacuation. Afraid of the approaching Russian Red Army, people started fleeing. Wagon after wagon with women and children were constantly rolling down the streets with people fleeing westward, all toward neighboring Bavaria and Austria. When the women desperately fled from their homes to save their lives and those of their children and the elderly, nobody helped them. Oh, what hardship they suffered!

After the war was over, the Germans wanted to go back to their homes. And some did, especially those who had a farm or some property there. However, half a year later, the expulsions and forced deportations of Germans in Czechoslovakia started. All Germans had to get out of Czechoslovakia. Some were transported to Mecklenburg, East Germany, some to West Germany. My parents went to Würtenberg, West Germany. Most of the people from our town ended up near Stuttgart, Schwäbish Gmünd. Only those very few Germans who married Slovaks remained in Glaserhau.

The name of our hometown, Glaserhau, has been changed to the Czech name Sklene. All German names have been changed to Czech names. In our town of Glaserhau (Sklene), we have a fenced in monument, donated by Germans. The only thing that is written on the monument is "Für die 187 Opfer des Krieges" [for the 187 victims of the war]. Nothing is said about who those victims were, nothing about the massacre, nothing about how they were killed in cold blood. At that time we were not allowed to put a monument there unless it did absolutely did not refer to the reasons of the massacre, just that 187 people got killed. The Slovaks wanted people to believe that the Germans did that, that the Germans killed 187 Slovaks. Imagine that! Last year [2008], there was, for the first time, a small section in a Slovak paper mentioning that it was Slovak partisans who committed the Massacre of Glaserhau.

Later we migrated from Germany to the United States. A lot of people from our home town are scattered all over the world now, in the former East Germany, West Germany, Canada, Australia, and the United States. All of us, no matter where we are, have lost our home forever.

Sometimes, when we meet in Germany with our friends from Glaserhau, we talk about our tragic forced expulsion from home and about the end of our beloved and more than six hundred year old German town back home. We were disinherited; we were expelled; we were forced to leave. We lost our home, our neighbors and neighborhood; we lost our city. Our Glaserhau is no more German. The Slovaks changed its name to Sklene. Even though we lived in Germany after the expulsion, and even though we have lived for decades here in the United States, home for us will always be our beloved Glaserhau.

Maria Antoni
Born 1926 in Glaserhau, Slovakia (now Sklene, Slovakia)

"After all that had happened, after moving to so many places, in our hearts we still think of Glaserhau as our home."

MARIA ANTONI

Interviewed June 23, 2008, in Michigan, USA

I was born and raised in Glaserhau, a small German town in the Carpathian Mountain region of Slovakia. I went to school there up to the eighth grade, which was at that time the official graduation of the German *Volksschule* [Grammar school]. Then I went to Germany to a Home Economics School. Slovakia was German friendly at that time. The reason I went to Germany was because of the people who came from Germany to Czechoslovakia to teach us about the German Reich. They encouraged us to go to Germany and they also helped us to get into schools in Germany. Through the Home Economics School I served in the *Landdienst* [mandatory rural service or land service]. It was the law of the Third Reich that young girls work in kitchens and in farms for a year. Later I became a *Landdienstführerin* [a leader of the rural service]. By that time I was nearly eighteen. So you see, I was in Germany already at the end of the war. That is why I didn't really flee from home. I had left earlier, after my eighth grade graduation, to study home economics in Germany.

It was in Germany in September 1944 that I heard about the Massacre in my hometown. I remember hearing on the radio that in my tiny hometown of Glaserhau, Slovakia, Slovak and Russian partisans killed 187 German civilian men in cold blood.

I remember a man who was a critic of the war. Already in 1943, he thought, like we did, that Germany would not win that war. He always walked back and forth in the city square and did not say a word to anybody. He always walked with a cane; at that time, many men walked with a cane. His steadfast, solemn walk, back and forth in the city square, with that cane in his hand, made an impression on me. Later on I found out that this German man had been put into the concentration camp in Dachau for a whole year because he questioned the war. He did not speak with anybody, most likely because he was afraid to be put there again.

When the bombs fell over Germany, I was in Melle, Osnabrück. That region of Germany was under British occupation, but there were Russian soldiers too. Oh, it was horrible when those bombs came crushing down, one after another. I remember that we had to hide from bombs that were thundering down, and we were scared. Yes, I remember that very well.

My family ended up in the city of Halle an der Saale in Sachsen, the Russian occupied and communist ruled sector of Germany, which became later the GDR. Josef and I got married there in Halle an der Saale in 1948. This is how I spent the first days of our honeymoon: As soon as I arrived at the West German border, I had to go to a camp where I was deloused. I was in that camp for about three days before I could join Josef. I was very lucky to be able to legally leave the Russian-occupied sector of East Germany and go to the West. The reason I was allowed to legally follow Josef to the West was because I was his wife, and he was living in West Germany. Later on it was much more dangerous to leave the GDR.

Every few years, we Germans from our home town of Glaserhau have a *Heimattreffen* [homeland meeting]. Most of the people from our hometown live now around Schwäbish Gmünd in Germany. Every few years we take a trip together to our old home town. We attend a mass in church there, walk the streets we used to walk, visit familiar sites, and reminisce. Yes, after all that happened, after moving to so many places, in our hearts we still think of Glaserhau as our home.

Isolde Zaschke
Born 1935 in Niemes, Bohemia, Czechoslovakia

"I lost my childhood; I lost my youth. Only at the age of twenty or twenty one did I begin to experience a little bit of my youth. Dance lessons or beautiful dresses did not exist. I was happy when I had something to eat."

ISOLDE ZASCHKE

Interviewed July 28, 2007, in Ingolstadt, Germany

I was born and raised in Bohemia. If you look at an old map from before 1918, you will see that Bohemia is located next to Czechoslovakia, not within Czechoslovakia. It was a separate region and belonged once to the Austrian-Hungarian Empire. During the middle Ages, the various ethnic groups in that region had a good relationship and got along just fine. After the First World War in 1918, that region was split up. Unfortunately, the German territory of Bohemia did not get to be a part of Germany; it became a part of Czechoslovakia. The Czechs had a strong national identity. That brought bad blood between those two national groups.

The Germans who were living in what had become Czechoslovakia, were now oppressed by the Czechs. In the 1930s, during the Great Depression when it was very difficult to find a job, there were about four Germans jobless as compared to one Czech. All positions that Germans held were transferred to Czechs. When Germans had a job at the post office or at schools or at the railroad station, they had to leave, and the Czechs got all those positions. The Germans had to live on a very small amount of unemployment money. That was about ten Kroner per family at that time. It was too little to live and too much to die. That caused some bad blood. I remember my mother telling me that when she went to a travel bureau to buy tickets to go visit an aunt in West Germany, she was yelled at by the Czech, who yelled at her in German, "What, you don't speak any Czech and you live here for so many years!" Next to her stood an Austrian who looked at her and shook his head to witness such animosity. That Czech was so loudly yelling at my mother, with such contempt in his voice that she cried. However, somehow Czechs and Germans still lived relatively peaceful alongside one another.

Then they sent us that Austrian who wanted to be a German [meaning Adolf Hitler who was born and raised in Austria]. The mistake was that Mrs. Hitler didn't have a miscarriage. If she would have had a miscarriage, we would have all been saved from all the tragedy and hell of World War II. But that is how destiny played out. Well, after the Germans had lived in what became Czechoslovakia under desperate conditions, without any jobs and without any money, Bohemia and the Sudetenland became a part of Germany again in the Third Reich. Some of the Germans in Czechoslovakia were, indeed, voicing their nationalism. That was a big mistake.

Hitler wanted to regain the German populated Sudetenland and did so after the *Münchener Abkommen* [Munich Agreement]. The British, the French, all gave their blessings. Everything would have been all right if it only would have stayed that way. But Of course the power-hungry Hitler did not respect that border. It was not enough for him. He invaded more and more countries. He had already Austria and then Bohemia, and that was the beginning of the end for us.

We come from Niemes. My father is a native of the Riesengebirge. He and my mother met in Niemes. He worked in Niemes, and then later he was self employed in Prague. In the 1930's it was possible for us to move to Prague because he was bilingual, spoke both fluent Czech and German, and had finished his Interpreter Examination. He had many friends who were Czechs. So we moved to Prague, and I went to school there for four-and-a-half years. Then in 1945, there was no schooling any more, and I stayed home.

All the German names of the cities in Czechoslovakia had changed into Czech names after 1945. One time I wanted to take a bus to Reichenberg. So I asked the agent at the ticket office for the schedule of the buses to Reichenberg. The name "Reichenberg" came so naturally out of my mouth. He looked at me and said, "What is Reichenberg?" So I quickly said the

Czech name for Reichenberg. It took quite a while to get used to that language and name changes.

In April of 1945, it all started. One heard several bits of news. You must know, we never listened to the radio station; we were afraid. But we had friends among the Czechs who told, us, "For heaven's sake, make sure you leave. You are not safe here!" But we felt sorry for the children. My brother was so small. He was four-and-a-half years old, and I was about nine-and-a-half years old at that time. We decided to leave Prague and drive to Niemes to our grandmother's house. There we thought we could hide out. So we left our place in Prague, furniture and all, and drove to Niemes. We only took a few clothes and bedding. Our house in Niemes, however, was occupied by two women and one child whose homes were bombed. So now we had to find housing for us, which we did. My grandmother, my mother, my brother and I moved into a two-room apartment. My father remained in Prague and continued to work there. He was not called to fight in the war because he was needed to interpret at the hospitals.

Earlier we had experienced the *Umsturz* [the fall of Germany] in Prague. It was absolutely awful. Those who suffered the least in Czechoslovakia took the most gruesome revenge. On the other hand, there were so many good Czechs. They even helped the Germans. They came to their aid, and they hid them from fellow Czechs who were very brutal. Yes, indeed. My father was stuck in the city at work and tried to stay with his Czech friends and co-workers. They said, "Yes, for one or two days you can stay with us. But we cannot keep you any longer because the neighbors will all be watchful, and people are eager to report." He stayed there for a day. When he went to the suburb of Prague, where we lived, to see how our house and property were doing, he was captured. While we were safe in Niemes, my father was now captured and severely beaten in Prague. He, together with all Germans, was interned to Theresienstadt [a city in Czechoslovakia with a large German population].

After two or three weeks came the command that my 60-year-old grandmother was going to be transported from her home in Niemes. Somehow the Czechs didn't have us on the list yet because our residence was not in the city limits of Niemes. So now my grandmother had to leave. We quickly baked a little cake for her. There wasn't much for us to bake with, but a little flour, sugar and milk. So at five o'clock in the morning, we brought her to the railroad station. We had packed a little suitcase which included that little cake and a loaf of bread so that she would at least have something to eat on her way. When we reached the railroad station, she had to go into a cattle-train. There were so many people in that cattle-train: old men, women, and children. They were all German. The cattle-train took them all the way to the Sachsen border. There they were ordered out of the cattle-train and had to do what they could to stay alive. They were walking with their little luggage toward Sachsen which had become the Russian occupied zone of Germany and arrived in the city of Siegnitz in Sachsen.

There was no refugee camp, nothing in Siegnitz. Germany had been bombed and destroyed. There were so many refugees and expelled newcomers; it was an impossible situation. They were hungry, homeless and so forlorn, without any food. To stay alive they literally went from house to house to beg. There was a woman who was generous and gave my grandmother some cooked potatoes. My grandmother was so grateful. Those people in Sachsen did not have anything to eat themselves, but they did have a roof over their heads. The expelled Germans from Czechoslovakia had lost everything. They had no food, and they had no place to sleep. They had become homeless. What to do? They slept sometimes in some barn somewhere; they sought shelter under trees in the forest.

The situation was so bad, my grandmother told us, that every day they brought the bodies of German people who had hanged themselves. Being deported from their homes in cattle-train wagons, now homeless and hungry and seeing ruins, beatings, and hunger all around them, some people simply couldn't go on any more and chose to die. Every single day there were bodies of men and women, especially old people. It was hard for everybody, and especially hard for the elderly. This is what my grandmother told us.

I absolutely adored my grandmother; I practically worshipped her. She was a most amazing woman and had such a golden heart. She was only thinking of others, never of herself. She wouldn't eat anything herself but leave what ever little there might have been for others. She was a golden woman.

Searching for another place to live, we went to our former home in Niemes. It had already been taken by the Czech administration. Interesting enough, the person who lived in our house was a Czech woman who went to school with my mother years ago. She, her husband, and their two children took our house right away from the Czech administration. Well, we went for a visit, knocked at the door, and who was standing there? It was my grandmother, the former owner of that house. Somehow, she had managed to escape from the Russian occupied East German zone with nothing but her little handbag. She said, "I couldn't stand it any more; I had to come home." So when she returned and knocked at her house door, my mother's former classmate replied, "Come, stay with us. We will hide you and will tell nobody that you are here, and we will feed you with whatever we will find." They searched for wild berries, mushrooms, and leftover potatoes after the potato fields were harvested. Nobody could know that my grandmother was there because she was German. It was against the law for any German to be there at that time.

We all were now in our old home in Niemes for a short time. Of course we could not be there very long and bc safe. However, where should we go? We were searching for another place to live, another empty place from which Germans had already been deported. We found a place where an acquaintance had lived. There we hid for about fourteen days before we had to leave again. All together, we changed places to stay four times, always a different place, so that we wouldn't be found out. It was always in Niemes and always in homes of Germans who had already been forced to leave their homes.

Whenever a Czech came who liked the house or the apartment that belonged to a German, he only needed to place a Czech flag in front of the house, and he could simply move in. Those were the gold grabbers; they were the first to inhabit the empty German homes. All the Czech needed to do is to place the Czech flag in the window of the house, go to the city hall and say, "I like this house. I want to move in there." Then he got a piece of paper, showed that to the Germans who lived there, and simply said, "I am living here now." Of course the Germans were forced to leave their own home. It also happened that once in a while there was an empathic Czech person who had a corner store and let the Germans stay for a little while in what has now become "his house." But they had to work in the store.

We didn't know how we could survive. There was no more money, there were no jobs and especially not for any German person in Czechoslovakia. My mother was forced to work in the fields and pick turnips and potatoes for the Czechs. It was terrible. She said there were so many women and girls working in those fields, and the Czech partisans were standing over them with their guns. Many times, when those women and girls didn't work fast enough, the partisans would beat them again and again. The girls were often bloody from the beatings. My mother, thank God, was not beaten. But some girls would come home drenched in blood. I must say, though, that one thing the Czechs did not do was to rape them. We regularly and often heard about the Russians raping German women and girls. The Czechs did beat the Germans, discriminated against them, forced them to work for them for nothing, but I have not heard of any Czech raping them in our area.

We had to do everything. I always went with my mother who used me as a companion for protection. You know, she felt a little safer with me on her side. I do remember one time in our yard there were some Russians, but they were of a higher rank and not the regular soldiers. They were officers, and they always said to my mother, "Schöne Frau, schöne Frau [beautiful woman, beautiful woman]". So I always stood in front of my mother as a sort of protection. Perhaps that did help. The Russians themselves had children, and one of the Russians put my little brother on his lap and said, "I have a little son just about your age." We were very lucky; those Russian officers didn't do us any harm.

But we had to labor hard doing all kinds of work. We and other Germans used to go to the forest to search for berries and mushrooms; our hands were full of bloody blisters from picking those berries. At that time, I was about ten years old, and I went from house to house with my basket of berries or mushrooms that my mother had nicely prepared. I knocked at the door and would say, "Please buy berries (or mushrooms) for one hundred Kroner." I did know the Czech language because I grew up with a bilingual education. However, I did not feel quite sure about the Czech grammar and was very careful not to show it in my sentences. The women would look at the berries, would look at me, and they would buy the berries or mushrooms from my basket. Then one time, imagine, I even went into the school, the Czech school, to sell my berries. I said to the Czech teachers, "Won't you please buy these berries?" They said, "All right, but where are you coming from?" I answered, "My father is in Prague, and he will come home soon." It was a great idea. However, I spoke very carefully, so as not to give away that I was German. I was lucky; they did not recognize that I was German. However, today, they certainly would. So many years and decades have gone by where I did not speak Czech any more, only German.

Soon we ran out of berries. Now what to do? My mother was very good at knitting and crocheting. So I went from one house to another and asked, "Do you need any needlepoint work to be done, any knitting, crocheting or embroidery?" One time, a Czech woman gave me some wool and said, "Yeah, if you can do something with this." I brought that wool home, gave it to my mother; and lo and behold, she knitted two sweaters from that wool. I went back to that house and sold each sweater for two hundred and fifty crowns.

Each German person, whether a child or a grown up, had to wear on their clothes a white band so that we Germans were easily identifiable. That white band meant that we were German but also that *der hat sich ergeben* [he or she has surrendered]. Any German who did not wear that white band would be fined and/ or beaten, or both. However, I thought I was so clever; I put the white band away and did not wear it because I knew the Czech language. Not only did I not wear it, but I even dared to walk on the footpath. No German was allowed to walk on the footpath. Germans had to walk in the streets. Whenever a German would walk on the footpath and a Czech would pass by, the Czech would push the German off the footpath. Imagine that; there I was, merrily walking on the footpath without my white stripe. If they would have found me out, I would have been in big trouble. Well, you know, I had to talk to so many people and go from house to house persuading the Czechs to buy my goods. The white band on my arm and walking on the street would have certainly made my necessary communications with the Czechs impossible. Also a little girl of ten or eleven who could speak Czech, did not wear a white band, and walked on the footpath would be more readily taken to be a Czech girl. I was kind of proud that I had it all figured out.

One time, however, I caught people's eye. I was going to a farm and asked the woman of the house if she would please sell an egg to me. My little brother was very skinny at that time and needed more nutrition. So I begged that woman, "Please do sell one egg, please just one egg to me." She did sell an egg to me for five Kroner. My mother waited a little distance away from me because she would not leave me alone there. Well, one time, they saw from afar that a woman with a white armband was waiting for me. When I came the next time to that farm, the woman yelled very angrily, "No, I will never, ever again sell anything to you. There was a German woman waiting for you!" That was the end of being able to buy an egg. My secret was out of the bag.

We were always hungry and always happy to get anything to eat. One time we got some wheat, but it was mixed with mouse poop and stones. So we cleaned it up very carefully, so very carefully. We put it in the coffee mill to get a flour-like substance from the wheat, and then we baked some sort of bread from it. Oh, that bread tasted so very good. One thing we had enough of was potatoes. Our meal every day was potatoes. It might be sour potatoes; potato soup; potato goulash (it was really only potatoes); potato salad, with a little bit of onions if we were lucky to get some onions; potatoes with a little margarine. We were lucky to have at least our daily potatoes. That was why we were all so slim at that time, unlike today.

You know, at that time, when you got a little piece of bread, it tasted so good it tasted like you had the most delicious piece of cake. I would sometimes beg, "Please, only a little piece of bread, please!" When they looked at me, I would say, "No, it's not for me; it's for my grandmother." I will never ever forget how much hunger hurts, how you have to beg for a crumb of bread. Yes, those were truly terrible times.

I was the communicator outside the house because my mother did not speak any Czech. All that time when we were in Niemes, we tried to find different places to live. Those were empty German homes which were not yet occupied by the Czechs. Again and again we were driven out of those homes; and again and again we would hide my mother because she did not speak Czech and was German. When someone came, I quickly hid her in the closet, and I would answer the door speaking Czech.

The war was over in May 1945, but we remained in Niemes until spring of 1946. People thought we were half-Czechs, and the very few Germans who were still there did not say a word. Then came the expulsion command, and we were forced to leave the country. We had to go to the camp where they gathered all the Germans. However, they would not deport my father because he was an expert in construction, and they needed his expertise.

My father was interned in Niemes. As construction master, he had to oversee various construction sights. The Czechs knew exactly how to squeeze the most out of the German people. As I said earlier, each German person, whether a child or a grown up, had to wear on their clothes a white band so that we Germans were easily identifiable. A letter "P" on that white band identified him as a German working for Czechs. My father had that letter "P" so that he was marked in such a way that the Czechs would not only know that he was working, but he might need to be working after it was dark. No German was allowed to be outside in the evening and at night. There was a curfew for all Germans after 8:00 PM. They would have no business being outside after 8:00 PM. However, some German people had to work the night shift. That is why whenever my father was found outside after curfew time and he could prove that he was coming to or from his night shift, he would not get fined or beaten. But if he would not have that letter "P" and just a white band without that letter, the Czechs could beat him and put him into jail. The photo below shows a "P" on a jacket of a young boy, indicating that he was working for the Czechs. Already at a young age, that boy had to work.

A German boy's jacket with mandatory white arm band and the letter "P "

In April 1946 we were brought to the camp, and our grandmother managed to go with us. They said, "She is not here on this list. They must have forgotten to write her name down. So let's just add her name to this list." We were lucky. But, remember, she was already over sixty years old and was earlier force deported to the Sachsen border. Nobody was to know that she had escaped earlier and returned home. Later, my father was also brought to that camp. So now we were all together there at the border. But where would we be taken next? What would happen to us? We had left everything behind and had nothing with us but two sacks. My father said, "The less you have, the lighter your weight to carry. If you load is too heavy, it will drag you down."

We lost everything. However, our future lay in front of us, we thought. My father was a construction master; my mother was still young; my grandmother was still able to get around; and most of all, we were all together. We were a few days in that cattle-train. But that was already in the autumn. It was already freezing cold, already minus degrees Centigrade, and people froze. My grandmother, my little brother and I were in the overcrowded cattle-train compartment where it was so crowded that we were not freezing. However, my father and my mother were in the regular compartment where it was freezing cold. It was night, and we didn't know where we were going. Next morning, in the daylight, we looked out and saw that we were transported at night to a former Nazi camp.

Oh, I am telling you that was some survival in that camp. They put one hundred people in one barracks, three bunks on top of each other. The toilets were community latrines outside. The hygienic situation was unbelievably horrid. You cannot imagine it. But as a child, you experience those things differently than as an adult. Oh, what my poor mother had to endure in those days! There were only the wooden planks; the back wall was all open. There were those latrines outside. It was freezing cold, and all was filthy dirty with human waste, which was covered with paper. It was awful.

We were the last transport that was brought to that camp. After us, they didn't take anyone else. Later there were not so many people any more in that camp. There were only sixteen or eighteen people left in one room. Women and children were separated from men. But the worst thing was that everything was full of bugs and lice. Oh, there were those darn bugs everywhere, and everything was itching. I itched like crazy. I woke up at night and scratched my itches, and I was full of bugs everywhere: on my face and my body all was red and full of bug bites. Then I got infected. There was no place to wash up or to take a shower or bath. It was horrible.

We were sent there to do forced labor in that camp. My father was ordered to work too. Our food consisted of potatoes or beans. In the morning we got a little bit of bread with a tiny bit of jam, and in the evening we got the same. One day a Red Cross Delegation from Switzerland came, and it gave every family some *Knackebrot* [cracked flat bread] and a little can of milk. Oh, were we happy! That was so delicious, especially the can of milk; it was so sweet.

We had to stay there until 1948. Then they allowed us women and children to leave the camp because they did not want to have to feed us. At that time my father was doing forced labor outside the camp. Although the people were allowed to leave that camp, they could not get out of Czechoslovakia any more. It was, as you know, heavily influenced by Communist Russia. People from outside the camp wrote, "You might want to stay where you are. At least you have something to eat. People are dying like flies here. Old people simply fall down and die." We decided to leave the camp. However, there was no transportation. Everything was stopped. At that time, my father had to work outside the camp. My mother said, "We will go outside to where your father is." So we got out of that camp. I must say, they did ensure that the families would stay together. At least that was good. It was also good that my grandmother, my father and I could speak the Czech language. That helped us quite a bit.

In 1949 we arrived in Prague, where my father started working in construction for an acquaintance. He did drawings and so forth. There was such a shortage of everything, especially housing. People lived in cellars, in washrooms, in old farm huts, anywhere to find a roof over their heads. There were no living quarters to be found, not for Germans. However, we found a place to stay in Prague in a warehouse where wheat was kept. It was full of mice, and those mice were running down and crawling around at night. There were two little rooms. So we were five living in those two tiny spaces. There was no bath, no toilet, nothing; but at least we did have those two rooms for the five of us. We slept on wooden boards on which we put sacks of straw. We really didn't have anything, and whatever little we had was in cartons. Oh, those were conditions!

Before we came to that warehouse, a guard had lived there. There was a hole in the floor because that guard had raised a pig below. We had to repair that hole, but at least we had now a little privacy. We were now out of that camp and its filth and all those bugs. While we were in that warehouse, my grandmother was working for the farmer in the fields. My mother was knitting for the people in exchange for food. I was lucky that I was pretty good in languages and I also studied hard. Even when we were in that awful camp,I got hold of a book and studied very hard.

You know, the Czech language is very difficult, especially its grammar. I read and studied it even in that filthy camp. Well, I did actually graduate with pretty good grades at the age of fourteen or fifteen.

Back in 1945, we had tried to get out of Czechoslovakia. But then everything was stopped; you could not get out any more. In 1949, my father tried everything possible to get out of Czechoslovakia. He filled out many forms to go to Austria and work as a mason. It was not possible. He tried Sweden; not possible. He tried Germany; not possible. He tried Switzerland to go there and work as a mason. Switzerland wrote, "Well, if you are a master contractor, then you certainly would not want to remain a mason." We tried all kinds of things to get out of Czechoslovakia. My father went to the British occupying forces and asked if there was a possibility to leave the country with their help. They were going to send him to work in Afghanistan. Yes, imagine, Afghanistan! Well, my mother talked him out of going there to work. Any neighboring country, like Austria or Switzerland would have been great, but not Afghanistan. It was too far away.

When I graduated from school, I had difficulty finding a job. I went to the employment office and had to take an exam. I was asked all kinds of questions from Czech literature (the questions were all a bit political), mathematics, and so on. I knew the answers to all the questions. Then the question was my ethnicity. The interviewer read from my papers, "Father: construction master. Ethnicity: German." That did it, that last word, "German." Also the papers indicated that we had owned quite a bit of property before the Czechs came, placed a flag on our villa and our property, and took it all away from us. Now that it was found out that we were German and had owned a lot of property, the interviewer changed her tone immediately. All of a sudden the interview and the questions were over. No more questions, no more interview. I was German and that was it. The Czechs knew everything about us. The secret police were everywhere, saw everything and knew everything about us. That was the Russian communist-controlled system. My father was self employed for many years, and that was considered negative in the now Communist regime. If he would have been a poor laborer and had not owned any property at all, that would have been looked at as more favorable, and it would have been easier for me to get a job.

Well, after trying very hard to get a job, I was finally told that they had a job for me. It consisted of removing animal feces. Yes, that was the job they had for me, animal feces remover. My mother told me, "No, under no circumstances will you do that!" Then, finally through contacts of my father, I was able to work in an office as an intern. I went to school and learned stenography in the Czech language while holding a job in that office. Later, I got a job in the outskirts of Prague. It took me two hours every day from Prague to where I worked. I took a bus, a streetcar, and walked a lot. However, as a young person one can do all that. I doubt if I could do that today. When I came home from work in the evening, after my two hour commute, the first thing was to fetch two to four buckets of water from the well. There was no running water. Next, my evenings were filled with studies. I took private courses in English and in Russian. My grandmother would be asleep, and I would sit at the table and study vocabularies in Russian or English. I wrote down every new word three times and spoke the word out loud. That is how I learned those languages. It was actually a good way to learn foreign languages.

In 1949, we were forced to take on the Czech nationality. We only had a temporary passport. So now we were told that whoever was a German needed to become Czech and have a Czech passport. So what were we to do? After a long discussion, we did go and get our Czech passport. Even though not much changed, it was especially important to become a Czech national because without being a Czech national, it was impossible to get a job.

At the Language School in Prague, where I studied English for three hours every day, I had an excellent language teacher. She was paying much attention to our pronunciation. I have so much respect for her and her method of teaching. They were private lessons, and my father and I paid for them. That was from about 1949 to about 1951. It all took a lot of work. I still had to work in the office. Sometimes I had to make up some work. Then I came home, after a two hour commute and fetched the water from the well. Then I needed to go to language school in the evening and study afterward until late at night. Such a thing as free time did not exist. I did not have any youth at all. Dancing classes did not exist. I lost my childhood; I lost my youth. Only at the age of twenty or twenty-one did I begin to experience a little bit of my youth. However, dance lessons or beautiful dresses, as other Czech girls had, did not exist for me. I was happy just to have something to eat.

Then my father tried very hard to find a job and found one with a construction company in 1954 in a small city in the Egerland region. We were even able to live in an old house. Because I had learned how to type and do stenography, I was able to find a job in an office. Later I worked in different places in the border area.

It was there where I met my husband. I was twenty-three years old then. He was a few years older than I, and his father had the same destiny as my father. He was forced to work in the pit in the coal mines. Just like my father, he was not allowed to leave Czechoslovakia either because they needed his coal mining expertise. They would not let experts go because they needed them. The borders were closed for them. My husband and I had a lot in common. We got to know each other, fell in love and married within half a year.

When our baby was born, I said, "That child is German and will be raised German." It was important to me that the first language in our child's early years would be the German language because a child learns a language much easier than an adult. So I always spoke German with her. My husband was working in the coal pit and later in an office while I was at home with my baby. I said, "I only have this one daughter, and I want to enjoy her." It was especially important for me to spend much time with her because of the language, so that I could speak German with her. I knew she would learn Czech later anyway. So her first language was German, and she was fluent in it. But now the question was what we would do when she had reached the age to go to school. Everything in school was in Czech. How would she be able to understand and follow? So I took it upon myself to translate everything from German into Czech. I would tell her a word in German and then translate that word in Czech. Then I repeated it about three times. Every word, every sentence, I asked her to repeat. She didn't like that at all. She was four years old; how could she be so drilled? But, there was no other way because it would have been impossible for her to go to the kindergarten and not know any Czech. So now she knew a little Czech, and children learn quickly from other children.

Our daughter went to a Czech school for about four years and was an excellent student. Her teacher said to me, "Yes, but she does not quite speak pure Czech because every once in a while, she mixes some German words in her speech." My daughter translated words from German to Czech, as she was used to when I taught her. She did not think in Czech; she thought in German. One has to think in both languages. You see, I thought in both languages, but she didn't. She could speak in Czech but had more difficulty writing in Czech, especially essays.

In 1968, the democrats in Czechoslovakia wanted socialism. It was the Dubczech era. Now we said, "We have to get out; we must find a way to get out of Czechoslovakia." My parents were able to leave because they were considered to be old, and Czechoslovakia did not want to take care of old German people. We, on the other hand, were young and able to work for nothing for the Czechs. They would not let us go that readily. When my parents were in Germany, they wrote again and again, "Please try hard to follow us." For a long time, we had the visa for Germany. My uncle had gotten it for all of us already back in 1949. That was almost twenty years earlier, imagine that! But we were not allowed to leave Czechoslovakia then.

So now we tried everything we could to be able to leave. During the new Socialist movement, the Czechs were a little more flexible than they were before. So it was easier for us to investigate all kinds of possibilities to leave. We filled out form after form and waited for a response. We were so eager to hear any response. We sat and waited like we were sitting on hot coals. A sister of my husband wanted to leave too. So I also got all her papers ready.

But then, lo and behold, the Russians marched in. Yes, the Russians marched in. It was in August, 1968. It was so terrible. The Czechs cried. The Russians wanted to prevent Dubczech from coming to power. There were shots. Tanks kept coming and rolling to Wenzel Platz. We were living the nightmare all over again. However, now it was the Russians against the Czechs. People were crying! Oh, it was terrible to see adults cry.

We thought we would leave for West Germany. We had already quit our jobs; we had given notice to leave our apartment where we lived. We had our visa to leave, but no permission to do so. How would we get out of there? My sister-in-law came and said, "We have nothing any more; we are like beggars." So I said, "I have to go to Prague because the visa was stamped in 1949 in Prague. However, before I left I went to City Hall and asked if our permission to leave had arrived. Imagine my jubilation to find out that it just had arrived the day before. I thought I would go crazy with joy.

But now I had to drive to Prague, so that they could stamp the visa up to date. I did not waste any time. It was dangerous because the Russians were everywhere. I had to travel by bus to Prague, but the Russians controlled each bus. I was afraid that if they took my papers away, I would have no chance of getting our visa updated. I could not let that happen. So what did I do? I made sandwiches and packed apples, pears, and underneath my lunch was my written permission to leave Czechoslovakia.

When I arrived in Prague, there was a long line of about three hundred people waiting in front of City Hall. I thought, "Oh, my God, I will never have a chance. What shall I do now?" So I walked around the city, and all of a sudden the shooting started, one shot after another. That was not all. From the windows they banged with pot lids and threw things out of windows. People were hiding. I ran quickly into a store to hide so that I would not be in the street. When I returned to the streets much later to make my way to City Hall, there were far fewer people waiting in line, thank goodness. I got my precious stamp on the visa and permission to exchange Czech Kroner for twenty German Marks. Relieved, I took the bus back home. My husband was anxiously waiting for me, afraid I would never be able to return. They knew what was going on. Then we drove to Karlsbad to exchange Kroner for twenty German Marks, and shortly afterwards we left for Germany.

On September 3, 1968, we left Czechoslovakia and crossed the border into West Germany. At first we had to go to a camp near Nürnberg where we stayed for three days. We were with eight people in one room, but that was totally all right. I must say, the Germans organized everything extremely well. We had a room, food, and even some money in that camp. We couldn't stay there longer because there were still many refugees arriving. But I must say that the Czechs were better received in Germany than we Germans, even though they came illegally. They were welcomed and hosted. We were German and came legally to Germany. It hurt a little, you know. It hurt a little that preferential treatment was given the Czechs, especially since it came from our own German people. Some Czechs could speak German, but most of them couldn't. But it didn't matter; they were all warmly welcomed and hosted. Many of them were professionals and well educated, and they were able to acculturate readily. They also sent their children to German schools, and they assimilated fully. Good for them and good for us that we were now finally in Germany and free.

When we were living at home in Czechoslovakia, we had many good friends and acquaintances who were Czech, and we got along well with them. But the government was a problem. The people were quite fine, except for those old ones who were grim because they were so extremely nationalistic. One time I went back to Czechoslovakia with a tour group to the Bohemian Forest. It was a reconciliation group. There were Czechs and Germans in the group, and they went back as a form of reconciliation. When we arrived in Czechoslovakia, there were speeches given. I stood on the side and watched. They didn't know that I could understand Czech. I heard the Czech people say, "Now they crawl again here into our land . . ." and many more foul words against Germans. It was definitely enemy talk. After I had heard enough I said, "Come, let's go. I can't hear it any more." Now, imagine. That was to be a "reconciliation visit!" Disappointed, we left right away.

When we moved to Schweinsfurt and enrolled our daughter in school, the teacher was amazed that she could speak such good German even though we were coming from Czechoslovakia. You know, there were absolutely no German schools after 1945 in Czechoslovakia. Soon after we arrived in Germany, my husband got a job in Nürnberg, Bavaria, where my parents were. Then he got a job with Audi in Ingolstadt. Audi was looking to fill positions at that time. So he could start right away in the mechanical division. That was very good. He had to learn a lot, but he assimilated fast. He was very happy to be there and worked there for twenty-two years.

We even got a three-room apartment in Ingolstadt since my husband was working at Audi. It was new, and we felt like we were in heaven. We had three rooms, a bath, a kitchen, and everything. It was wonderful after all that which we had endured. I got a job at a bank in Ingolstadt, and worked there for seventeen years. I could write German, but to type German on the typewriter was something I had to get used to. Now and then I did make a mistake, and because of that mistake I had to start all over again. At that time there was no computer where you can delete your mistake. So sometimes my co-workers did let me know nonverbally and verbally that I was not from there. That hurt and was not easy to take. I had to swallow it and keep quiet. But all is well that ends well. I am so thankful to Germany that it welcomed us. The State Employment Agency found us the jobs.

We experienced a lot until 1949. We were discriminated against in Czechoslovakia. We were not allowed to speak German except at home. My mother did not speak any Czech. Whenever she and I would walk on the street and a Czech would come by, we would stop talking. Whenever that person was further away, we continued to speak German. I would speak only Czech in public. My mother could read Czech, but she could not speak it. She didn't learn it as a child, and if you don't learn a foreign language when you are a small child, your speech will reflect it. Even if you learn to speak the language fluently, most likely you will speak it with an accent. Certain letters give you away. That even happens with different dialects. For example, I have the Prague German; I cannot change it. Here in Bavaria, the Bavarians look at me in the stores. They know right away that I am not Bavarian. On the other hand, they love to hear my Prague German.

When we were in Niemes, I only had one pair of shoes, and they hurt so much. They were too small for me because I was a child, and children grow out of shoes quite fast. But I only had that one pair of shoes. What was to be done when I grew out of them? So my parents gave me shoes belonging to my aunt, who was transported by the Czech and not with us any more. Those were such high heels. Everybody laughed at me. Imagine. I was a child walking around with those high heels. In the winter there was a pair of men's shoes which were far too big for me, but at least I did not run around barefoot on that snow. I am telling you, those were tough times. Then I remember my father brought some material, some cloth, which he had bought with the money he had earned. We took that cloth and made cloth shoes, putting rubber souls at the bottom of the cloth. Oh, were we happy; we had shoes that were comfortable. We didn't care that they were made out of cloth. We could walk in them. How can you explain that to the youth of today? They can't imagine it. They do not know how good they have it today. Whoever had to experience that can simply never forget, and will look at things differently. I can cook, I can live with very little, and I do not need to spend a lot of money. Nature is free. I can take walks in nature. It does not cost anything; it is free. Many wonderful things in life are free. There are many museums and libraries that are free. How wonderful it is when people are free to use them.

Elisabeth Siebert
Born November 17, 1927, in Odrau, near Fulnik, East
Sudetenland, Czechoslovakia

"Yes, indeed, I do believe that nationalism and religious zealousness are truly something
dangerous."

ELISABETH SIEBERT

Interviewed July 31, 2007, in Ingolstadt, Germany

I was sixteen years old in 1944 when the war-front was already close to my home town, Fulnik, in East Sudetenland. The center of the town was burned down by the drunken Russians. They drank too much Schnapps, and then they burned down the center of our town. All the inhabitants of our city were ordered to leave their homes. So like all other women with their little children and the elderly, we had to leave everything behind and flee. Hurriedly my mother, my two little brothers, my sister and I packed a knapsack and a suitcase and left for Prague. It was very difficult to get there by train. Luckily, we got a ride with an army transport. My little brother, Hartmut, called each soldier "Daddy." After arriving in Prague, we met up with my father's brother, who was later killed by the Czechs.

We made our way further to Eger which is already at the Bavarian border. I went to the *Gymnasium* [German High School] in Eger for three weeks because I was not up to par with the other students in the English language. Apparently at my school in Prön, we had poorer English instruction than at the school in Eger. Prön, where my mother had lived, was located right at the border of Poland and Czechoslovakia. It was a language island of Czech, Polish, and German-speaking people. Later, all the schools were closed in Eger.

My uncle (another brother of my father) took us in. Since he was a pharmacist, I helped him and worked as a pharmacist assistant. My mother, who was also a pharmacist, was married to a physician. She had to bear the main burden in our family.

Later, we bought an apartment with the help of my uncle, who was relatively well off.

Then the Americans came. The American soldiers were very friendly and an elite group of soldiers, and they gave the children all kinds of sweets and goodies. Of course the children went to them all the time. We went through the garbage pile of the Americans and picked out nylon stockings that were thrown out because they had a hole or so. We fixed those stockings, sewed them up, and wore them.

When the Americans left the Eger region, the West wanted to keep that region in its block. Eger, Karlsbad, and Mariendbad is the natural and very beautiful mineral bath triangle. But politically, the West did not keep it. Unfortunately, it was the East Bloc, the Russian,s who got it. Yes, that was unfortunate indeed!

It was then that the Czechs came to Eger. We had to endure many hardships because of the Czechs, especially from young boys. Perhaps they were fanatics or had experienced hardships during the Nazi regime. There were many very young Czech soldiers in Eger; they were about sixteen or seventeen years old with their guns over their shoulders. They only wanted to get something, steal something. So again and again, at gunpoint, they kicked entire families out of their homes and put them out on the streets, with only what the people were wearing. It was a lawless time then. My mother was a very smart woman. She turned the furniture in our house around and covered it with old cloth, so that it appeared to be in poor condition. So whenever they rang the bell, the house looked poor and undesirable. Therefore, they did not throw us out on the streets. So many people were thrown out in the street by those young Czech soldiers.

At that time we were really starving and almost starved to death. We got one loaf of bread for a whole week for all of us. That is all the food we were given in Eger, even after the end of the war. It was revenge for the food stamps the Czechs got from the German authorities during the war. Of course we got no meat. But we stood in line for hours at the butcher store, starting as early as seven o'clock in the morning, hopeful to be able to get some blood from the butcher. Yes, blood! Many a German, if they were lucky to get some blood, would carry that blood in a container and make something eatable out of it. That is how desperate we were.

I remember that in Eger, all Germans had to wear those identifying white arm bands as soon as the war was over, very much like the Jews had to wear the Star of David for identification. We Germans were not allowed to go out after dusk. We were allowed to be out in the daylight only. The Czechs were extremely strict. Once, a young boy of my age was hanged in the city square in Eger because he stole a little butter. His body hung there for a long time. It was to be an example for all to see. Yes, that is how it was. People were very hungry, and that poor boy was just trying to provide for his family.

The Czechs confiscated my uncle's pharmacy as well, but my uncle was allowed to continue working there. The new Czech manager of the pharmacy was very nice. Her husband, however, was dealing in the black market. He got alcohol and all kinds of drugs, whatever he could get his hands on. My uncle took as much time out of work as he possibly could, and I took several sick days as well. We would sneak across the border from Eger to Wallsassen, which is already in the Oberpfalz [upper territory] in Bavaria. It was not far away, only about three hours by foot, and we wanted to bring some of our things to the West so that we had them when we finally left Czechoslovakia. We went through the forest but had to be very careful. The first time we went at night with a man who knew the way. It was winter, and it snowed. We covered our bodies in white bed linens and walked through the forest so that we could not be readily seen in that snow-covered forest. Our guard walked in front of us. Whenever the patrol came, we hid and then continued on our way.

I was sixteen years old, and for me it was not only stressful but also adventurous. For my courageous mother, who felt responsible for us all, it was not at all adventurous. She was full of stress and fear. The man who led us had a bicycle with a trailer on which he carried carpets and other items. Our uncle had given him a few of his possessions to smuggle across the border. Our guide was a professional border guide who knew what he was doing and knew his way around. Later, after crossing the border for the first time, I crossed the border frequently by myself to sneak some of our things across the border. That was the only way we could keep some of our belongings when we got to the West. But, I only went during the day. One time, however, a soldier was shooting at a girl in the forest. Then I went back a little distance, hid in the forest for two hours, and then I continued on the same path when the soldier had gone.

Later, my mother and I sneaked across the border, from Eger to Waldsassen. It was in the summer, and we wore many winter coats and as many layers of clothing as we could to bring those clothes to the West. A Czech policeman caught us. He said in Czech, (I did not speak Czech, but my mother did), "What are you doing? You are not allowed to leave Eger." My mother said, "Yes, but people take everything away from us and we want to hide something at a farm nearby." That was, Of course a lie. He let us go. As we returned from Waldsassen, after five or six hours, that policeman was there again. Of course he recognized us. There were no other people on the way; nobody was allowed to be there. He demanded to know, "Where were the coats that you were wearing?" My mother, who spoke fluent Czech started to cry and said, "We have two little children, one three and one four-year-old, and they have nothing to eat; people take everything away from us." I thought, "Oh my, what will happen next? They will put us in prison and what shall become of those two little toddlers and my sister!" But then it was quite amusing. The Czech border guard started talking to my mother about miserable conditions in Prague where he came from.

That guard was about forty years old and a kind, empathic man. There were city officials among the Czechs that were reasonable people, unlike those youngsters who went plundering and terrorizing. At any rate, then my mother told me, "This kind gentleman lends you his bicycle. Take it and ride home. In the basement I still have some cognac from your Uncle Karl. Get that cognac and come back here again." I was so scared. I was German and therefore, not allowed to ride a bike through town. That was forbidden for Germans. But I did take that policeman's bicycle and pedaled away as fast as I could. Luckily, I was not stopped by anyone. I went to the basement of our home, got the cognac, and returned by bike as fast as I could. There I saw my mother sitting with that Czech policeman deeply engaged in conversation. That man had two little children of his own in Prague, and he missed them very much. After that incident and meeting, he visited us every week and played with my two little brothers who were three and four years old. He even brought us bread stamps so that we had enough bread to eat. Yes, among all the bad people, we found again and again good people who did good deeds, good people who helped us.

The 300.000 inhabitants of Brünn, where my mother comes from, consisted of two—thirds Czech inhabitants and one-third Germans. One day in 1945, a car with a loudspeaker was driving on the street of my grandfather's house, where my mother was born. The loud speaker announced that everybody must leave at once, within one hour, and wait in the street. Later a Czech neighbor, whom we visited in Brünn, told us that all Germans in that street and in all streets had to get out and had to walk on foot to a camp. That was the anticipated Brünner Death March. These German civilians had to walk for months from Brünn all the way to Prague. That is about 200 kilometers. Of course many old and frail people died on the pavement. On their way, these German civilians were distributed to Czech farmers for whom they had to work hard with little food. That went on for a while, and many died of starvation and over-exhaustion. My aunt, who was quite tall— about 1.75 meters, was a musician and music teacher at a *Lehrerbildungs Anstalt* [Institute for the education of music teachers]. When she arrived at her sister's home in Vienna, she weighed only about seventy pounds. Imagine, being 1.75 meters tall and weighing 70 pounds. She was barely alive and looked like a skeleton. That was in 1945, after the war was over.

The survivors of that Death March were sent into labor camps. Unless they died there, they were held there for two years. They never talked about it, not a word. Some Germans, whose skills were of great use to the Czechs, were not allowed to leave Czechoslovakia. The Germans who were skilled workers, for example, mechanics, pharmacists or medical workers, were not allowed to leave the country. Many strong German men were also not allowed to leave. For example, I know a Mr. Fuchs who was sitting with his brother on a suitcase in the street because they were supposed to be deported. But, they were not allowed to leave because the Czechs needed them to work in construction. That Mr. Fuchs remained in Czechoslovakia for twenty years. The Czechs kept those German people in towns and in the country-side because they absolutely needed them, and they made them work very hard for nothing. Those poor Germans were stuck; they were not allowed to leave. That is how it was.

One night at three o'clock, our doorbell rang. We opened the door, and the Czechs took my cousin away. They also wanted to take me, but since I was working in a life saving company—the pharmacy, they did not take me. My cousin was only fifteen years old, one year younger than I. He was from Prague, where his father had fallen in the war, and he could no longer go back to Prague. His mother was interned in Prague. His brother had also died. My cousin lived with us in Eger, where he was forced to work in construction. One day, the Czechs took him and many other young people and put them on a train. That train was to bring them to Bohemia where they were forced to work hard as mineworkers or as wood choppers.

The area of Oberschlesien [Upper Silesia], Kathowitz and vicinity was a coal mine region. The Germans from that region were not deported. Those who did not flee early in 1945 had to remain there as forced laborers and were not allowed to leave.

In Langemosen, where we once lived, there was a priest who came originally from Oberschlesien, which after the war became part of Poland. He told me personally that he could not speak Polish when he had to go to school as a six-year-old. The school was Polish because that Eastern state, like all states east of the Oder Neisse Line, was given by the victors of the war to Poland. In that now a Polish school, that little six-year-old boy was constantly beaten because he could not speak Polish. He went on to higher education and studied theology, but all that time, again and again, the Poles threw buckets of cold water on him or over his head because he was half-German. After the war he came to the village to which we were transported, near Ingolstadt in Bavaria, and shared his experiences.

We were very lucky that we did not end up in a camp, thanks to a Red Cross nurse in the town of Neustadt and der Eich whom my father knew well. As a favor to my father, she made it possible to arrange for a *Zuzugsgenehmigung* [permission to move into the country] to Germany. In order to do this, we also had to get permission from the Czech officials. It took half a year until all the papers were cleared. My mother could speak Czech because she grew up in Brünn, where the population was one-third German and two-thirds Czech. She went to a farmer and rented a horse and buggy, and we drove to a cloister and hospital in Waldsassen. The nurses received us and we spent Christmas of 1945 there. Here in the West, we were free. What a priceless Christmas present!

Then we landed in Langemosen, a little village near Ingolstadt with a population of 800 people. My father, who was earlier a prisoner of war, worked as a physician in Langemosen after he was released. My brothers, and all the other refugee children in school, were constantly bullied by shouts of, "*Du Flüchtling, du Flüchtling*" [You refugee, you refugee]! The boys had a hard time, but they survived. Immediately after our flight, we came to Mittelfranken. There was very little to eat after the war. My brother Hartmut was so malnourished that he had the kind of high stomach that only the starved, severely malnourished children possess. So my sister and I went to the farmers and begged for food. But the rich farmers hardly ever gave us anything; the poor ones did.

Then I worked for one year with the refugee camp. There were three hotels in the town of Gerhardshofen in Mittelfranken. Each of their meeting rooms was packed with thirty people, men and women. The only things that were in those rooms were beds and a chair for everyone. That was all. The elderly women who were all alone, many having fled from East Prussia, had absolutely nothing. They got underwear and only one dress from the prisons. That was all they had. Many simply lay down in the bed in that overcrowded ballroom. Every week at least one person died. When we saw a woman that was too frail or too weak to move, we talked with her. When a woman died, she was brought to a barn, where her body was kept until the funeral. That happened again and again, week after week.

My worst experiences were when I worked at the refugee camp. One day a teacher couple arrived. The man was truly a distinguished looking older gentleman who resembled my grandfather. My grandfather died in 1943 and did not have to go through that trauma of being expelled from home. At that time, we had a meeting room in the camp with only twelve people in it because so many had already died. That gentleman lied down, did not eat or drink anything, and in ten days, he was dead. He could not go on any more. His wife was very courageous. She had a daughter and a son who was a little mentally-challenged. That was why the Nazis did not order him to fight in the war. Perhaps that family lived in a small village, where his challenge was not so noticeable.

It was a terrible time, I must say. I myself suffered greatly from depression. Working in that refugee camp was one of my worst times because I witnessed first-hand what happened to those who had lost their home, were now homeless and had to live in that refugee camp. It was especially depressing to see the old and frail people suffer so much.

I was especially sorry for the farmers. During the war I had to work in farms during summer vacations, as we all did. So I worked for the farmer Brossmann in Wolfsdorf. They had a huge farm. He was drafted to fight in the war, and his wife was left running that huge farm. The grandfather in the family was seventy years old. I worked mostly with him in the fields and in the garden during the harvest season. They lost absolutely everything, were deported to Bavaria where they all became unskilled factory workers to make a living. For them that was extremely hard, especially for the old people. There were old folks of highly advanced-age, women, many of them widows, who were so depressed and had such hopes to return to their homes and their hometowns and regions. The young ones were better off; they could more readily integrate, and they could work. But for the old people who were in grave sorrow, it was almost too much to bear.

One of my jobs was to delouse the refugees as they were coming to the West. I had to sprinkle DDT powder on their heads. I worked much with that poisonous DDT powder. Then their entire clothing was soaked for twenty-four hours in a disinfectant solution. I also assisted nurses, including Sister Bertha. There was also another assistant to the nurses. She was about sixty years old. She was of royal blood, had lost everything and had no social insurance. She was not used to working and was really not of very much help. Because of this, she often got the third degree and disapproving looks from Margret, the head nurse. I shared a room with that unfortunate woman, who was used to royal treatment and the life of royalty. However, now she was penniless at the age of sixty, homeless, terribly unhappy and depressed.

Let me tell you a lighter story now: Once a month the head of the refugee department of the city hall came to that refugee camp from Neustadt an der Eich, which was the region's capitol. His name was Mr. Schwarz. He came to check on the food and the living conditions of the refugees. He was a very nice man, tall and handsome man. Whenever he came, the nuns would prepare him a special dish. He was an owner of much land in East Prussia, which of course was now all lost to the Russians. Mr. Schwartz asked me, "Do you know that you could actually go back to the *Gymnasium* [German High School]?" He had heard that I went to a *Gymnasium* before and could not continue school because of the war. "Your mother would get 25.00 DM per month for school money to support your education."

I was used to giving my mother 60.00 DM, the money which I earned monthly from working in the camp, to pay for our expenses. But, when I told my mom about the possibility for me to go back school, she said immediately, "Of course that's what you will do! You will go back to the *Gymnasium*." She had hidden a little bit of her jewelry from home in the shoulder pads of the children's coats; and with the help of that jewelry and the German government's 25.00 DM, I was able to go back to high school. After one-and-a-half years, I graduated. But I had to really study hard during those one-and-a-half years, especially in Latin, where I was behind and had to catch up. The nuns and the elderly people at the refugee camp congratulated me on my graduation. Thanks to Mr. Schwarz, I was able to go back to school.

I remember when the American soldiers arrived in Eger. Many of them were such handsome men. Unlike most around us, they were well-fed and well-kept, not fat, but athletic. They were also friendly, and they were apparently soldiers who did not have to fight directly on the front. We were happy when the

Americans marched in. We were happy that that terrible war, which cost us so very much, was finally over. We were also relieved that the war was over because many countless bombs fell, even in Eger and all around us. The railroad station and other parts of the city were destroyed. The country was destroyed. We were driven away from our homes. But the war was finally over.

I mentioned earlier that my father was a physician. Well, he was ordered to work as a physician in a camp, a kind of concentration camp. We had heard rumors about such camps. He absolutely did not want to go. He tried to find all possible ways and alternatives not to be sent to work in a concentration camp. The only alternative was to work at the war front. So he was sent to the war front in East Prussia. But after that experience, he never talked a single word about the war, not a single word, and my mother did not talk much about it either. I did notice that whenever my father came home for a short vacation from the war, he was so disoriented. With every visit he was more and more disoriented. He always listened to the Swiss radio stations. However, we were not allowed to listen to stations from Switzerland or the BBC. It was severely punishable and very dangerous to listen to those stations, but my Dad risked it anyway.

My father was wounded at the front. Finally, thank goodness, he landed in the West as an American prisoner of war. He was in Nürnberg Langwasser, and we went to visit him there a few times at the fence. One time at the fence, he gave me a big atlas of the world from 1890. He exchanged cigarettes for that atlas in the prison camp. He was always interested in the world, in topography and geography. I still have that atlas. Then after a while, he was released. He was lucky that he was in the American zone, imprisoned under the Americans. If he would have remained in the Russian occupied zone, he would have been treated horribly since he was at the front, even though he was not a soldier but a medical doctor.

After my father was free, he could not work as a physician just anywhere he liked. At that time, you had to fill out all kinds of forms required by the government. They would send him wherever a physician was needed. He was offered a position at two villages. One of them was Langemosen, so that is how he came there. The priest of Langemosen was especially nice to him. He rode on his bicycle almost 100 kilometers from Neustadt an der Eich to Langemosen to welcome my Dad. The priest hosted him, got him a place to stay, and was so happy to have him. It was a rural area. My father also made house calls by bicycle to his patients in the nearby villages.

I was so lucky to go to school in Neusatdt an der Eich. We had such a good teacher there. We all adored her. Unfortunately, she died at the age of sixty-five. She was our German, Latin, History and Geography teacher. In German classes we learned about Antigone; in History about all kinds of fascinating historical events; she was the best Latin teacher. We had no books because there were no books available. We had to take notes to remember. So we had to learn to write very fast to take our notes. I even learned a little shorthand.

All books were infected with Nazi propaganda. Therefore, they needed to be rewritten. That was called then *Moralische Aufrüstung* [moral re-armament]. All the books in school had to be approved by the American government. I don't know exactly when the American government started to authorize our books. Not only history books, but all books had to be approved by the Americans because, in all of them, Hitler and his party had managed to insert their propaganda and their views of the world. For example, even the natural science textbooks were infiltrated with propaganda of the "incredibly great accomplishments of Adolf Hitler and the Nazi Party." Yes, indeed. Hitler didn't leave a stone unturned to spoil even the minds of school children. In science, there were the *Rassenlehre* [Race Studies], those nonsense and idiotic "race teachings." In biology we also had *Rassenlehre*. So we were constantly asking the question, "Well, who then actually is really Germanic?" Hitler himself, who was Austrian, was not "Germanic." Actually, we are not either. We are also no "pure race," whatever that is.

From 1933 until 1945, the Nazis had enough time to infiltrate Hitler's concepts into school books. For example, I had a music book, entitled, "Die Garbe." There was no music of Mendelssohn in it because he was Jewish. Imagine that the great Jewish composers would not be studied. Imagine that Jewish people had no musical talent, according to that absolute intentional exclusion of books of the greatest composers and musicians. Imagine that! But Richard Wagner, Of course him we had to study. He was Hitler's musical idol. Wagner "was everything." He was revolutionary; he was extremely nationalistic; and he was also an opportunist who was living above his means. He lived in villas in Vienna, and when he moved out, he left an enormous amount of debt behind. Nevertheless, him we had to study, but not any Jewish composers, no matter how great they were.

For one of my research term papers, I chose to write about *Das Zeitalter des Nationalismus* [The Era of Nationalism]. It dealt with the origin of nationalism. I had hoped that finally, after that barbarous World War II which shook and changed the entire world, the world would finally be cured of nationalism. I hoped that nationalism would be dead, and I expressed that in my research paper. Well, that was only wishful thinking. It did not happen that way. Since then we had ethnic and religious cleansing in the former Yugoslavia and in Sudan; we have strife in Israel between the Palestinian Arabs and Israeli Jews; and I can go on and on.

When I grew up back at home in Fulnik, we had a Czech housekeeper. Her name was Mila. She was my age, spoke German, and she was like a friend to me. She and I went to the same German school back home in Fulnik. During the Communist era, I returned quite often to my hometown to see my childhood friend, Mila. You were actually not allowed to go, but I applied for a special visa and went anyway. At the border the guards were extremely strict. They searched absolutely everything. There were certain things that were strictly forbidden to bring across the border to Czechoslovakia, which had become a Communist bloc country.

On our visit back to Brünn, my mother wanted to see her father's home where she grew up. The people who lived in our home did not let us in. My grandfather and my Aunt Elsa and my mother had lived there. Later on, my uncle with his wife lived upstairs. Now, there were three different Czech families living in our house. Our house, as all the houses that belonged to Germans, was now the property of the Czech government. All those villas—it was a region of beautiful villas which Germans had built and lived in, became property of the Czech government.

Anyway, the people did not let us inside the house. Perhaps they were a little ashamed because the house was not kept up at all during those forty years of Communist rule, and it was very much in need of repair and care, as we could see from the outside.

Our former Czech neighbor had bought the villa next to ours from the government. She lived there with her parents. Her father was a brewery director, and her mother was a pharmacist. They had enough money to buy that villa from the Czech government. They let us into their home and were very friendly and hospitable to us. Her mother could not speak German, but she and my mother, who was also a pharmacist, had a great time speaking Czech. The husband, who was educated as brewery specialist in the Stephan brewery in Bavaria, Germany, spoke very good German. He showed us around our old hometown and translated everything for me because I could not speak Czech. Many Czechs, especially on farms and rural areas, were afraid that we Germans might want to get our properties back.

There are travel groups consisting of Germans from the Sudetenland and those from Silesia that visit, as a group, the regions of their lost homes and hometowns. They know every house, every street; and they know the history. Well, of course the Czechs are a little afraid that they might have to give up the places where they live now. That is why I believe that we will have difficulties in the future, just like the end of every war. For example, there was a law at the end of the war in which President Beneš of Czechoslovakia gave amnesty to Czechs who were lawless perpetrators during the war. All German villas, farms and property were confiscated, transferred to the Czech government and shared among the Czechs.

The Americans left Eger because of a political agreement. There were many negotiations between Russia, the United States and Great Britain. They agreed that all the German regions east of the Oder and Neisse rivers would go to Poland and Russia after the war. That is very much like it was in Thorgau where the Americans came first but then left it to the Soviets. Perhaps the Americans simply did not know or care, or perhaps it was naïve, but the Americans left entire large German regions. Apparently that was not important to them. The war was over.

They simply went back to the United States and left those regions to the Russians. Oh, and the Russians were cruel beyond words when they first came. They occupied the important big cities. Perhaps there were also Russians in Eger, but perhaps in such a small number that we did not notice them except in the very beginning of the occupation. At any rate, it was unfortunate that the Americans gave up entire regions, very much to the benefit of the Russians.

Traudel Schüttig
Born 1935 in Bohemia, Czechoslovakia

"It was those women, those incredibly courageous women, like my grandmother, who made
the impossible possible. If one would read their stories, one would not believe it."

TRAUDEL SCHÜTTIG

Interviewed July 31, 2007, in Ingolstadt, Germany

It was about 5:00 AM in May 1945, when our door bells rang. Czech partisans were there holding a stop watch. They ordered us to leave our home within ten minutes. We were allowed to take with us only what we could carry. Now imagine you had three children. You had to hurry to wake up the little children and carry them out of bed. Often all you could carry was your child. Then the Germans were ordered to go to a huge gathering place in Depetz. There, whatever they had carried with them, every bundle, was searched, and whatever the Czech partisans liked, they simply took away from them. Now those poor people who had been driven out of their homes had to climb on foot over the huge Erzgebirge Mountains to West Germany. It was really awful. If one has not experienced it, one can hardly imagine it. We had no choice but to leave the neighborhood and country where we were born and had lived for generations. The only way to make our way to neighboring Bavaria, Germany, was to climb over the Erzgebirge Mountains.

From the hilltop near my grandmother's place, we could see the war front. That was where we saw the Russian Red Army with all their tanks rolling in, coming closer and closer. There were shots, one shot after another. I remember my cousin was visiting us, and we saw soldiers marching. Of course we children went to have a closer look at what was going on. We saw the soldiers. They were Russians. It was the Russian Red Army that was marching in, and it was horrific. That was in the beginning of May 1945. The *Umsturtz* (fall of Germany) was around May 5.

The Russians marched in a little earlier before the fifth of May. They went from house to house, shot through the keyholes of the doors and raped the women. It was a catastrophe. Although I was only ten years old at that time, I remember it very well. If you have ever experienced great trauma, especially as a child, it will always be burned in your memory.

My grandmother, my mother and I (my father was not there) were very lucky that we had Czech people in our house. We had helped those Czechs during the Third Reich's expansion into our area of Bohemia. At that time when the highest officials from Germany came, they had no idea how life was in our region. They wanted to throw the Czechs out and put Germans in. My mother, who was a smart and quick-thinking woman, said, "You can't do a thing to me. My husband is serving in the war, and as long as my husband, whose house this is, is fighting in the war for Germany, just as you are, you will not do anything with us in this house." After all, my mother had the store, and it was a German store. After the other stores were all closed, it was in their interest to keep it open.

It was those Czechs whom my mother had protected who helped us when the Russian Red Army marched in and searched German houses to rape German women. It was those Czechs who told us, "You come right away to our house. When the Russians are coming tonight and break into your house, they will be alone. You will not be there." So you see, one hand washes the other. Those Czechs that my mother had protected from the German officer protected us now from the Russian Army. Thanks to our Czech friends, we were the only ones in that street who were saved from the brutal Russian rapes. We were so very, very lucky.

Living alongside the Czechs in Czechoslovakia was not as it is presented nowadays. There were three and a half million Sudeten-Germans and about seven million Czechs. One could not in full conscience say that we were a small minority. The really bad blood among us started with the overthrow of the Czech government in 1938 by the Nazis in the German Reich. They got the power for a while. Again, those *Reichsdeutsche* [Germans living within the German Reich] had no idea about the life of us *Volksdeutsche* [ethnic Germans] in Bohemia. The one and only good thing about their coming to power was that we could speak German again. Before that, after 1918, when our region became Czech, everything there was in the Czech language. Anyway, the living together with the Czechs earlier was a lot better and much more positive than what came later during World War II.

While most Germans were thrown out of their homes in our region and deported in May 1945, we were not able to leave until late 1948. The Czech government officials realized that their social structure disintegrated after they had thrown all the Germans out of the country. Therefore, all Germans who had a store or business which was useful to the Czechs were not allowed to leave any more. We had a milk store. That meant that we offered needed provisions. Therefore, the borders were closed for us. We were in some odd or crazy way protected. Most Germans were evacuated, actually thrown out of Czechoslovakia, yet we were not allowed to leave. Most store owners had to stay because they provided needed supplies or nourishment.

In addition to her home, my grandmother had a little apartment about forty kilometers from Depetz, which she had always kept as a second residence. So my grandmother said, "We have a place to stay; we can go there. But, how do we get there?" Then she had an idea. One morning she went to the police station, told the police her name and said," I have been here only for a visit and would like to return to my home with my daughter and my grandchild." Well, to make the long story short, the officer did give her a stamped paper which indicated permission to go back to her residence. So one night in 1948 we simply disappeared with only the multiple layers of clothing we were wearing, no handbags and nothing in our hands or on our shoulders. We were able to reach my grandmother's little place and stayed there. We had a roof over our heads but nothing else.

I am telling you, it was those women, those incredibly courageous women like my grandmother, who made the impossible possible. If one would read their stories, one could not believe it. Earlier, when refugees came to our home, we also could hardly believe their stories until we were ourselves homeless and on the streets. It is a totally different thing to hear about those atrocities compared to actually having to live through them.

When I asked my mother how all those atrocities against German people could have happened, she said to me, "It is quite simple. We would have perhaps even run after an ape if he would have said, 'You can speak German again.'" It was not a monstrosity against any one person, it was simply that one ethnic group oppressed the other, and no one was literally able to understand the language of the other. The mistake was that we should have been educated in two languages, Czech and German. At that time there was hardly a German who could speak Czech. Look at Switzerland. The Swiss may not all get along, but most of them speak all of the three languages of Switzerland, and they all can understand and communicate with each other. That was one of the main mistakes in our region, that we were not bilingually educated, that is in Czech and in German.

After we finally arrived in Bavaria, Germany, we were not welcomed with open arms either. In their defense, I have to say, the people here in Bavaria didn't have anything themselves. The war had caused so much destruction. Everybody had to take refugees into their homes, whether they wanted to or not. I knew that firsthand from my husband who is from Würzburg in Bavaria. The locals had to have a certain number of people in their homes. One can imagine that they were not enthused to have so many outsiders in their homes, but living space was a most scarce resource in a ruined post-war Germany.

We ethnic Germans from Bohemia were not typical Germans. We were actually more Austrian/Hungarian. We had a different mentality, a different cultural way of being than the Germans in Germany. In the beginning it was hard to live in Germany. However, I think the Germans from Czechoslovakia were blessed in a way because they were able to adjust and to acculturate wherever they landed. My mother always said, "We are only tolerated here; we have to live through it." That was typical of Bohemian Germans because we were already used to that in Czechoslovakia.

When we first arrived here in Bavaria, which is a Catholic region in Southern Germany, we stood in a long line at the marketplace for the soup kitchen. However, before we got any soup, we were first asked if we were Catholic or Protestant. Yes, indeed, that question was asked at the marketplace by the women who were standing behind the tables and giving out soup. We were totally appalled and thought we didn't hear right. Whoever did not answer "Catholic" was overlooked and did not get any soup. That is absolutely true. The Protestants either had to lie and say they were Catholic or they stopped standing in the soup line. We were so very appalled. At home in Bohemia nobody really cared if anyone was Catholic or Protestant. That was each person's personal choice. Well, we learned quickly that that was certainly not so in Bavaria at that time, and we certainly learned that we were not of the right religion to deserve a bowl of soup.

It was a challenge to go to school in Germany. At home, I went for three years to the Czech school. There I was called "the German;" here in Bavaria I was called "the gypsy." Yes, at that time, the Germans from Czechoslovakia were considered in Bavaria to be gypsies. That's what even one teacher said in class. When I heard that, I jumped up and said, *Herr Studienrat* [Mr. Secondary School Instructor], I am from there." Then he did apologize. I will never forget it. Well, they just simply did not know how we Germans lived in Czechoslovakia.

My father came out of Stalingrad with the very last tank. It was his luck and also a coincidence, thanks to my mother's previous thoughtfulness. My mother always put cigarettes into the packages that she sent him. Every single day she sent a package of cigarettes. Many packages did not get there, but some did reach him, and he shared them with others. My father's superior officer, who appreciated the rare cigarettes, always said to him, "Heinz, if ever I can do something for you, I will be happy to do so." When he saw after an attack that my father was wounded and was lying in the dirt on the ground, he got out of his tank, dragged my father out of the dirt and put him on top of his tank. When they got over the hill, Stalingrad just happened to have a break in fighting. He was literally in the very last tank that came through there. After that, no other German tank ever came across from Stalingrad again. Next day, Stalingrad was closed.

My father had tuberculosis and went to a hospital in Vienna. He was just skin and bones. The cousin of my mother went into the hospital and asked my father if he knew where the husband of my mother was. She did not recognize him; she did not know that she actually talked with my mother's husband. My father said, "I am he." You can imagine how he must have looked for my cousin not to recognize him. Then my dad went to Belgium and had to take part in the Belgian war campaign there. He became a prisoner of war. It was his luck that he was sent to Scotland as prisoner of war. We say that the Scotts are the "British Bavarians" because of their easygoing nature, like Bavarians. Even their reactions are close, we believe, to Bavarians.

My father said that it was terrible in England. The prisoners of war were treated terribly. When he went from England to Scotland as prisoner of war, he said it felt like he was in paradise: "We were invited to church, and families invited us into their homes." The priest said to his congregation, "I see that we have prisoners of war here. I hope that you invite them to your table." And they did. You must know that those Scottish people had very little themselves, but they shared it with the German prisoners of war. They really did have a different mentality from most people. My father told that story quite often. Of course the Germans were prisoners and had to work in the fields. My dad was not used to that kind of physical labor. He had a splinter that moved from one side of his body to the other side, and he needed an operation to remove that splinter. When he went into the hospital in Scotland, he was operated on and treated as if he were one of the natives, not at all like a prisoner of war, or like an enemy. He said again and again, "Really, you don't believe how good the Scottish people were to me. Those people in Scotland had the watch over us prisoners of war. That was the very best experience any prisoner of war could ever have."

One of my dad's fellow prisoners of war was a jeweler. He wanted to make some jewelry out of the British coins, which were pure silver. However, he had no tools. So they stole some tools from farms, with the intent to bring them back eventually. Of course that was found out, and the camp was searched, and they found those tools. When the authorities were returning the tools, the farmers said, "For heaven's sake, don't take them away from those poor people. They stole the tools only because they were hungry." That jeweler made jewelry and all sort of things out of those coins. My dad said that as a prisoner of war, his experience in Scotland was remarkably positive. It was a totally different experience from that with the Russians. The Russians didn't treat the prisoners of war any better than their own people because they did not have anything themselves. My father said that the Russian soldiers only went out into the war because they were poor; they had nothing. He used to say, "What can you expect from them?"

I must say, I was always lucky that those people who did something good for us, I had a chance to do something good for them in return. For example, my Czech girlfriend wrote one day that both of her parents in Czechoslovakia were very sick. So I wrote her back and asked her what they needed. She wrote back that they needed medicine which they didn't have in Czechoslovakia. I asked her to ask the Czech authorities if I am allowed to mail this medicine to her. For many years we were able to send that medication. I want my grandchildren to know those experiences we had. It is important to also remember the positive. All of us got somehow stronger, much stronger. It is amazing what a human being is able to endure.

Regina Schnell
Born January 1944 in Thammühl near Hirschberg in North
Bohemia, Czechoslovakia

"The expelled German people had to stand in line, and the rings would be ripped off their
hands. The earrings and any jewelry items they were wearing or that were found in their
pockets, handbags, or rucksacks were taken away from them."

REGINA SCHNELL

Interviewed August 3, 2007, in Ingolstadt, Germany

My family came from Thammühl near Hirschberg, where Count Waldstein had his residence. It is the area between Reichenberg and Prague, near the cities Niemes and Prachatitz. It was a popular summer vacation spot because there was a beautiful lake nearby. My grandparents, who had many daughters, had a hotel there. Their youngest daughter was my mother. My father was forest master at Count Waldstein's property. He came originally from the south, from Moravia. So I say I am an early Sudeten German; my father was from the Moravia, and my mother from North Bohemia, in Czechoslovakia. So I have the best of both regions.

The death of my mother in 2005 made such an impact on me that I wanted to know nothing about all that had happened to us Germans in Czechoslovakia. I didn't want to think about our dispossessions and expulsions. I didn't want to talk about it; I wanted to push it aside. My mother had shared traumatic experiences of her expulsion from home with my daughter, who wrote a paper about it. My daughter gave her paper to me as a Christmas present last year, but I did not want to have it. I thought, "How can my daughter give me such a painful thing as a present!" I took that paper and put it away. Later, when I read that paper, it opened my eyes to all that my mother, with me as a young child, endured. I cried and thanked my daughter many times with heart-felt hugs.

In late July1945, we began to experience the beginning of the so called *Wilde Vertreibungen* [wild expulsions]. We lived in

Hirschberg and heard that in a neighboring city German people were shot on a bridge during those expulsions. That hit quite close to home. In Thammühl, where my grandmother lived, the expulsions of Germans happened a few days earlier than in Hirschberg. My grandfather was weakened by a heart attack and could not walk, but they were forced to leave. Now what to do? So my aunt, who lived with my grandparents, pulled him from his bed on to a wooden stretcher. She also had her two children with her, a three-year-old little girl and a nine-year-old girl. They all walked across the steep mountain while pulling that stretcher on which my grandfather was lying. On the other side of the mountain was the suburb of Siegnitz in the Russian-occupied zone of East Germany (which in 1949 became the GDR). My aunt and her little group rushed down the mountain to that suburb and hurried to bring my grandfather to a hospital in Siegnitz, where he died a few days later.

My aunt was totally exhausted and suffered a nervous breakdown. She was a thirty-five year-young woman and was hospitalized for a long time there in Siegnitz. We were lucky that my grandmother had sewn money in my aunt's coat and that it was not found by the Czechs. So with that money, they could afford to stay in a hotel and pay for the funeral of my grandfather, which was in August.

My grandfather and my aunt were expelled three or four days before my mother, who was now alone at home. My father was no longer alive; he had fallen in the war. There were only German women, children and the elderly left because the men were all in the war. On the night of July 30, 1945, Czech policemen knocked at our door and said to my mother, "Tomorrow morning at three o'clock, you have to be at the railroad station. You are allowed to take thirty kilograms of luggage with you, and that is all." So my mother hurried up and packed up things of necessity. She also took, thank goodness, some valuables. She took many of my father's papers and some photos. She put her wedding ring and a baptism coin, which I was given at my baptism, in a little doll and placed the doll in my hand. Later on she told me, "If I would have known the risk I was taking, I would not have taken those valuables." Then she got dressed, three or four layers on top of the other, whatever she could wear. The most important things she had in her suitcase were the photos, the documents, and towels to keep me clean. I was at that time about one-and-a-half years old. She also took the gloves and those things that she had most recently bought when she was invited to stay overnight at the Waldstein Palace because of my father's position at the palace. She recalled that time with great pride and took those along for remembrance. She also took along the baby carriage and the rucksack and went, as ordered, to the place near the railroad station.

When she arrived at the railroad station with her suitcase, rucksack, and baby carriage, the first thing that the Czechs ordered her to do was to show what she had brought along. She had also packed the ring of my father who had died in the war. When my mother received the news of his death, together with his ring, she had left the blood on the ring. She did not remove it, and I still have it today. She also had a watch which she did not sew into clothes because it was too big and the Czechs would have felt it immediately and taken it away. Well, the Czechs took everything out of her handbag, and pointing at the watch, asked what she had there. My mother could speak the Czech language, and so she said in Czech, "It is the watch of my husband who died in the war. His blood is still on it. Please let me keep the watch." They answered, "Who knows where you got it from, and now you want to take it with you." They took it away from her and threw it on a pile of things, mainly jewelry. The expelled German people, mainly women, had to stand in line, and the rings would be ripped off their hands. Earrings and any jewelry that they were wearing or that was found in their pockets, handbags, rucksacks or suitcases were taken away. There was literally a mountain of jewelry, watches, earrings, rings and gold. The Czechs took all the jewelry from the German people and threw it all on that pile, mountain high. Many people had sewn their valuable jewelry into the seams of their clothes because they knew anything they wore would be taken away from them. However, when The Czechs found that jewelry, they took not only the jewelry away from those people, but they whipped and beat them. The Czechs had such strong whips, and they whipped those poor German women and children in whose clothes they had found any sewed-in valuables.

My mother had me in a baby carriage, and they wanted to take the carriage away from her. My mother saw a young officer, about thirty years of age, who was standing nearby. In her despair she said to him, "What shall I do? I have my rucksack, and I have this little child; I cannot carry both my child and my rucksack at the same time. Please let me at least keep this baby carriage!" He said, "Go, but if the others in the train have something against the carriage, you'll have to give it up." So she could take the carriage with her and was thankful that she had that at least. My mother had a cousin and an aunt who were also expelled with her. The cousin was alone since her husband was also in the war, and she helped my mother carry some things.

We were all shoved into a cattle-train, and then at about six or seven o'clock we were transported. We were squeezed together with many others in that cattle-train without a roof over our heads. We were deported from Hirschberg am See in the direction of the *Sandstein Gebirge* [Sandstone Mountains]. On the other side of the mountains was *Siegnitz in Sachsen* [East Germany]. The cattle-train brought us near the end of the mountains, and then we were ordered out. Under armed supervision we had to walk quite a long distance. I was one-and-a-half years old, and my mother had to push me in that baby carriage and carry her knapsack. The people who were elderly or who could not walk fast enough were beaten. Some who were left behind were lying on the ground. No one was allowed to help them. They most likely died there on the street.

Earlier that day, at three o'clock, my mother had had to leave her home, and about twelve hours later she was up on top of the mountain looking down at a suburb of Siegnitz in Sachsen in East Germany. Down below in the valley, she saw a few lights. So she ran down the hill with me to a house where the lights were still on. That house had a porch with a bench at the entrance. She went inside and asked if she might be allowed to sit on that bench for a little while. The East German people in the house asked her to come in the house and rest. They gave her water so that she could give me a bath. Of course I was a toddler of one and a half years, and I needed that bath badly from head to toe. The next day, my mother said that that kind East German woman even went and got some milk for me. Yes, there were such good people too at that time.

Then a girl came along. My mother could not believe her eyes! It was my nine-year-old cousin. She was sent by my grandmother and her mother who had heard that a transport with expellees from Hirschberg had arrived. So they sent her to look if we were among them. My cousin, who knew quite a few people from our town that were also transported, asked around. That was how she found my mother and me. We walked from that place where my mother saw the light a few kilometers further to Siegnitz, where we had a union with my grand parents and my aunt. We stayed there with them in the hotel where they were staying until my grandfather's funeral in August.

There was a severe shortage of food in Siegnitz. We got food stamps and rations. In addition, because I was a little child, my mother was able to get one-and-a-half liters of milk for me per day. But the milk had to be picked up, and we had no container in which to pick it up. A good woman, the owner of that milk store, Frau Brumme, gave my mother a present. It was a beer mug to carry the milk. I still have that beer mug. Frau Brumme was, indeed, a kind and helpful person. Yes, I must say, there were some good people who would help you. On the other hand, some individuals whom you personally trusted could also disappoint you. For example, my mother gave an Austrian woman her fur coat to keep it safe until we might someday arrive in the West. That woman was able to travel freely because she was an Austrian. Later on, when my mother asked for her fur, she simply said that she did not have any fur. So you can also be disappointed. There were also people who said, "We will help you; come to us." Then we stood in front of their doors, and as soon as they saw two women who looked hungry and needed help or a place to stay, they wouldn't even let us in.

We couldn't afford to stay in the hotel in Siegnitz for a long time. My aunt, who had suffered a nervous breakdown was in the hospital. She had two children. There was also a third aunt who also had two children. Now we were all together five children. I was the youngest among them. My aunts Grete and Hilde left my grandmother with us five children in the hotel and tried to look for a place for all eight of us to stay. They searched from Siegnitz in Sachsen all the way to Altenburg in Thüringen, bordering on the state of Sachsen in East Germany. Their modes of transportation were hay wagons or their own two feet. Sometimes they also took a train. Since they had no money, they went to the railroad mission. They also asked women whom they met on their way if they could stay overnight at their places. There were some women who said, "Yes, my husband or my son is not here. So you can sleep in his room. But when my son comes, you have to leave right away." Of course they were always afraid of being awakened in the middle of the night because the Russian presence was very much felt in that Soviet-occupied zone of Eastern Germany.

Well, those two sisters made it all the way to Altenburg in Thüringen and then went to Ehrenberg. In Ehrenberg was an empty villa of a former wool fabric owner who had to flee. The city had made that villa available to refugees. My mother and my aunts went to city officials and asked if we could stay there. With their permission, we stayed in Ehrenberg near Altenburg. Now we had a roof over our heads.

When my aunts Else and Grete heard that both of their husbands were released as prisoners of war, one by the French and the other by Americans, my aunts and their children left. Aunt Grete moved with her children to her husband in Austria, and Aunt Else, who was sick earlier, moved with her children to her husband and his parents in Reichertshofen near Ingolstadt, Bavaria. Her parents-in-law were expelled from their home and transported to Reichertshofen, where they were given a place to live.

Now my mother, my grandmother and I were alone. My mother received 35 marks per month for me as orphan pension. That was not enough for the three of us to live on, but it was all we had. Neither my grandmother nor my mother received any widow's pension. They had heard that in West Germany the situation was much better. Widows in West Germany did receive a certain amount of monthly monetary aid, which was a big help. But that did not happen here in East Germany.

We had been in the Russian-occupied zone of East Germany for two years, and its Communist rule was drastically intensifying. It was now 1947. My mother and grandmother longed to go to the free West. However, at that time that was only possible if there would be three people from the Ingolstadt area in West Germany who would be willing to move near Altenberg in East Germany. We needed three people to exchange with the three of us because of the "one to one person exchange" law between the Russian zone and the American zone in Bavaria, due to the extreme shortage of food and housing.

My aunt in Reichertshofen near Ingolstadt wanted us to move to the West and did not waste any time. She put an advertisement in the Ingolstadt local newspaper, *Donaukurier,* asking if anyone would be willing to trade residencies. For a while no one responded; it appeared that nobody wanted to go to the Russian-occupied zone of Germany. However, finally it so happened that a couple and their son who were now living in Ingolstadt but had some property in Thüringen showed interest in going back there. They read the announcement in the newspaper and answered the advertisement, indicating that they were willing to trade residencies. My mother was overjoyed to trade with them.

It took a lot of effort to come to Bavaria, West Germany. Since only an exact city-to-city or town-to-town exchange was allowed, my mother had to visit many offices and had to do a lot of paperwork. In order to get the necessary paperwork done, she had to cross the border from East to West Germany. That was, of course, illegal. She had to overcome her fear and the danger of crossing the border illegally. The only way to get written permission for our move to the West was to go there personally. It had to be done. She wanted to be in West Germany, and she did make it happen. At that time it was easier to cross the border than it was later after the GDR was founded in 1949. Years later she said, "I don't know how I did it. I would never have the courage to do that alone as a woman at night today."

As soon as my mother got the written permission, she organized our move and departure from the Russian-occupied sector of East Germany. My mother, grandmother and I traveled by train. When our train reached Moschendorf, at the border between the Russian zone and the American zone of Germany, we had to go to a refugee camp where we were de-loused and quarantined for four days. That was required before we were allowed to enter the American zone on the other side of the border. There were about twenty people in that refugee camp. After we were de-loused, we were physically examined and received a written permission to register in the American zone in the West.

Now we were able to board a train going west, and on June 27, 1947, we arrived in Ingolstadt, Bavaria, and looked forward to our three-room apartment. At least that was what the written permission had said. However, again my poor mother had to fight for us, just to have a roof over our heads. We had come that long way, and had finally arrived in the West only to find out that the family who agreed to exchange residencies with us had changed their minds. They had given us a written agreement that they would move back to Thüringen, but now they had simply changed their minds. My mother pleaded with the woman. My mother explained to her that she had come a long way with her little child and her aging mother, and that all of us now would have no roof over our heads. However, the woman of the house had not an ounce of empathy and told my mother that it was not her concern. My mother should go to the City Housing Office; it was their problem.

My poor mother went to the Housing Office in Ingolstadt and was told by an official that the city was suffering from severe housing shortage. There was simply no apartment, no room available, and that there was nothing they could do. This city official told her that she had come at her own risk and they could not give her a place to live because they simply didn't have one. However, another city official who heard all this had pity upon her and suggested that that house in which we were originally promised three rooms should be inspected to see if there would not be a room available.

So my mother went back to that house, but this time with the city official from the housing office. He pointed out that there was plenty of room in the living room for us. However, the woman of the house, in no uncertain terms, objected to that suggestion. Only after the city official said that if she refused the city would be forced to move her family out, did she reluctantly agree to have us stay and use the living room as our bedroom. At that time, the natives who had living space needed to share their space with the swarm of homeless refugees that were coming in. My mother could understand their situation, but it also lay very heavily in her heart that we had to live where we were not wanted. It was not easy to live there psychologically and economically. The rent for that room was 30 German marks per month. That was the entire amount that my mother got from the Office of Social Services.

A year later, in 1949, my mother found a one-room apartment with a kitchen, and we were delighted to move there. In 1954 we were able to move into a private three-room apartment in one of the new buildings that had been built. From then on everything looked much better.

One might think that all the hardship and loss would be left behind when we came to West Germany and had a place to stay. But my mother was affected for the rest of her life by the forced expulsion and deportation from her beloved home and her home region and all the difficult years that followed. All those traumatic events and years of hardship lay very heavily on her soul. She had gone through so much, and she had suffered so much. She had been disappointed by people whom she had trusted. She missed her home, her friends, the neighbors and neighborhood she had lost.

My mother wanted to see her beloved home one more time. So in 2001 she and I went back to Czechoslovakia to the home that she had lost and so much longed for. We went in the reverse direction from which we were expelled from our home. We went from Ingolstadt to Dresden, to Siegnitz, then across the border to Hirschberg in North Bohemia, Czechoslovakia. All the German names had been replaced by Czech names. Our centuries-old hometown and region was German no more. We have lost it forever, and how very painful that was for my dear mother.

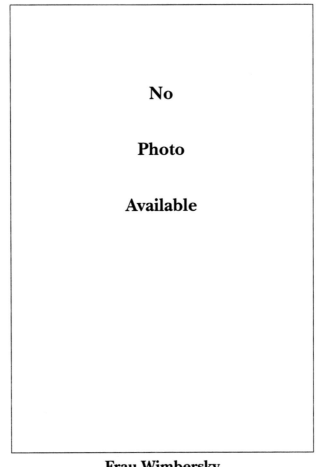

Frau Wimbersky
Born near Prachatiz, the Bohemian Forest region in
Czechoslovakia

"To be expelled by force from your home and home region and to lose all rights is one of
the worst things that can happen to you. We will never be able to go home again."

FRAU WIMBERSKY

Interviewed July 31, 2007, in Ingolstadt, Germany

We come from the *Böhmerwald* [Bohemian Forest] region in Czechoslovakia, which borders on Bavaria. We were expelled by the Czechs from our home and home region and lost everything. I don't want to think about it. I never talk about it. I would like to push it away, but it's not that easy. Thank goodness, we were able to survive it all. With the help of the Germans here in Bavaria, we were able to go on and start all over again.

The Czechs had wanted for a long time that the city of Prachatitz and the entire German Sudetenland region would become Czech. That started back in 1919 when the First World War was over and our German Sudetenland region became Czechoslovakia. The Czechs wanted all the Germans to leave and wanted only their people to live there. But that didn't yet happen. At that time, Mazarett came to power, and he was of Germanic background. So the Czechs agreed that the Germans in Czechoslovakia would have the right for self-rule. However, that right was not implemented. One time there was a rebellion. The Germans wanted self-rule, and during that rebellion, eight Germans were shot. From then on, we were the tolerated Germans in Czechoslovakia, and the Czechs oppressed us. All Germans who occupied positions lost their jobs, and their positions were given to Czechs. That went on from the end of World War I in 1919 until 1938 when Hitler's troops marched in.

Before the Germans marched into Czechoslovakia in 1938, the German men were ordered to join the Czech military. Now it was like this: "I am a German, and now the Germans come marching in, and I am ordered to shoot at my own fellow Germans?" No way could the ethnic Germans do that. So they hid in the forests and waited. Then, in October of 1938, the Germans marched in. We were happy because it meant liberation from Czech oppression for us. We took photos, and the Czechs must have taken note of it. At any rate, the Czechs knew exactly in 1945, when the war was over, who had been hiding in the forests to escape serving in the Czech military. They took all those German people and put them in prison. What the Germans had to endure in that prison was really horrible. There were not only men but also women put in the prisons because the women had earlier been in the German Organization for Women. Those German men and women were brutally treated. But, I must say that rape of German women did not seem to happen in Czechoslovakia. At least I have not heard of one such case. However, there were constant reports of so many horror stories about beast-like rapes of German women and girls in the eastern states of Germany when the Russians marched in. Compared to those Russians, I must give the Czechs credit; they did not seem to violate German women. In that regard, we were still lucky.

After Hitler reclaimed our region in 1938, my future husband was standing in front of a big house. Upstairs in that house a Czech city employee and his family had rented the apartment between 1919 and 1938. They were now living in that nicely-furnished apartment. When Hitler and his troops marched in, that Czech city official was fired because he worked in the city administration. He left right away and went to his hometown in Czechoslovakia. He gave the key to my future mother-in-law and said, "I give you the key. I cannot, at the moment, take everything with me. But if it is possible, I will come back and pick up my things." Three to four months later he returned to pick up his belongings. Nobody took any of his possessions, and he was able to take his things and drive away. He was a very friendly man, and we always got along with him. You see, we had no hate or disrespect for the Czech people. However, the power-hungry men who led us into that horrible war, they were half blind. They had no sense. Before doing such terrible things in various regions in Europe, one has to think first, one has to work in unison with one's conscience. But perhaps they had no conscience. Young German men, boys practically, were ordered to fight, especially toward the end of the war. If they didn't, there were most severe life or death consequences. Oh, when I think of how many of them from my own circle of friends and acquaintances died in the war! It was horrible. There were all the time, again and again, memorial services. Mothers lost their sons. I went with those boys to school; I knew them. They were my classmates. It hurt so much. How agonizing it was for the mothers who lost their sons.

You must understand that for us, who were under the thumb of the Czechs, Hitler's victory to gain back our Sudetenland was a relief. It seemed to mean freedom for us, and who doesn't long for freedom? The Sudetenland, which included the entire border region of Czechoslovakia, beginning from Silesia to the Egerland, down to the Boehmerwald on the border of Austria, was not under the Czech rule. It was Sudetenland, where mainly Germans lived, where German was spoken, and where we had German schools and German culture. We were Germans in our region, but we also accepted the Czechs because they were born there. Many Czechs were born there in the Sudetenland. We got along really fine with the Czechs that were born in that region, but with those that came from other parts of Czechoslovakia, there was anything but a friendly relationship. Unfortunately, after 1945, it all fell apart. It was all broken down.

At the fall of Germany, in May 1945, I was twenty two years old. I didn't come to West Germany with the transport that expelled many Germans from Czechoslovakia. The men were all in the war, and there were hardly any men left in our town. We left our home earlier because the rumor was that German women and young girls who were able to work would be gathered by the Czechs and taken away as forced laborers.

On the day when Germany fell, the Czech partisans came immediately with their weapons, and with them came also the Americans. I must say, the Americans behaved in an exemplary manner. The Americans were only looking for the Germans in Czechoslovakia because they knew that we were oppressed by the Czechs. I worked with Americans. Nobody did me any harm. We were also lucky. Thank goodness, we did not have to experience the Russians. It was not so bad for us because we were so close to Bavaria. It was not as horrible as in the East, where the Russian Red Army marched in. However, the Russians came very close to our border of Czechoslovakia. Then the word always was, "When the Russians get here, run for your life and leave as fast as you can!" We were so lucky the Americans came instead of the feared Russians, and the Americans really did support us. But that was a thorn in the eye of the Czech people because they knew that we Germans would get some food. We got some salary when we worked, and the Americans did not aid the Czechs in that way. There was an American officer who helped us a lot.

Then, of course, all kinds of things happened. The Germans had to give up their radios, their bicycles, their sewing machines to the Czechs. Everything that the Czechs wanted from us, we had to give up. That, of course, included our homes and all our land and property. We were forced to immediately leave our homes. The Czechs took everything. It started in May 1945, and it lasted until the expulsion of Germans from Czechoslovakia. The word was that the Germans had to be eliminated. They had to leave Czechoslovakia, even though they had been there for centuries and had built prosperous communities in their regions. But how the expulsion should happen, we did not know.

From December 1945, when the Americans left, until March 1946, I was working in a Czech butcher's household as a maid. I washed, baked, and did other household work all week long, seven days a week. I had to be there all that time, from six o'clock in the morning until eight o'clock at night. You know, they had a butcher store, and they were used to getting up early and getting to work, so it was expected that I do that too. Now when I look back, I wonder how I was able to do all that seven days a week.

I got a lot of information there. They lived in the middle of town, and when I looked down from the window upstairs, I could see how the transports kept coming and what was going on. Oh, my goodness, there were so many old people sitting there on their bundles, so forlorn, so hopeless. It was such a sad sight. Many couldn't walk, so they had to be carried to the cattle-trains that were waiting to deport them. There were so many old people. It really was painful to watch what was happening. The reason that mainly old people were being transported was that the Czechs did not want to have Germans around who could not work for them. So after expelling them from their homes, they deported them. Where they brought them, I didn't know. Here I was, looking down from the window, and I saw all that tragedy happening. I witnessed a terrible history unfold in front of my very own eyes. It was a very sad sight. I was at that time twenty-two years old and didn't quite grasp the monstrosity of it all.

In February 1946 the first transports to expel the Germans from Czechoslovakia took place. The Germans were first gathered into a refugee camp, which was earlier a barracks, then a hospital, and finally a refugee camp. From there they were transported in cattle-trains to Germany. Early in January of 1945, many refugees, who fled from Silesia in Germany, which is located east of us, came to Czechoslovakia. They had fled during the war, trying to escape the approaching Russian Red Army. Therefore, many of those refugees were already housed in our German region of the Sudetenland. Now when the Czechs came to expel all Germans from Czechoslovakia, all those poor refugees were deported as well in cattle-trains. There were about thirty people in each cattle-train compartment. All were taken to the border to a refugee camp.

My parents were among those who were expelled and transported. They were kept in that refugee camp for fourteen days. During that time, all of their bedding or the few things they had taken with them were searched to see if the Czechs could use any of it. Yes, many a time, even those few necessary items that they had gathered to survive were often taken away from them. The Czechs could simply take anything they wanted. There was certainly no law against it and no law that Germans could go to for help.

Now I have to tell you the situation with the transport. There were, as mentioned, thirty people with their luggage in each boxcar of those cattle-trains. The train had twenty box cars. So there were all together about six hundred people at each transport. They were simply shoved into those boxcars like cattle. They were given two buckets for their bathroom needs and something to drink, nothing to eat. The train stopped at the border station in Kopenwalde. There was the American Army with many trucks already waiting for those refugee transports. The Americans directed where in Germany each transport truck should go. That was in February 1946. My parents arrived in Germany in May of 1946. As soon as they arrived, they were de-loused with the help of a powder. Then they got something to eat.

When the German expellees arrived in the West, they were still wearing the required identification bands on their arms. As soon as the war was over, all of us Germans were forced by the Czechs to wear a band on our clothes to identify us as Germans. Most bands were white. I had to wear the youth star on a yellow band on my left arm which every German teenager from fourteen years upwards had to wear. So when the expellees arrived in Germany, they threw all those armbands away. I am sure that it felt good. Then they were transported in trucks to Ingolstadt, Bavaria. The city administration of Ingolstadt had registered children into different schools. Because of all the influx of refugees and deportees, the schools were crowded. There were at least fifty children per classroom at that time.

While I was still in Czechoslovakia, some young acquaintances and I risked going illegally across the border to Germany. We did that so that we would have some necessary things when we arrived in the West. Even though it was illegal and dangerous, I dared to do that not once, but three times. Once in the winter, in the snow, and another time we took our bikes and packed things on them and brought them over so that we may have the most needed things after leaving Czechoslovakia. The third time I remained in the West. We only had that which we could wear. But I tell you, after each escape, I was totally *kaput* [a wreck]. I had to walk fifty kilometers to the border and then at night come back in the dark, quiet as a mouse, careful not to be caught. One had to escape at night because the Czech guards were everywhere on the watch for any escapee. They knew that people were crossing the border illegally with things, and they were able to take those things away and keep them for themselves. Yes, it was difficult. Again, the only reason to go across the border twice before finally staying in the West was to bring some of our most necessary things across so that we had them when we got there. It was difficult. One could not take much, only a little at a time.

The first time when we were crossing the border, it was winter and high snow. We went with a big sleigh. We put quite a few things on that sleigh. Two boys and my sister-in-law were with me. The whole sleigh was full of stuff. Then we got lost. We couldn't find the way in the snow. We knew that we were close to the border because there was light in the houses. But, we could not enter them. We didn't know whether Czechs were living in those houses. So we took a detour. We finally made it across the hill and across the border. We were so terribly nervous that it was impossible to rest or sleep. The people who helped us on the Western side made the beds ready for us, but we could not sleep. After a while, we had to start our fifty kilometer trip back again. Toward the end, you had to go uphill. That was six kilometers or so. Then we ran down the hill. We couldn't even stop and stand because we were not strong enough. Our legs were simply automatically running. Today we can't even imagine it. You can only do that when you are young. When I returned home, it was midnight. My mother said, "You have to get up at six in the morning and wash clothes" (at the butcher's house). Yes, and that after having run and hidden from the Czech guards for about one hundred kilometers. That was in the winter. I will never forget it.

The second time I crossed the border, it was not winter time. I went with my bicycle. It was easier because I did not have to carry anything on my back. It was all on the bike, and I could ride the bike some of the time. Oh, yes, and then we had to cross a river where the water was flowing because the snow had melted. There by that river the Czechs were watching to catch any German who might try to cross. How did we do it? Very carefully! We looked and we watched. There were people like us who were returning from the Western side. When we met them our only conversation was, "Did you meet any? Did you see any?" When the answer was, "The air is clean; you can go," we went on. The river was not very wide, about three meters or so at that point, because it's not far from its origin. So we did not need a ferry, we only used tree stumps to walk across. One time on our way across the border, we heard shots and everybody jumped in a ditch. It was risky to cross the border.

A friend of ours went across the border alone one time. He did not go over the bridge because he was afraid to be caught. So he decided to walk across the river. It was later in the year when the water was not so cold anymore. But just as he was in the river . . . . Oh, my! the Czechs were coming! Fortunately, there was a stone in the middle of the river; and he sat on that stone and hid for three hours until the Czechs left. The Czechs were standing on the bridge, but he was about twenty meters away. They did not see him because there were so many stones. Yes, such things happened. He waited on that stone until they were gone.

My husband was badly wounded in Finland during the war. He was shot, and the shot landed in his lung. Half of his lung was infected and full of puss. Then he was flown from Finland to the Black Forest in Germany and had an operation. Four of his ribs were taken out, all on the right side. He had suffered a lot. He was only nineteen years old then. This teenager was in the war until he was injured in Finland. That was before we got married. The third and last time I crossed the border was with my husband who had risked coming back from the West to bring me across the border. So in March 1946, I finally escaped across the border from Czechoslovakia to West Germany with my husband. Now that we were both in free West Germany, we got married on May 18, 1946. My parents were already here in West Germany and my husband's mother and sisters were here, too.

We came right away to Ingolstadt in Bavaria, and had to look into how we could find something to eat. We slept on the floor. Well, what should we do? We had nothing, and there was little room available for all those refugees that were flooding into the city with the daily transports. Later we got some army beds to sleep on. That was good. People tried their very best to give us the most essential things to survive. I must say, it was extremely well organized, considering the grim situation, the destruction of Germany which was severely bombed, and the large influx of refugees. The refugees and deportees had to look wherever they could to find a place to stay. There were many with children who had to seek shelter in a small space with the little ones. The city of Ingolstadt had a barracks. There were, again, about thirty people in a huge room. It was quite a catastrophe. That influx of refugees continued for many years until the 1950s.

Everything was destroyed in Germany. The question was how and where to start building it up again; and on top of that, how to accommodate so many truckloads of refugees coming in every day. It was terrible. But the local people who had to take in the refugees and deportees were extremely humane. It was not at all easy for the locals to share their homes and living space with the refugees and deportees. In our case, it was for about four years that we had to go through their kitchen, use their bathroom, and so forth. There was really no more privacy as the locals had known it before. I cannot imagine how we would feel about that today.

My husband was unemployed, but because I was able to sew a little, I was able to earn some money. There were refugees who came from the Eastern regions of Germany. They were better organized in the beginning because they were not such a huge group. They got a little help from someone, and whenever I sewed for them, they brought me some food. Yes, that is how good these refugees were. They knew firsthand how badly off we were and that we, like them, had nothing and had lost everything. That little bit they had they shared with us. That is how they were, very generous, very empathic.

There were also food stamps. It was very little, but as the saying goes, "It was too much to die and too little to live." We were not at all very picky. After four years, in 1950, our child was born. Now we had that small child in that tiny space to live, and we had no bed for that child. Someone gave me a straw suitcase. We screwed the lid of the suitcase off, and that suitcase was my baby's bed. When my boy was born, I was distracted from thinking too much about the terrible tragedy that had happened to us. I had to deal with the urgent necessities of everyday life. Later we were finally able to get an apartment in Ingolstadt.

Here in Bavaria at the border of Czechoslovakia, we had much in common with the Bavarians, culturally and linguistically. We speak a similar dialect. The local Bavarians were also very much affected by the war. They had to suffer a lot too. I must say, I had not a single exchange of bad words, no fighting with the natives of Bavaria. One had to keep to oneself and try not to be in the way of the local home owners. I was happy to have a roof over my head and that I was finally out of the oppression in Czechoslovakia. Yes, I must say it was oppression and hardship that we were finally free from. I don't want to say that the Czechs were bad people. Anywhere in the world people are good and bad. Most of the time one remembers the worst, especially when one had to suffer traumatic hardship at the hands of those people. That was an experience that is forever burned into our memories. To be expelled by force from your home and to lose your home, your home region and all your rights, is one of the worst things that can happen to you. We will never be able to go home again. However, we arrived here in Ingolstadt, Bavaria, and I can thankfully say that what we experienced here was extremely humane and well organized.

In 1948 the *Währungsreform* [German monetary reform] came, and the Reichsmark was changed into Deutsche Mark, DM. Now we were able to buy a few things, and how happy we were about every little thing! Well, you see, we lived through it all and we survived. We can never go home again, and we had to start all over again with very little. I know how hard it was to get anything. Up to this day, my husband says to me, "Throw that stuff out; throw that stuff out!" But you know I can't throw it out. I remember how hard it was when we had nothing. He says, "What do you want with all this? You are eighty-some years old." But I can't throw away perfectly good things. The furniture and other things that you can buy today are not half as good quality as our old ones. Anyway, no ten horses will bring me to a store to buy new furniture. My grandson, who studies business at the University in Munich, comes and visits us and says, "Oh, that closet. I would love to have it." "Yeah," says, my husband, "You are welcome to it, but it seems not possible to move it out of here!" Ha, ha, ha. Big smile! We bought that wardrobe when we moved into our first new home in 1958.

We were not the only ones who suffered. It was the entire German nation that had to suffer immensely. I have to tell you, we who are refugees and expellees, we can be proud. After losing our homes, our home regions and everything, we came here and worked very hard with everyone to build up this destroyed country and to restore our bombed cities. It became an economic wonder. Yes, we refugees and expellees were very hard workers. I remember how someone said, "From the refugees one can learn how to work; they can make something out of nothing." Also you know, work distracts you from your sorrow. That is not a bad thing.

Isabella Müller
Born June 20, 1937, in St. Aegyd am Neuwalde, on the border
between Czechoslovakia and Austria

"How the women were able to cope and make the best out of the worst, I just don't know.
One can only marvel at their ingenuity."

ISABELLA MÜLLER

Interviewed July 30, 2007, in Burgberg, Austria

W e are originally from Erdberg. It's not far from Obersdorf. Near our house was a telegraph pole, and we would climb on top of it and look far out. My mother shouted, "Now they come again, those silver birds [air planes]!" Yes, it had started. The bombs crushed down, one after another and the whole city began to burn. The entire city was on fire, and it was such a beautiful, very clean city. All the houses, everything was on fire.

Whenever they show a film of that on television today, I turn the television off. I cannot see it; I can't hear about it. I want to forget it. I tried very hard not to think about that horrible time, to push it aside. I don't know how I shall explain it. As soon as I hear about or see a part of that tragic history, an electric current goes through me. It goes through my skin and legs. It really hurts. When one has experienced so much, one tries to turn it off, doesn't want to be reminded. It's too painful, and yet, one cannot forget. The children were robbed of their childhood, of their youth. One cannot talk about those times with everyone. It is impossible for people who have not gone through it to even begin to understand. So it is better to keep quiet.

When the Russians came, they drove out all the animals. It was quite a horrible sight. Every animal that could walk or run, they chased out of the stalls. Then I witnessed something incomprehensible. One of the Russians took his gun out and started shooting at the cows; but as he did that, he shot himself in his stomach. So then he lay in the middle of the street; but nobody went to help him. He asked for a little water, but the other Russians who were with him told him to go and get some himself. I know it was war time, but how can one human being, one fellow soldier, treat another that way?

I don't remember my grandmother. I only saw her one last time when we were still in Graz. However, I have great memories about my Opa [grandfather], the father of my father. Opa always called me "Gisela." I was his Gisela. I went to him every day in the barn where he was milking his cow and let me get cream from the milk. When I returned to the house, my mother would say, "Oh, you don't need breakfast; you were in the barn again." Yes, my grandfather and I, we were good buddies. He let me do just about anything. When the Russians came, he said, "They will not get my cow!" He was determined not to give his cow away, so he hid it. He loved that cow. Did you know that that cow saved his life? No, it didn't just provide milk and very much needed sustenance, that cow saved my grandfather's life. It protected him from a gunshot that he would otherwise have gotten. Opa was sitting down and milking his cow, when gunshots flew through the barn window. They hit the cow while he was milking her. By the time he got up from his milking stool, the cow was dying. That cow saved his life but lost hers. My grandfather was never quite the same after his cow died. He became very quiet and hardly talked anymore.

My father was not in the war. He was working with the railroad. He did not like the trade union and was pretty vocal about it. All the union members had a membership number. Well, he had no number, no party book. And because he was not in the union, he was somehow not forced to go to the front. It so happened that my father's favorite foreign language was Russian. He had studied it all on his own. That was why his youngest child was named Olga, a Russian name. He taught himself Russian and could speak it quite well. He was working in the office of our City Hall and translated into German what the Russians wanted him to translate.

Some Russians used to come into our home because they knew that our father could speak some Russian. Since he could understand what they were saying to one another, my father said, "When these Russians come into the house, it is very dangerous for the women. We have to hide them." You know, the Russians were extremely dangerous when it came to women. There were a few Russians who would come often and sit around in our home and talk with my father. We had an accordion and we three little kids and my father even sang with them. However, my mother was hiding. Whenever we saw the Russians coming, my mother would hide quickly behind the closet in the bedroom. She would not come out until they had gone. It was good that the Russians who came into our house did not do any harm to us girls.

On the other hand, one learns; one learns quickly. For example, when a Russian was standing in front of the door of our home and asked for my father, I knew that I could let him in. But I had to depend on my instinct in relation to whom I could or could not let into the house. Those Russians needed my father for translation, and so I let them in. Of course as soon as I we saw a Russian coming, my mother quickly hid. My father always said to the Russians, "My wife got killed by the bombs." That way they would not look for her. They knew there was no woman in the house. Dad said to every Russian he met that the bombs killed his wife and that he was now a widower with three little kids to take care of. There was only a thin place between the wall and the closet where my mother would hide. It's a good thing she was slim so nobody would suspect that my mother could squeeze in that tiny space and hide for hours. It was awful. When she came out of hiding, she was stiff, and her body hurt. Once she almost fainted.

Another time, when the Russians came to our house, my mother hurried to hide. I will never forget how she looked after she returned. She fell in a ditch full of burning nettles. You know, we had our hiding places. Mom said to me, "When I have to hurry up and hide, you know where I am." That time she hid in such a hurry she fell in a ditch which was full of tall, burning nettles. When the Russians left and the coast was clear, I carefully sneaked out of the house from the backdoor and looked everywhere in all directions to make sure that nobody was watching me. Then I went to my mom and told her that she could come out again from her hiding place. My two siblings, Olga and Annie, were far too small; I couldn't send them out. So I did that every single time, all by myself. That was how we saved Mom from being raped. Better to tolerate the burns of the nettles and the bites of the bugs than the brutal rapes of the Russians.

One day some Russians came to our house and demanded something to eat. I said, "We don't have anything." So they took me with them into the village. I will never forget that. I had to go into a house and get some ham for the Russians. That house had a lot of ham hanging in the cellar. From every ham I had to eat a little piece so that they knew the ham was not poisoned. Then they shook my hand and told me to disappear. Do you think I could swallow those pieces of ham? After they were gone, I spit those little pieces of ham out from the back of my mouth. Ha, ha! These Russians were afraid that they would be poisoned, so they used me as a guinea pig. I was lucky that I was small and eight years old, and one of the few girls they didn't harm. It's a good thing I was not older and looked younger than my age. So many girls, so many teenagers and so many women had to suffer the unspeakable [rape] over and over again.

When the Russians first marched into our village, they came from the railroad station to the main street. They looted and took two sacks full of things, absolutely everything that they could find. Then they drove away. Those were all things that I had to experience as a child, and I will always remember them.

One day, in 1945, a car with a loud speaker went from street to street, and the loud speaker blasted, "*Raus, raus!* [Out, out!]" We were allowed to take only fifty kilograms with us. If you had a baby or a toddler, you hastily took diapers and a blanket. Otherwise, we took absolutely nothing except the clothes we were wearing. All of a sudden, without any time to waste, we had to leave our home and were ordered to wait on the street in front of our house. All over the city German people were driven out of their homes and they all stood on the streets. A truck came and picked us up.

It was quite a chaos. We were very lucky that the four of us—my mother, my two younger siblings and I, were all together and not separated. My mother tried very hard to keep us together, to make sure that one child was not in front and the other in the back of the truck. I still remember. It was the time when the cherries were ripe. We were in the back of the truck and picked some cherries from the tree. We were put in that truck and were driven to the railroad station where we were shoved into a smelly cattle-train.

The cattle-train stopped many a time and stood somewhere in the middle of nowhere. It would just stay there for a long time. We sat on the floor inside that train, crowded and all locked up in the dark with the little child [my sister] who was with us. When the doors of the cattle-train were closed and locked, it was dark, and we could not see anything. There was no window, no bathroom. There was a bucket of water but otherwise nothing. There was straw in the corner for us to lie on, as if we were cattle. Finally the train continued, and we were brought to a large, overcrowded refugee camp.

That camp was actually a barn filled with German refugees. There were no beds. Each family had just one straw sack to sleep on. We were a family of four, my mother and we three children: my younger sister Annie, born in 1941, and my baby sister Olga, born in 1944. All four of us had to share one straw sack. How can one sleep with four people on one little straw sack? There was no space to lie down; we could only sit on it.

We were in that refugee camp for quite a while. I don't know where that camp was, but I remember clearly that it was infested with bugs. To protect us from those awful bugs, my mother did the following: she had small bags and stuffed them with herbs which she gathered from the field. I don't know what kind of herbs they were. She took those herbs in those bags and put them all around our straw sack. We sat inside on the sack, and as a result, the bugs did not bite us. The other people, however, were full of bug bites. Their bodies, their faces were so red, and the poor little children suffered. But we were lucky; we had no trouble with bugs. What a clever woman my mother was!

One day there was a white horse lying in front of the door of our refugee camp. That poor horse was sick and full of pus, and the man next to him was also hurt and full of pus. Perhaps they were both shot; I don't know. At any rate, I was afraid of them; but my mother sent me to that man all the time to bring him some food. Whenever there was a little food left over from lunch she would send me to bring it to that poor unfortunate man who was lying on the ground in front of the door with all his wounds open and infected. Nobody cared for him; yes, nobody cared.

After leaving that refugee camp, we again were transported in a cattle-train. Again, there was no toilet or anything in that cattle-train. During the day, when the train stopped at a railroad station, the hole in the ground of our compartment was opened, a bucket of water was put inside, and that was it. That hole was our toilet. My father's sister, Rosa, was a little finicky when it came to that hole. She went out of the train to do her toilet business every time it stopped at a station. Now the Russians looked at her suspiciously. They thought that she wanted to spy at the railroad station. Just the thought of our Rosa being a spy was pretty funny, indeed. But the Russians did not believe that she was not a spy, and they beat her so badly that her whole back was raw. They kept on beating and beating her because she did not tell them for whom she was spying. Well, she was not a spy. What could she tell them? They didn't believe that she just wanted to go to the toilet. All her life she suffered back pain, most likely due to those brutal beatings. She was a young girl of fifteen years, just that age where you don't want to go to the bathroom in front of everybody, especially if it is a hole right in the middle of everyone in a crowded cattle-train. When the train stopped for the last time, they just ordered us out and the train left. Now what to do? We started walking and walked all the way to Scheuring, Kreis Landsberg, in Bavaria.

We arrived in Scheuring at ten o'clock in the morning, but we had no place to stay until four o'clock in the afternoon. We had three kids and no place to stay for all those hours. Finally we did get a place with two little rooms, a kitchen and an upstairs bedroom. I slept upstairs. Since I was the oldest child, I always put the little ones first. They, of course, were allowed to sleep downstairs with my mother.

From then on we had a better life. In addition to two bedrooms, we had a relatively large kitchen and a wash house, where we could wash our clothes on Mondays. In the back of the house, we could take baths. The two rooms that we lived in belonged to a business household. We were not allowed to touch anything. Our landlords thought themselves to be so much better than any of us refugees. Well, although they thought of themselves as elegant, and modern, their bathroom was an outhouse! If you had to go to the bathroom, you had to go outside to that outhouse. How elegant, indeed!

In Scheuring we boiled our clothes in a kettle on the stove with water and a little washing powder. There was not enough water available in the apartment to complete the washing of our clothes. So I had to go outside to a brook, even in the winter, and wash and rinse the washing powder off those clothes. The water at the brook was so very cold. My hands were freezing, but it was the only way to do laundry.

Each of us had one pair of boots for the whole winter. There were no shoes, no boots to be gotten anywhere. Otherwise, you ran barefoot until the frost came and it got too cold to go barefoot. We had to use our pair of shoes sparingly. We only wore them when we really needed to. Thank God, we did not have far to go to school, so we did not have to use up our shoes too much. That was to our advantage.

One time my mother went to a place where clothes were given away. She came home with a green motorcycle coat. In the back of the coat was a slit. Out of that motorcycle coat, she sewed three coats for all of us children. She did not have a sewing machine, so she sewed it all by hand. Can you imagine? How the women were able to cope and make the best out of the worst, I just don't know. One can only marvel at their ingenuity. My mother also sewed my first dancing dress, all by hand.

We did not have any access to medical help for my cousin Rosa's hurting back. First, we had no money. Who would help a refugee for nothing? Secondly, the natives of the village spoke of us refugee and deportee women as the "whore refugees." Yes, they called us, "the whore refugees." Perhaps they thought so because so many German women were raped by the Russian army. Many women refugees fleeing from their homes in eastern Germany to escape the Russian Red Army were brutally raped. Those unfortunate and traumatized victims of the Russians had to tolerate now in Bavaria insults from fellow Germans on top of those atrocities done to them. Imagine that!

Those horrible and frightening memories of our forceful expulsion will be with me all my life. One can't imagine what could be worse. Oh, God in heaven, all of the things that have happened to us! Still, it was much easier for me as a child than for my mother. When I think what the women at that time had to live through, I can only shake my head in admiration. Today I doubt anyone would be able to do what they had to do to stay alive and to keep their children alive and together. They had to do it all alone and often bear also the dreadful news that their husbands or sons were killed in the war and would return no more.

My grandfather never quite got over his cow being shot and killed. He had a hard time getting over the entire trauma of the war: being expelled, losing his home and all his property and all the hard years that followed. The loss of his cow was probably the last straw for him. He became very quiet after his cow took the fatal shot for him. He just stopped talking. I saw him for the last time when my mother died. At that time I could not understand why he did not come to the funeral. I went to him in the barn and asked him. He said, "To see your child in the grave is more than I can bear. No, I cannot do it." I did not understand it then, but now I do.

In 1955, my father, who worked at the German Railroad, got a company apartment in Kaufering. So we moved from Scheuring to Kaufering in Bavaria. Our father went to work at five o'clock in the morning, riding his bicycle for five kilometers, even in snow storms or rain. But he was never sick. He sometimes returned home frozen stiff, but he never got sick.

We were living in free West Germany but I missed my old childhood home and neighborhood where family and friends had gathered for generations and where I have so many childhood memories. I longed to go home again. So fifteen years later, I went back again to the home and region we lost. My aunt said, "Don't go back home." But I was aching to go back; I had to see it again. So my husband and I did drive back to Czechoslovakia. We had at that time a white BMW and were afraid that our fancy car would draw attention. When we saw what the Czech people had done, or rather not done, with all our land and property, we could have just cried. All the once-beautiful German vineyards and all the wheat fields were now all decayed. Everywhere we looked things were in bad shape. Nothing functioned at that time. Even the traffic signs were full of rust. It seemed as if nothing was taken care of in our German region, fifteen years after all Germans were thrown out.

Of course now Czech people lived in our home. One of my cousins went inside the house that had been ours. I didn't know if I could stand it, going inside our home, but my cousin entered. The people living there were nice to him and did let him in. It was sad and hurt much to see our family home in such bad shape, not taken care of at all. Yes, it hurt seeing my beloved home and neighborhood so run down. I could not help but cry. How different it looked now compared to then. It was the home, the land we lost by force forever, through no fault of our own. I learned the hard way that you can never go home again. That painful loss will stay with me forever.

Elisabeth Eckl
Born March 3, 1932, in Munich, Germany

"I will never forget when the Americans came to Pernbach. We heard so many shots, one after another after another, and you could hear the artillery. So we knew that the Americans would come that night."

The Perspective of a Local Bavarian on the Flood of Refugees

ELISABETH ECKL

Interviewed July 29, 2009, in Ingolstadt, Germany

The situation was awful, especially for those refugees who came from far away and spoke another German dialect different from Bavarian. They were not welcomed with open arms because in 1945 everything was destroyed in Ingolstadt, Bavaria. The bombs were dropped here, too. Many buildings and cities were destroyed. There simply were hardly any living quarters to be found anywhere. Then the swarm of refugees came into a bombed Ingolstadt. Those poor people who had lost everything and were now homeless needed a place to stay. The city tried to do everything it could. City officials inspected homes, rationed living space for each family, even in their own homes, to make any space available for the incoming swarm of refugees and expellees.

I remember the house at the Nördliche Ringstrasse in Ingolstadt where we lived. We had rented three rooms there. One day a big truckfull of refugees came and stopped in front of the house. Two older people and their daughter stepped out of the truck. They were told to live in a tiny attic room in that house. Most likely they were not welcomed very lovingly by our landlord because his house was already overcrowded. We originally rented three rooms in that house but now, when the flood of refugees came to Bavaria, we had to give up two of those three rooms. My mother, my sister, my brother and I were in one room; in another of our rented rooms was a Polish man, a former guest-worker, who simply was told by the city authorities to live in one of our rooms. We had nothing to say about it. In the third room lived a woman with her physically-challenged son. Our little three-room apartment was absolutely overcrowded; we were left with only one room for our family, even though we had rented a three-room apartment.

So when those three people came out of that truck, they were reluctantly led by our landlord to a tiny attic room in the already-overcrowded house. They had no toilet. This poor elderly couple had to climb all the way down from their attic to the first floor and ask for permission to use our toilet. They were Germans from Poland. I will never forget that woman, Lukilis. She and I got to be good friends. She and her husband, a basket weaver who had sold his baskets in Warsaw, suffered immensely. They had to flee from their own home leaving everything behind, and now they had to live in a tiny attic room with total strangers, and had to ask those strangers if they could please use the toilet downstairs.

There were also thousands of displaced Sudeten-Germans from the city of Prachatitz in the Sudetenland in Czechoslovakia who were expelled and came to Ingolstadt and other cities in Bavaria. They came daily by the thousands. They too had absolutely nothing but the clothes they wore and had somehow to go on in that new and strange place. All of the refugees were very industrious people and did find work fast. That elderly man wove baskets. Everybody needed things, and baskets were needed. We always say now that one-fifth of Bavaria consists of Sudeten-Deutsche [Germans from the Sudetenland in Czechoslovakia]. It was they, together with the native Bavarians, who helped build Bavaria up again, out of the rubble and utter destruction of the war. Gradually, those Sudeten-Germans integrated into Bavarian life. The Sudeten-Germans worked hard alongside of the locals. One forgets sometimes that they were an important part of the rebuilding. You know, there were hardly any men here to rebuild; most of them were killed in the war.

We here in the West had a roof over our heads, which the refugees from eastern Germany and the displaced people from Czechoslovakia did not have. We were not forced to flee in the bitter cold winter in order to save our lives and that of our children. Without any fault of their own, they were forced to leave everything behind to save their lives. When the survivors finally made it to West Germany, which was severely bombed and destroyed, they were still not safe from bomb attacks.

At the corner of our street, a family had built themselves an air-raid shelter. Nine people lived in that air-raid shelter. One of them was a woman from whom we bought milk. Her family thought that they would do something safe and special when they built a huge bunker in their garden to be safe. Unfortunately, deadly bombs fell exactly in that garden at their self-made bunker, and all nine family members were killed. What a tragedy! We knew them well; they were our neighbors. All of them had left their house to seek shelter in their bunker. The bunker was bombed, and they in it. None of them survived. The irony is that their house was one of the very few houses that was not destroyed.

A similar fate happened to a beautiful church in Ingolstadt, the Antonius Church. Children and their teachers were seeking shelter in the cellar of that church. One bomb after another fell on that church and every teacher and child died in those the bomb attacks .Not a single person survived. All that remained of that beautiful Antonius Church were ashes and rubble.

Oh, and I will never forget that terrible day when the British totally bombed Dresden. There was a bunker where the City Museum is located now. Whenever we thought the bombers were flying over Ingolstadt, we ran into that bunker because it was the closest to us. You could tell the direction in which they were flying. There were a multitude of airplanes flying over Ingolstadt, one after another, after another. We thought it would not end. It was very scary. We heard on the radio that these bombers were on their way to Dresden. Somehow they could determine where those planes were flying. That particular day, on their way to bomb Dresden, they did not drop a single bomb on Ingolstadt. Everything, all the ammunition, all the bombs were dropped on that beautiful city of Dresden. That beautiful city, which was often referred to as the "Venice of the East," was totally flattened and completely destroyed. It wasn't only the citizens of Dresden who were killed but thousands and thousands of refugees. A continuous large stream of refugees had arrived in Dresden who had fled under the worst conditions from the most eastern provinces of Germany. All these unfortunate refugees found their death in that horrific and total destruction of Dresden. The British literally bombed and bombed endlessly the entire city, literally flattened it, and destroyed everything in it until only rubble and ashes were left.

My grandmother, my father's mother, lived in the Bavarian Forest in Pernbach, a very small village consisting of only five farms. There rumor was that the Russians would come at night. So the people of those five farms dispersed and hid in the forest. Only my grandmother, who was single at that time, was willing to risk sacrificing herself. She remained in the village to milk the cows because they could not take the cows with them. But, thank God, the Russians did not come; the Americans did.

I will never forget when the Americans came to Pernbach. We heard so many shots, one after another after another, and you could hear the artillery. So we knew that the Americans would come that night. We knew they were the Americans because the Russians came from the East, not the West. All night long before that, my grandmother frantically dug trenches with the help of some young boys. Early in the morning the boys were all gone. So we knew they were hiding. Since the Americans were coming, we took a white bed sheet and hung it outside. Then we were told, "For heaven's sake, take those sheets off! If the Nazis come and see those white sheets, you will be shot. So please, don't hang those sheets up too early; it'll make you a *Vaterlands-Verräter* "[fatherland betrayer]." We did not want to be shot, so we took all those bed linens off and brought them back into the house. At that time German soldiers were hiding from the enemy somewhere in the forest.

Early the next morning the first tanks rolled in. They were indeed American tanks. With weapons ready to fire, an American soldier ran into my grandmother's home. My little four-year-old sister started to scream. Oh, that child screamed and screamed so loud and so fearfully, I can still hear it today. That American and three other Americans who were behind him saw a pair of men's boots at the staircase. My grandmother had gotten those boots as a present from someone because we had no shoes. The American soldier demanded to know where the German soldier was whose boots were standing there. My grandmother said, "There is nobody here but the four of us whom you see. We are women and children living in the house, and these are our boots. We women wear them because we have no other boots. There is no soldier here." He did not believe us and kept pointing his gun at us while talking about those boots. At that time we hardly spoke any English. Oh my goodness! Then he saw the cross that my grandmother had hanging on the wall and said, "Catholic?" So I understood that had to mean whether we were Catholic. He must have been Catholic himself because after seeing the cross, he stopped pointing his gun at us. That cross, I think, saved us. Then he went into the cellar and looked if there was anyone hiding. Yes, those men's boots were the boots of my grandmother. You know, at that time you took any shoes that you were able to find or get because they simply were none available.

Everybody was glad that our part of Germany became an American and not a Russian-occupied zone. There were countless daily reports of barbaric and heinous deeds done by the soldiers of the Russian Army as they marched in and occupied all eastern provinces of Germany. Among all four occupied zones in Germany, the American zone was the best. As you know, all of Germany was divided into four zones, which were occupied by the four victors of the war. So there were the Russian, the French, the British, and the American zones. The French did not have anything either; they were themselves poor. And because of the Americans and their Marshall Plan, everybody who was in the American zone was glad to be there rather than in the other zones. But those poor people in the

Russian zone really had to suffer the worst of unimaginable brutalities, especially the women.

When the Americans came, they occupied many houses. Around the corner of our place in the *Nördliche Ringstrasse* in Ingolstadt, there was a big house. The Americans chose it as a place for their officers to live. The officers wanted to live in private houses. The people who lived in that big house had to get out of their home within two hours so that the American officers could occupy their home. In that house lived a woman whose child was in a wheelchair. That boy was in the same grade as my brother, Reinhard. They were both ten years old. That mother did not know where to go when they were forced to move out of their home to make space for the American officers. My good mother said, "Come stay with us." So they moved in with us.

My brother and the boy in the wheelchair always kept going to that house where the American officers lived. The two boys found the Americans interesting, and they always got something to eat there. One day, I remember it very well, my brother came and said to my mother, "Give me a pot." My mother asked, "What do you want to do with the pot?" He replied, "I will get some beans." Sure enough, he brought a pot full of white beans with tomato sauce. Oh, was that a feast! Another day my little brother said to my mother, "One of the American officers always washes his own shirt. I told him that you could do that for him. That way we will be able to get some soap." The next day he brought the soldier's shirt and my mother washed it. Now we got some soap for that work. You know, we really had nothing, not even soap. Anyway, those American officers to whom the two boys always went obviously liked the boys and treated them very well. Perhaps those soldiers remembered their own children. Those two boys spent a lot of time with those Americans.

GERMANY

BRIEF HISTORY OF EAST PRUSSIA AND SILESIA, GERMANY AND THE EXPULSION OF GERMANS

By the end of the eighteenth century, the Holy Roman Empire of the German Nation was simply a loose association of numerous territories and fiefdoms which lacked central political authority. Real power, exercised with absolute authority, was held by the European great powers, Prussia and Austria (Historical Exhibition, p. 25). During the War of the Austrian Succession in 1742 most of Silesia was seized by King Friedrich the Great of Prussia and became a Prussian province. Thus Silesia became part of the German Empire in 1871.

The provinces of East Prussia and Silesia were parts of Prussia within Germany until the end of World War II (see Map of Germany 1914). Before that, the former German state of Prussia consisted of thirteen provinces: East Prussia, Silesia, Pomerania, Brandenburg, Berlin, Saxony, Saxon-Anhalt, Schleswig-Holstein, Rhine Province, Hesse-Nassau, Hohenzollern, Hannover, and Westphalia. Posen-West Prussia was sometimes considered a fourteenth province. Friedrich Wilhelm was the absolute ruler of Prussia from 1640-1688. For centuries many kings ruled over

Prussia and participated in various wars in Europe (Historical Exhibition, 1998).

Until 1848 all German states, including Prussia, exercised a great deal of autonomy. The liberal and democratic revolution of 1848 in Germany had two aims: The union of all German states into a single federal German state and the creation of liberal constitutions in all German states. In April 1849, the Frankfurt parliament offered the Imperial crown to the Prussian King, Friedrich Wilhelm IV (1840-1861). However, not wanting to be a part of a revolution, Friedrich Wilhelm IV rejected the offer. Prime minister and foreign minister Otto von Bismarck demonstrated that a monarchical and military Prussia could achieve German unification. However, Prussia formed its own North Germanic federation state with the annexation of Schleswig-Holstein, Hannover, Hesse-Nassau and Frankfurt. The war with France of 1870-1871 made the southern German states join the North Germanic Federation. This federation became the newly elected German Empire, and the Prussian King, Wilhelm I, became German Emperor in 1871 (Historical Exhibition, 1998).

After the founding of the German Empire, Prussia exercised great influence in Germany. This was the Prussian period in German history. The King of Prussia was not only German Emperor but also commander-in-chief of all German forces. Bismarck created a parliament elected by universal suffrage and introduced liberal economic laws which brought about opposition parties and the social democratic movement of the working class in the empire.

The German defeat in World War I led to the revolution of 1918-1919. Prussia continued to exist as the chief member of the Weimar Republic. The Federal government consisted chiefly of the Reichstag and a president elected by all Germans. Prussia introduced universal suffrage and elected parliaments with democratic majorities. After the Nazis came to power in 1933, the Prussian government was subordinated to the chancellor and the individual Reich ministries. Ironically, Adolf Hitler, who wanted to restore the Prussian military spirit, actually destroyed Prussia completely.

East Prussia, Silesia and World War II

At the end of World War II and the collapse of the Third Reich in 1945, Germany lost all of the territories east of the Oder-Neisse line (all of them were in the former Prussian state) to the Soviet Union and Poland. The northeastern part of East Prussia, with the old capital of Königsberg (now Kaliningrad) was annexed by the Soviet Union, becoming an exclave of the Russian Soviet Republic. The German province Memel was integrated into the Lithuanian Soviet Republic. Poland got the rest of East Prussia, all of Silesia, West Prussia and Pomerania, including Stettin, and a section of Brandenburg.

On the western side of the Oder-Neisse line, the Soviet Union occupied the former Prussian states of Saxony, Saxony Anhalt, Mecklenburg, and most of Brandenburg, as well as a portion of Berlin, Germany's capitol city (see Map of Germany 1950). On February 25, 1947, the Allied Control Council proclaimed the final dissolution of Prussia (Zentner, 1998). In 1949 all of those Soviet-occupied states west of the Oder-Neisse line became a separate communist country named East Germany or German Democratic Republic (GDR) under subjugation of the Soviet Union. The GDR issued its own currency, different from that of West Germany, and did not allow its people to go across the border to the West (Kleindienst, ed., 2001).

Flight and Expulsion of Germans from East Prussia

When word got around about the atrocities committed by the Soviet Red Army, many Germans wanted to flee from East Prussia. However, the regional leaders of the eastern territories of Germany delayed the flight of German civilians until the Soviet and allied forces had defeated the German forces and the Soviets were about to march in. That was because Hitler's Nazi regime gave strict "no retreat" orders in Germany's Eastern provinces to show no signs of defeat (Schieder, 2004).

After January 20, 1945, panic stricken German refugees from Germany's eastern territories fled, desperately trying to make their way westward through snow and ice, to escape the fast-approaching Soviet Army. Two million of them lost their lives. Many women did not survive the heinous brutalities of repeated mass rapes by entire Russian battalions, often followed by bodily deformation and assassination. No female was safe from Russian mass rape, whether she was a young child or an eighty-year old woman, not even women found unconscious after an anesthesia in an operating room. Many civilians were rolled over by marching tanks, killed, or they left to freeze to death, especially children and the elderly (Clough, 2006).

After the Soviet Army had cut off the route between East Prussia and the German western regions, the only way for the civilians in East Prussia to flee was to cross the frozen Vistula Lagoon which was subjected to repeated attacks of fighter plains. Many people and their horse-pulled wagons never made it across the lagoon. When the load of the fleeing trek was so heavy that the ice began to break, the lagoon was filled with dead people, dead horses, refugee wagons, and goods left behind (Clough 2007, p.130).

Soviet reprisals against German civilians were barbaric. An eye witness reports that in Nemmesdorf, "Women were found naked hanging on barns, nailed through their hands like a cross . . . In homes we found seventy women, children, and a seventy-four-year-old man, all murdered like beasts, with the exception of a few who were killed by shots in their necks" (Reuth, 2007, p.9). The Soviet brutalities against civilian Germans were so heinous that Aleksander Solzhenitsyn, who served in the Soviet military in 1945 in East Prussia, condemned the Soviet crimes in his private correspondents with a friend. For his crime of sympathizing with the enemy, his own Soviet regime sentenced him to eight years of forced labor in the Russian *Gulag* (Schieder, 2004, Vol. I).

In the February/March 1944 census, East Prussia had a civilian population of 2,519,000 Germans, and the neighboring German Memel territory had a German civilian population of 129.000 (Schieder, 2004, Vol. I/ 1 p. 5E). After the Soviets took complete control of East Prussia and Memel in May 1945, the German population in these provinces was completely wiped out. The Germans fled, were evacuated, were killed or expelled. About 311,000 civilians died during the flight and expulsions after the war; about half a million German civilians died during the war as a result of heinous deeds (Schieder, 2004, Vol. I/ 1). These numbers do not include the thousands of helpless German children, called "the wolf children," who lost their parents, were unattended, froze to death and/or died of starvation (Kibelka, 1999). Eight hundred thousand East Prussian Germans who returned to their homes after the war were expelled by the Soviets and Poles who occupied their homes and property (Schieder, 2004, Vol. I, p.5E,). By January 1950, the Soviet Union had cleansed Germany's East Prussia and Memel provinces of their German population. None of the German civilians who lived in East Prussia at the February/ March 1944 census were left in East Prussia and Memel (Schieder, 2004, Vol. I/1).

Flight and Expulsion of Germans from Silesia

Forty percent of all Germans who lived east of the Oder/ Neisse line were in Silesia. In January of 1945, the German civilian population in Silesia, Germany, was 4, 6 million (Schieder, 2004, Vol. I, p. 51E). Silesia had been their home, and that of their ancestors, for centuries. They had built up the agriculture, industry, coal mines, cities, villages, and culture of the land. In the bitter cold winter of 1945, the civilians in Silesia, like other Germans East of the Oder-Neisse line, had to flee from the approaching Soviet Red Army, leaving everything behind. As soon as the German call for evacuation came on January 19, 1945, the mass of the civilians hurried to the trains, trucks and buses to be transported westward to the neighboring Sachsen province in Germany and the Sudetenland in Czechoslovakia. However, there were not enough modes of transportation for the 4.6 million people. Therefore, most of them had to make their way by foot or by wagons carrying small children and the necessary basic provisions. The streets of Silesia, just like those of other Eastern German states, were filled with refugees (women, children and the elderly) trying to escape the Soviet Red Army. It was the German provinces of Silesia, together with the other German provinces east of the Oder-Neisse Line, which became the "Land of Death" at the end of World War II when the Soviet Army marched in (Reuth, 2007). Millions of women and girls were mass-raped in public over and over again, disfigured, and then killed. (G. F. 2004, p. 453; Jungk, 2005; Weidner, 2008; Streibel, 1994)

In Silesia's capitol city of Breslau alone, with its population of 500,000, more than 100,000 civilians had to flee on foot. Many of them gave up their harsh flight, due to the deep-freeze snow storms, lack of provisions, and lack of safety in the open streets. When they secretly returned to their homes, they found dead people all around them. When the Russians arrived in Breslau, in the middle of February, 200,000 civilians who were left in the city became victims of the most gruesome unimaginable atrocities at the hands of the Russians. Forty thousand civilians of the city of Breslau perished (Schieder, 2004, Vol. I, p.54E; Breslau, 1950). Others were transported to the Russian occupied zone.

At the end of World War II, the entire German provinces of Upper and Lower Silesia were cleansed of their German population. The German population was replaced by the Polish population, the German language by the Polish language, German names of streets and cities by Polish names. Silesia, like Pomerania, West Prussia, Danzig (now Gdansk) and a great part of East Prussia had become part of Poland. The northern part of East Prussia, including the city of Königsburg, became part of the Soviet Union.

Personal Narratives of the Flight from Silesia, Germany

Ruth Hoffmann
Born May 1924 in Breslau, Silesia, Germany.

"We were two human beings, two women in need of each other.
We are all human beings, all having the same needs. Why on earth do we have wars and
create enemies!"

RUTH HOFFMANN

Interviewed July 29, 2009, in Ingolstadt, Germany

I have to admit that my family and I were extremely lucky. Fleeing from our home in Breslau was relatively easy for us as compared to most German women who had to flee from their homes to escape the Russian Red Army.

In the Third Reich it was mandatory for all young people to do *Dienstverpflichtung* [public and government service] whether they wanted to or not. After I graduated from school, my father got a letter notifying us that I had to fulfill my service requirements. Those notices came to my parents and not to me because I was not yet 21 years of age and thus was not yet considered an adult. I served as a clerk for half-a-year, followed by half-a-year of war assistance service. I was happy when I had finished that half-a-year with the war assistance service. I thought that I had done my duties, that now I was free. So I went home.

I arrived home in Breslau on a Friday evening. The next morning my father received a letter via registered mail which said that I had until 6:00 PM Wednesday to report and serve at the harbor barracks in Stettin. The city of Stettin is located on the *Ost See* [East Sea]. I was not at all pleased to receive those orders. But at that time you had to do what you were told. One was not allowed to disobey, or else! Resistance to the Third

Reich was not allowed to exist in those days. If someone dared to resist, there were dire consequences to self and one's family. We also did not belong to a particular political party.

In Stettin I was trained to be a *Funkerin* [telegrapher]. It was actually quite interesting. Each letter in the alphabet had a different code and tone. We had to differentiate if the tone was short, long, and so forth. It was quite interesting. However, one had to blank out everything else from one's mind. When one was wearing the head phones at the telegraph instrument, one could not think of anything but to fully concentrate what message was coming through via the tone and then translate each tone into alphabetical letters. That really did need a lot of concentration. Every letter was then decoded. That decoding was not done by that same telegraph operator who translated the tone into the letter. It was done by another person. That was the process of translation from tone to letter and then decoding those letters into total meaning of the message. I was trained and able to decode the meaning. That is why I was able to know what was really going on. We were not allowed to speak to anyone about the content of those telegraph messages. It was top secret. That is why we had been assigned to work many kilometers away from our home city. That way, we would not have any contact with our family and friends.

After my training I served as telegrapher in Nürnberg at the *Generalkommando* [main military command station]. Whatever was really happening in the war effort was different from what the news media reported. The news that was reported via the radio or the newspapers was no longer the truth. What we telegraph operators heard in the news and what we had decoded were quite different in relation to the war situation, how much ammunition Germany had left, how far the front was, how the war was progressing, and so on. We continuously decoded bad news. So it became quite clear to us telegraph operators that we would lose the war. The German mass media, however, portrayed a very different picture. In the cinema, on the radio, and in the newspapers, you heard only about victory and how well the war was progressing.

The uniform that I had to wear consisted of a grey suit, grey blouse, black shoes, grey stockings, and a grey coat and cap. We wore some medals on our blouses and a ribbon around our arms that would indicate nonverbally that we were the women auxiliaries for signal duties. Because of our uniforms, we were noticed in the city. Wherever we went, people noticed us. They felt sorry for us because we had to keep to ourselves and were not allowed to mingle. We had to adjust to the situation.

In December of 1944, the first refugees arrived from the furthest East German states. By 1945 everything was happening so fast. The war was going so badly, but the German media continued to talk constantly about victory. The Russian Red Army came closer and closer to our home in Breslau. Finally, the people of Breslau and its vicinity were urged to hurry up and leave their homes and cities on foot because the Russian troops were marching in. It was one of the coldest winters ever. We heard that in their flight westward, a large number of people died. Many of them froze to death, especially babies, children, and the elderly.

In the middle of January 1945, I received a letter from my parents in Breslau. They wrote that they would not leave home; they would remain in the city that they loved. My position at work allowed me to know what was really going on with the war effort. I knew what the Russians were doing, how fast the Russian Red Army was marching into Germany, what was happening with the poor refugees who were forced to flee from Poland, Upper Silesia and other East German states. They were helpless, defenseless women with small children, pregnant women about to give birth, and the elderly, all of them forced to flee. Their plight moved me so much that I could not get it out of my mind. I was worried about my parents and decided to do everything possible to get to Breslau and warn my family and friends about the grave situation. I could not let them stay in Breslau. I went all the way up the chain of command to the general to get the permission to go home to Breslau and was so thankful to be granted that very rare permission.

I was wearing a uniform at that time, and that uniform saved my life. I needed three days by train from Nürnberg, through Dresden, to get to Breslau. I got as far as Dresden, and in Dresden I had to wait one day until I got the permission to go on to Breslau. You need to know that at that time, no civilian trains were running any more, only *Wehrmachtszüge* [military trains] to support the war effort. So wearing my uniform allowed me to take a military train from Dresden to Liegnitz. In Liegnitz I had to report again at the military station, and from there I went on to Breslau.

My parents had no idea that I was coming. Now I am telling you something relevant: as a child, I used to ring our doorbell in a unique way so that my mom would always know that it was I who was at the door. I used to ring it so loud that my mother often was angry with me. Well, now I arrived and rang that doorbell the same old way. My mother said to the others who were in our home, "That can only be Ruth." There were always people in our home because there were many meetings and talks about, "What are you doing? What do you think we should do?" I hurried up to tell all of them that it was out of the question for them to remain in Breslau and that they needed to leave as soon as possible. There was no time to waste or even think about it. I told them that the situation was extremely grave. I also told them that what we telegraph operators knew already, the public did not know. I urged everyone, "Pack your suit cases; wear as many layers of warm clothes as possible. Tomorrow morning we will go to the train station and try to get a train to get out of Breslau." I am so very happy that they listened to me and that we were able to get out of Breslau. How very lucky we were! It was my luck to be a telegrapher which most likely saved my life and that of my family and their friends. The only reason I risked going to Breslau was to inform my parents and my sister of the impending danger that would befall them if they would remain in Breslau and to get them out of there before the Russian Red Army arrived.

Well, the next morning we were on our way. At that time my father was more than seventy years old. Therefore, he was not ordered to fight in the war. That is why we were able to go through the barricades at the main railroad station. The railroad station was over-crowded, full of refugees. The train was so crowded that you barely got a place to stand. We were packed like sardines. Because there were no regular trains any more, we had to get on the *Viehwagen* [cattle-train]. We wanted so desperately to get out of the city and move on westward. We had taken what each person could carry, nothing else. We took food so that we would not be hungry. It was ice cold, one of the coldest winters ever. The train took us to Dresden. At that time, the end of January 1945, Dresden had not yet been destroyed by the bombs. In Dresden we were transient for a few hours before we could take a connecting train. Then we were separated in different trains. We tried everything possible to remain together, my parents, my sister and I. My sister was eleven years older than I. We drove a few hours after we got out of the train. Then we were taken care of. We were brought to a sort of school building where we got warm food. There was a big goulash kettle, and we all had warm goulash to eat.

While I was working as a telegrapher in Nürnberg, I had the opportunity to make very good acquaintances in that city. They had told me that we could stay with them if and when I was able to get my family out of Breslau. These people had a big home. The husband was working at the courthouse. However, we were only there for about one week; then Nürnberg was bombed. On January 2, 1945, Nürnberg was bombed, and the entire beautiful city of Nürnberg was destroyed up to eighty to ninety percent. We were so very lucky. That particular building where my parents stayed was one of the very few that was not destroyed. I was at that time still working in Nürnberg at the *Generalkommando* [main command station]. Thus, I continued to live and work as a telegraph operator in Nürnberg. After the bombing of Nürnberg, the friends where my family stayed tried to find them a place outside of the city. They were successful in finding a home in Altenfürth, near Nürnberg. At that time Altenfürth was a small suburb of Nürnberg; now it is a part of Nürnberg. My parents and sister lived in a house where the homeowner lived with his mother and two small children. Their home had been bombed as well. However, they still had one extra room, and that room they gave to my parents and my sister.

Oh, there were so many bomb attacks in Nürnberg, and I was right there. The thundering bomb attacks that I lived through in Nürnberg were horrible. I wanted to close my ears and eyes and not think about that burning horror. One particular bomb attack is especially burned into my memory. During the war there were many forced laborers from Poland, France, and other countries in Germany. During that bomb attack on January 2, 1945, I happened to be close to the main railroad station. I ran into a bunker when I heard the first bombs thundering down. I was in uniform. I had found a place to sit in the bunker. But soon the room got filled with so many people; I stood up from my seat to give it to someone else. We were taught from childhood on to be good examples and to get up when older people needed a seat. So I got up and was standing next to a female forced laborer from another country. With every bomb that thundered down, that woman shook and hugged me tighter and tighter. She needed someone to lean on. Both of us stood there hugging each other, providing support for each other. Even though I was German and wearing my uniform, I was not a negative force to her. She needed someone, and I was glad that I was there with her and that we both hugged each other tightly during that horrible bomb blast which destroyed much of the city. We were two human beings, two women in need of each other. We are all human beings, all having the same needs. Why on earth do we have wars and create enemies!

I continued to work as a telegraph operator in Nürnberg until the Americans came at the end of April 1945. We got word that the telegraph station should not be destroyed; it should be moved instead. So we closed the station in Nürnberg. At night all the equipment and instruments were put on trucks and brought to Ansbach in Bavaria where the telegraph operating station was to resume. But I got away! I did not want to do that any more. We telegraphers, there were twenty-seven of us, were organized into three groups. Among ourselves we all talked about getting away from that kind of work because we knew what was going on. One helped the other; we all helped each other. When the time had come for us to be moved, we were told, "Tonight at about 2:00 we will be moved." I told my fellow telegraphers, "Do not look for me; do not search for me; I will also be on the truck." But when time came to leave the building, I hid around the front of a house, waited until they left, and no one looked for me. I stayed behind. They did reach Ansbach and were working there for a few days until the Americans came. Then the telegraph group was moved to Austria. In Austria they did continue their work until the very end of the war.

Now I was all alone. I packed my little suitcase with my belongings, bread and cheese, and cigarettes, which I had received from my sister. I was told to save the cigarettes because they would come in handy when I needed them. For nourishment, I did have my bread and cheese. Then I walked in the direction of the main railroad station. I did know in which direction to go in order to go to Altenfürth, where my parents were living. I just stood there on the street and waved. I was trying to hitchhike a ride. Fortunately, some German soldiers stopped and took me with them. When I arrived near my destination, they drove around Altenfürth, not into the town, because the streets were already closed. They continued to drive in the direction of Feucht on the Autobahn. They said they could bring me as far as Feucht, and then I had to continue to Altenfurth on my own. So they dropped me off at Feucht, and they continued on.

Between Feucht and Altenfürth was a forest. It was a rich area, full of thick trees. I was very eager to get away from the street as soon as possible and into the forest.

Now I had a pleasant surprise. In the forest I met four Frenchmen, former prisoners of war. Near Nürnberg was a large camp for prisoners of war. During the war there were Russian, Polish, French, and other international prisoners of war held in Germany. At the time when I was walking in the forest, the camp had already been closed, and the prisoners were freed. Now those four Frenchmen were coming toward me. I must confess I was a little scared. However, they were so very good to me. They asked me where I wanted to go and told me that I should not be scared, they would not harm me. I told them that I wanted to go to Altenfürth to my parents. They told me that they were glad to be free. They spoke fluent German, but I could not speak any French. They showed me pictures of their families, their wives and their children. They were so happy to be free and to be returning to their families in France. Yes, I was very lucky, indeed. Those Frenchmen were so good to me. They told me not to wear those medals on my coat. It was too dangerous for me to wear them. That would have never occurred to me. They even helped remove the medals from my coat. Instead of harming me, they helped me, and I am very thankful for that. In my suitcase I had those cigarettes from my sister, and bread and cheese. So in the forest on our way, we sat down and had a little picnic. They enjoyed the cigarettes as well as the bread and cheese. After our little picnic, they accompanied me all the way home to Altenfürth, all the way to the house where my parents lived. That was at the end of April 1945.

A few days later, the Americans came, but there was no fighting. The Americans were a little afraid of bomb attacks because even at that time the Germans still dropped bombs. We women were seeking shelter from the bombs in the cellar at night. We hid at night in the cellar, but the Americans stayed outside. They would not come into the house at night. I think they must have been afraid of the bombs. Even though they would have been safer from bombs in the cellar, they did not come down to the cellar at night. Only in May did we find out that Hitler was dead.

When the Americans came into the house during the day, they brought us food. They brought us chocolate, cake, and other goodies. We were so happy to get the food. One of the Americans could sing the song "Oh, *du lieber Augustin.*" He said his grandfather was German, and he had taught him that song. So with great enthusiasm and joy he sang for us whenever he came, "Oh, *du lieber Augustin.*" They were good people, those American soldiers; they helped us by bringing us food. Without them we would have had nothing to eat. They helped us a lot.

When the Americans left and the soup kitchen was no more, the hunger returned. We got food stamps from the mayor's office. Everybody was allotted a very small amount of food. At that time, because I was so thin, I got a ration of milk, half a liter every week. Milk was very hard to get. Those people who had something to trade could trade that in the black market for some food. Those who had money could also somehow buy some food. But we refugees had absolutely nothing to trade. One could also go to a farmer and beg for a potato. Somehow we survived.

One thing Germany had plenty of was rubble, ruins and destroyed buildings. We worked on gathering bricks from the rubble and cleaning them. We had to clean the debris of cement so that the bricks could be used again in construction. That was how we received our food stamps. We had to prove that we worked. I found some work doing the brick cleaning at a brick factory. It was taken for granted that we worked in the brick factory. We were gathered all around the wider region of Nürnberg to build the city up again. Germany was destroyed. Ruins, rubble, and destroyed buildings were everywhere. One way to build up again was to clean the old bricks and reuse them. We were in desperate need of housing. So it was a given that we gather the old bricks from the ruins and knock off the old cement. Those were normal bricks that were not damaged. We gathered them, sorted them out, and put them in a pile. I did that work until around July 1945 when I got a job in a kindergarten.

I was not a kindergarten teacher. Let me tell you how I got that job. A minister saw an empty kindergarten which belonged to a former political party. He noted those rooms were empty and knew that there was a need for little children to go to kindergarten again. So he wanted to open that kindergarten; but he had nobody to teach in the kindergarten. Since he got to know me, he asked me if I would be interested in working with little children in his kindergarten. He told me that I could go to Feucht into the cloister where nuns had been leading a kindergarten for years. I should go there first, look around, and see if I would be interested in doing that line of work. After checking out the cloister, I agreed to work in the kindergarten. Let me tell you, it was a whole lot better than the brick cleaning. So I directed the kindergarten until September of 1945, when professional teachers arrived.

There in the kindergarten, I learned many humorous things. You know, at that time where there was great hunger, people would go to the country to the farmers for food. I worked with the children and we performed "Kasper Theatre," in which Kasper went out to the country because he was hungry. So I tried to weave our every day life into their theatrical performances and integrate the children's experiences into the performances. But as soon as I opened my mouth, everybody knew I was not Bavarian. People would often say, "The Prussian, the Prussian." The children in the kindergarten knew right away that I was not Bavarian. I learned the Bavarian dialect with the help of those little kids in many humorous ways.

Now I have to tell you something that is very difficult to talk about, even difficult to think about. However, again, I was so very lucky. It was in March 1946. I needed to go to a dentist. In Altenfürth, where we lived, there were no dentists. The closest dentist was in Feucht. I was able to take a bus to Feucht, but there was no bus returning to Altenfüerth in the afternoon. Therefore, I had to walk back home. At that time the entire area from Feucht to Altenfürth was a forest region full of trees. There were cars and bicycles on the street, but to the right and to the left of the street was a tree-laden thick forest. I was a young woman at that time. Near Nürnberg, in the former Nazi barracks, there were American soldiers, black and white Americans. When we women walked during the day on the streets, we were not dressed as usual. We tried to look old and ugly. For example, I had gotten an old coat from my mother and an old scarf to cover my head. Well, on that day when I came back from the dentist, I was not dressed like that. I did not cover myself up. My mother had noticed earlier that my stockings were worn out and that they showed too many signs of having been repaired. So she gave me a pair of good stockings. That day I wore those stockings because my mother said to me, "Now don't take the bus to Feucht with those old worn-out stockings; wear the good stockings that you wear on Sundays." In those days you wore whatever good clothes you had only on Sundays. So I took my old stockings off and wore the good ones when I went to see the dentist. I also wore regular clothes and did not cover myself up. That may have been my demise.

Returning from the dentist who had put some fillings in my teeth, I was walking on the side of the street and was already halfway on my long way to home. At the other side of the street, from the other direction, came an open jeep with four American soldiers. They stopped and waved at me and told me to come into the forest with them. Yes, they did. Quickly I responded, "No, I know what you want." I knew that in Altenfüerth, where American soldiers were stationed, quite a few women were raped. So I thought, no, under no circumstances will I go into the woods. So I let the American soldiers know that I would not come with them into the woods, that I would continue to walk on the street. Then everything happened very fast. One of the soldiers jumped down from the jeep and took his gun while another called again for me to go to the woods with them. The others pointed their guns at me from across the street where I was. However, I remained firm, and I let them know again that I was not going to go into the woods and that I was going to continue walking on the street. As I took the next step, one of them shot into my legs. I was not able to walk any more. I had two bullets in my left leg which are still there today. Then I got a long *Streifschuss* [grazing shot] in the right knee and another *Streifschuss* on the left hip. Now I was totally unable to walk or even move. After they had shot me, they drove away because behind their jeep, there were a German motorcycle driver and a bicyclist who had stopped. They had witnessed everything that had happened within those two to three minutes. The American soldiers drove away quickly, but the motorcycle driver came to help me. He helped me to sit on his motorcycle in the backseat and drove me back to Feucht to a doctor. The doctor called the Red Cross in Nürnberg. The Red Cross came right away to Feucht to pick me up with the ambulance and brought me to the hospital in Nürnberg where I was hospitalized for two months until my wounds healed.

Yes, many German women were assaulted and raped. It was a catastrophe. Acquaintances told me the more they tried to fight back, the more they were assaulted before they were raped. In our American-occupied zone, it was not the Russian Red Army that raped the German women; it was American soldiers. Yes, indeed, it was Americans! I was extremely lucky that I did not need to defend myself physically. Since the men were on the other side of the street, they did not physically touch me, but they shot me instead so that I was unable to walk. After a few months I could walk again. In spite of all the suffering from those shots, I was extremely thankful not to have been raped. The American soldiers must have seen the motorcyclist and the bicyclist behind their American Army truck, which might have prevented them from their beastly intentions after they had shot and immobilized me. I will always be thankful to those two men on the bicycle and motorcycle.

These two witnesses reported my case to the police, who made a report. I received a note saying that I should fill out a form for *Schadenersatz* [compensation]. That claim form for compensation needed to be filled out within one year of the incident; otherwise, it was too late. It was the German government that would give that compensation. Well, the compensation which I received was 1,388.88 Reich Mark. I also received a letter from the U.S. Claims Commission. The letter read as follows:

U. S. CLAIMS COMMISSION NO. GA-21
AMERIKANISCHE ANSPRUCHSKOMMISSION NO. GA-21
U. S. ARMY
AMERIKANISCHEN ARMEE

AWARD
ZUSPRUCH

U. S. REF: US/7728/2247/G2   C. C. DOC. NO: US/CC/GA-21/475

TO:
AN: Ruth HOFFMANN   (CLAIMANT)
(ANSPRUCHSTELLER)

ADDRESS
ANSCHRIFT: 190, Altenfurt / Nürnberg / Germany

The Claims Commission, having duly and thoroughly considered all the evidence submitted in connection with the above claim, finds:

That it is a bona fide claim, that the damage for which claim is made was caused by U. S. military personnel and/or Civilian Employees of the War Department or of the Army and falls within the provisions of Letter AG 150 GAP-AGO, Headquarters, U. S. Forces, European Theater (Main), 17 October 1945, Subject: Claims against and in Favor of the United States Arising in Germany and Austria, as amended; that the damage so caused was under circumstances justifying compensation therefor under that Letter, and current policies and directives. The Commission awards the claimant above named the sum of 1,388.88 RM, payable from funds chargeable to Germany/Austria as part of the cost of occupation, conditioned upon the acceptance of this award in full and final settlement of this claim, and approves the same for payment. Payment will be made only on presentation of the original voucher. The decision of the Commission is without appeal.

Auf Grund eingehender Berücksichtigung aller auf den Anspruch sich beziehenden und vorgelegten Beweise erläßt die Anspruchskommission die folgende Entscheidung:

Der Anspruch ist begründet. Der Schaden, für den Ersatz beansprucht wird, ist durch Angehörige der Amerikanischen Armee und/oder Zivilangestellte des Amerikanischen Kriegsministeriums oder der Amerikanschen Armee verursacht worden und unterliegt den Bestimmungen der Anordnung in abgeänderter Fassung AG 150 GAP-AGO, Hauptquartier der Streitkräfte der Vereinigten Staaten im Europäischen Kriegsschauplatz (Hauptstelle), vom 17. Oktober 1945, betreffend Schadenersatzansprüche gegen und zugunsten der Vereinigten Staaten, die in Deutschland und Österreich entstanden sind. Deshalb besteht wegen des so entstandenen Schadens Anspruch auf Ersatz gemäß der genannten Anordnung und der geltenden Bestimmungen und Direktiven. Die Anspruchskommission spricht dem oben angeführten Anspruchsteller den Betrag von 1,388.88 RM zu und genehmigt die Auszahlung unter der Bedingung, daß die Annahme dieses Zuspruchs und dieses Betrages als endgültige Erledigung und Bezahlung angenommen wird. Der Betrag ist zahlbar aus den Geldern, die von Deutschland bzw. Österreich als Teil der Besatzungskosten zu tragen sind. Die Auszahlung erfolgt nur gegen Vorlage des Originals des Zahlungsauftrages. Der Beschluß der Kommission ist endgültig.

DATED THIS
DATIERT AM: 12th   DAY OF
TAGE: June   194 7

SIGNATURE
UNTERSCHRIFT:

TYPED SIGNATURE: WILLIAM D. VAN ARNAM, Major QMC
UNTERSCHRIFT IN MASCHINENSCHRIFT: (Rank) (Titel)

COMMISSION NO: GA-21
KOMMISSION NO:

AGPD-4078-12-46-18 M 82786

Again and again I was so very lucky. I was lucky that the American soldiers shot me and did not do me any worse harm as had happened to far too many young German girls at that time. When I look back I can only say again and again how often luck was on my side.

I was also lucky to find a job in the office of a health insurance company in Nürnberg. That office building had been bombed. However, there was a little corner where we could work. It was such a small space that you would hear everything that everyone was saying. When I came for the interview, something funny happened. All the people working in the office were Bavarians. One woman said to another, "Stop typing and listen to how that woman there speaks." She, like all of them, Of course was Bavarian, and was not familiar with the German language being spoken in any other way than the Bavarian dialect. The interview went well, and after a few days I got a letter that I could start working soon. I did not know how to type. At that time, it was not necessary to know how to type in an office. It was important for that position to be good in bookkeeping and mathematics.

My parents remained in Altenfürth. There was a great deal of hunger. My father was more than seventy years old. My mother was thirteen years younger than my dad. The government had established the *Arbeiterwohlfahrt* [workers' welfare]. That was a welfare system for people who were working, thus the name "worker's welfare". That worker's welfare had a food shelf which was near the office where I worked. At lunch I was there with a food container and joined a long line of people waiting for food. For ten *Pfennige* [pennies] we got soup, which was carefully measured with a ladle into our container. I used to go twice in line to get the soup. In the evening I took the little container of soup to my parents in Altenfurth. The two visits to the welfare food shelf cost twenty Pfennige. I earned at that time only thirty Pfennige a day. That little bit of soup from the worker's welfare was the only nourishment my parents received. My lunchtime was spent standing twice in a rather long line at the worker's welfare, and my lunch consisted also of that bowl of soup. That is why when the worker's welfare asks for donations today they do still get a generous donation from me. However, now they do plenty of more sophisticated things, like building houses for people, and so on. Yes, that was the hunger time. Everybody was so very thin then.

That hunger period lasted until a new German currency was adopted. Before the currency change in the spring of 1948, everybody got, I think, forty Reich Mark. I don't remember the exact amount, but I think it was forty Reich Mark, and with that you could buy something. All of a sudden there was food on the table, there was bread, and there were vegetables and fruit. Everyone, even those who did not work, received forty Reich Mark. Then on June 20, 1948, the Reich Mark was changed into Deutsche Mark (DM). After that currency change, the Reich Mark was not worth anything any more, not even a penny.

In that one room where my parents, my sister and I lived in Altenfürth, there was no heating; we froze. It was very cold. There was one stove, but it was not enough to heat the whole room. When we got up early in the morning, the washcloths were frozen. All of us carefully saved as much money as we could. The first thing we bought with all the money that we all had carefully saved was a stove. It cost one hundred DM. We all pitched in together to buy it. Now we had the stove, but now the question was how to transport the stove all the way from Nürnberg to Altenfürth. We certainly did not have a car or anything. On foot I pulled the stove behind me on a little wooden hand-pull wagon all the way to Altenfürth. That was already in August or September when we were able to buy that stove. We did not want to freeze any more on cold days in the autumn or winter.

The stove was the first item, and then came the second item. It was a used sewing machine for my mother. She said that she needed a sewing machine because if she would have a sewing machine, she could start buying material and sew clothes for people. So my mother started sewing clothes for people. The third on our list were feather beds. We bought meters of bed-ticking and sewed it together. We knew a woman whose relatives were farmers in the country, and those farmers sold the feathers to us. My mother and I put the feathers in the bed-ticking, and then she sewed it all together into warm cozy feather beds. Even though it was a used sewing machine, my mother was so happy to have it and to be able to sew all kinds of things for us and for other people. That was the beginning of a new life for us.

Now working in that health insurance office, I earned roughly about 100 DM a month. Coffee was available at that time, but we could not afford it. The clothes we wore were very simple then. I still wore the blouses and the suits from my job as a telegrapher, but I had no winter shoes. I had to take the train every day from Altenfürth to Fischbach and then on to Nürnberg to work. Here is something funny that I remember: my parents and others went into the forest where the Americans were because the Americans were generous not only with food but also with their clothes. They used to throw away shoes and clothes in the forest. That was why my parents went every once in while to spend time in the forest, close to the area where the Americans used to be. They brought home, among other things, shoes and boots. Imagine that, shoes and boots! Those were so very hard to come by in those days. There was a pair of boots that didn't quite fit me, but they almost did. So I wore them during the winter. Since the boots were too big for me, I stuffed them with cloth in front where the toes were supposed to be so that they would fit me better. After I used them for a while, the tips of the shoes pointed into the air. In Nürnberg, one of my colleagues, who was a lot of fun, said," Oh, here comes Fräulein Hoffmann with her *Himmelfathrstschuhe* [ascension shoes pointing to heaven]. Ha! Ha! Ha! Yes, I wore those boots every day for many a long and cold winter; I was so happy to have them. Those were my American army boots. Indeed, they were generous, those Americans. They quickly threw away in the forest many things we could use. How often I heard from my fun colleague, "Now comes Fräulein Hoffmann with her *Himmelfathrstschuhe*." We all laughed. One had to have a little humor in order to keep on going.

I continued working at the Health Insurance Company until November 1950. It was important for us to get an apartment. However, because Nürnberg was totally bombed, it was very difficult to find a place to live. Therefore, among the first who got housing were the city's native citizens, not we, the refugees. My sister had worked before the war in Breslau as a bookkeeper at Brinkmann's, a tobacco and cigarette factory. Well, that factory came to Ingolstadt, and that was how my sister also came to relocate in Ingolstadt. We always had said that we would get a place to live in Ingolstadt and that we would settle there. In Ingolstadt, the firm Brinkmann arranged for apartments for their employees. So first my parents moved to Ingolstadt. Next, I followed them.

Once again I was lucky. I went to the employment office and reported that I was looking for a job. It was my luck that the employment office itself needed several temporary employees. I filled out an employment form, got an interview and was hired. At first I worked as a temporary employee. Later I got a full-time position and received education and training to be a career advisor. My father died in 1961, and my mother died in 1968. My parents were happy that my sister and I were doing well and that we now had a good life. I worked there as a career-advisor until 1984 when I reached my 60th birthday and retired.

Our beautiful hometown of Breslau and all of Silesia (as well as other East German states) became part of Poland after the war and were then no longer Germany. However, my sister and I longed to see our beloved home town again. In 1979, both of us had special permission to go to Breslau. It was the first time since our flight from home twenty-four years earlier. It seemed strange that Breslau was in Poland now. Since Poland was behind the Iron Curtain and under the East Bloc communist regime, Westerners were not permitted to cross the Iron Curtain. We had arranged for very special permission to be able to cross the border. We were there for about one-and-a-half weeks and stayed with a Polish woman who spoke German. We had to pay a certain amount of German money to the Polish government for each day that we were in Poland. We went to the mountainous Riesengebirge, which was once our home region. We went to places where we hiked and played, where we grew up in our childhood and youth. Those were all now Polish-speaking places. By now all the street names and all the cities and towns were changed from German into Polish names. The German language was replaced with Polish everywhere. The German people were now replaced with Polish people. We were told not to speak German in the streets and in public. So since we were not allowed to speak German, and since we knew no Polish, we could not communicate with the Polish people. Also we were very careful to be quiet and not to attract any attention. The inner city of Breslau was totally destroyed. It was only rubble and ashes. That was the first thing that hit us. It took the Polish people a long time until they cleaned things up again. The fields that once were rich and full of wheat were now barren, and weeds grew everywhere. Our family home, where we grew up, was totally bombed. Our elementary school was no longer there, but the middle school was still standing. That middle school was now a boarding school. The nuns who were teaching there were the ones who organized our stay with the Polish woman who spoke German.

Now I must tell you a funny story related to the poor nuns at that school. My sister and I had brought with us some chocolate and other goodies. When we arrived in Poland in the evening, the nuns invited us to have tea and buns. We had not yet unpacked our suitcases. Later in the evening when we went to our quarters where we stayed, we heard one cloister nun say to an acquaintance, "I wonder if they have brought some chocolate." Chocolate was not available then in Poland; neither was good coffee or cocoa. That woman told us, "You have not given anything to those nuns. They are waiting for your chocolate." Oh, the joy was huge when we unpacked our suitcase, and gave the nuns what we had brought for them. I tell you, there are again and again those little things that come our way in life that make all the difference, those little things that one remembers. Oh, and the good coffee and the cocoa! Little things like that made a big impact and gave so much pleasure because they were not readily available there in what is now Poland.

It was such a joy to still find a familiar building in our hometown of Breslau and to walk several times on Breslau's Main Street, the street on which we used to walk regularly to go to the theatre and so on. Even though everything had changed, including the name of the street, which has now a Polish name, it was still a joy to be able to walk that street of our home once more in the city that I love, the city that I still call home. Unfortunately, that once stately street did not at all resemble what it once was. It was now uncared for and dirty. We visited the pond, where we ice skated as children. All those were dear old memories. We walked along the river Oder of which we have the fondest memories. That was the center of attraction, our beloved river Oder.

Visiting our *Heimat* [home land] that we lost forever filled our hearts with all kinds of emotions. It was wonderful to be there but it was also very painful. Breslau is my hometown, and I love it like no other. But there were no friends, no family, no more neighbors; they all had to flee in January 1945. Many of them lost their lives during the flight. Many babies froze to death during what is known as the Death March of Breslau. Those who did not flee were deported. One after another, they had to leave their homes, their possessions and everything behind; they were forced to get out. Between 1945 and 1946 Breslau and all of Silesia, which was in Germany, was literally ethnically cleansed by the Poles. The Germans were driven out of their own land. They had to get out. That part of Germany, together with many other eastern states of Germany, became Poland. Polish people moved in, got rid of the German people and all German names, and replaced them all with Polish people and Polish names.

I went back to Bresalu once more, around 1989 or 1990, right after the fall of the wall and the Iron Curtain. The Judicial World Congress was held in Breslau then. That time I went with an acquaintance because, unfortunately, my sister had died. I had said to myself, "I am from Breslau, and whenever there should be a Judicial World Congress in my home town, in the town where I was born and raised, the town that I love, the town that I still call home, I shall go." So of course I went. When my sister and I went to Breslau the first time in 1979, we got to know a Polish family. We had stayed in touch with that family. Now my acquaintance and I also stayed with that family. That is why we could attend the World Congress in Breslau. It was bitter-sweet to be in my beloved Breslau again. My heart was again full of emotions.

There was a tragedy in Ingolstadt with the refugees that had arrived from Stargatt. Those refugees had barely arrived at the Ingolstadt city hall when the air alarm siren went off. The siren was blasting loudly; and the newly-arrived refugees all ran into the *Franziskaner Kirche* [Franciscan Church] to seek shelter. Under the church there was a cellar, so they sought refuge in that cellar. However, that church was bombed, and the unfortunate people who sought shelter there died. Among them were many priests and those refugees who had fled all the way from Stargatt, had made it to Ingolstadt, and then had to die under the bombs in the church cellar while seeking shelter. That beautiful Baroque church was totally destroyed. However, there was a miracle. Among the ashes and rubble of that totally destroyed church, the Madonna of the *Franziskaner* Church, the "rubble mother," as she got to be called, was found under the rubble. Like a miracle she was whole and undamaged. Yes, indeed, that Madonna was dug out manually from the mountain of rubble and ashes of what once was the beautiful church, and by some miracle, she was totally undamaged. The church itself was totally destroyed. Now that miraculous "Rubble Madonna" has her special place in the newly rebuilt *Franziskaner* Church in Ingolstadt.

There were very few men left after the war. Many young women remained single. The men that I could have married were all lying under the ground. All of those handsome young men, they did not return. The war had swallowed them. I could not marry any of them. I am eighty three years old now, and I am telling you, a war, any war, is a terrible, terrible thing.

Elfriede Laske, née Brendl
Born in Wittelsbach, Lower Silesia, Germany; 83 years of age
in July 2007

"Even though we suffered immense horror under the Poles and the Russians, we have met a few good people among the Russians, and we have met a few good people among the Poles. Everywhere, there are good and bad people."

ELFRIEDE LASKE

Interviewed in July 2007 in Gohfeld, Germany

I was born in 1924 in Wittelsbach, Lower Silesia in Germany and was raised there. Unfortunately that part of Germany was given to Poland after World War II and is no longer ours. My family members from way back were born and raised there. My father was born there in 1896, and my mother in 1899. When I was a small girl, before all the horror of the war happened, I was called Friedchen. Unfortunately our whole world was turned upside down toward the end of the war, and we lost everything.

I don't like to talk about what happened to us toward the end of the war and the years that followed. I have hardly ever talked about it. I get so depressed when I think about all that horror which we had to live through. It was truly hell. I don't want to fall into deeper depression. That's why I keep quiet about it. However, no matter how hard I try, I am unable to forget that hell which I had to live through. At night, in my nightmares, I have to relive it over and over again.

Please forgive me, I can't tell you the utmost worst, about the flight from our home and the evil that was done unto us. It is a terrible nightmare, and I don't want to go there. But I will tell you this: My parents had a farm in Wittelsbach. All of a sudden in January 1945, we had to leave everything behind and flee westward. We quickly got two horses ready, hurriedly put some things on the wagon and left our beloved home and farm. We were gone from home for three days, and the Russian Army was already rolling in. You could hear shots everywhere. They began to shoot at us already. Russian tanks were rolling in, one after another, shooting at us. They shot our dear horses. We had to leave our horses and everything in our wagon behind. Other refugees passing by shouted repeatedly "Leave fast and flee as fast as you can! Leave fast and flee as fast as you can!" Those warnings still ring in my ear today. I had a little suitcase in my hand. Before I could look around, a gun was pointed at me, and I had to give the suitcase up to the Russians.

Even though we suffered immense horror under the Poles and the Russians, too horrible to talk about, we have met a few good people among the Russians, and we have met a few good people among the Poles. Everywhere there are good and bad people. But you know how it was; most of them stole everything we had, every little thing. But it is all over now, and it is better to forget it all. It is better not to talk and think about it.

I lost four brothers in the war, and one of them is still missing. Gerhard, Erich and Erwin, they all lost their lives in the war, and Reinhard is still missing. Oh, what agony for my mother! The loss of all her sons was almost unbearable for my mother, for both of my parents. Gerhard was my favorite brother, but I loved them all. Our family was very close, and that is very important in life.

My mother, my grandparents, my sisters and I were together. All of us were, day in and day out, the work horses for the Russians; we were work horses for the Poles. We were not able to escape from them and come to the West until 1957. All those twelve years after the war had ended, we were slave laborers without any rights. We were forced laborers for five years under the Russians and for seven years under the Poles. We had to work very hard every day from dawn to dusk, often under gunpoint. When it was the time of the year when the potatoes were infected with bugs, we had to get up very early every Sunday morning and pick those bugs from the potato leaves with our bare hands all day long. They ordered us: "You better do it or else!" There was no way out. No, we had no rights, no one to turn to.

In spite of the fact that we had to slave so hard under abominable conditions, we were starved and had practically nothing to eat. They took us out to work at gunpoint. After we worked in the fields all day, we had to clean kitchens. The worst thing was that we were so very hungry and we had to watch and smell how they were cooking ground meat and other food, but we got nothing, and our stomachs were growling. We ached with hunger, and hunger hurts so very much. That was very hard. Later, when the Russians and Poles realized that we could be forced to stay and work for them for a long time, we got half a loaf of bread to eat and a little bit of margarine which we had to share among all of us: my grandparents, my mother, my sisters and I. were together; we had to share that half a loaf of bread and that little margarine among all of us. That was the only food we got for the whole day. I really don't know how we were able to survive on that and do that hard forced labor from dawn to dusk seven days a week, but I certainly know all about hunger and starvation.

To make sure we would not escape at night, Polish guards would stand with their guns in front of our door. Like slaves, we were not allowed to leave. We German slaves had to be kept to labor hard for the Poles. But we had windows. The guards were standing in the front of the house, and they didn't seem to know that there were windows in the back. Desperate to escape this slavery, my brave mother threw her knapsack out of the window one day and pretended to go for a walk. That is how she escaped bondage in 1947.

Later on, the years with the Poles were a little quieter. We didn't have to work as hard any more as during the early years after the war. We worked on farms. Now we even got some money and we could go and buy some food. As a matter of fact, during the last year or so with the Russians, we already got a little bit of money. They would come and ask, "Who wants money?" But, in order to go to the store and buy anything, we had to walk six kilometers all the way to Sportau. That was difficult. However, the very first two years after the war were horrible. We worked so very hard, and we got very little food for it. We were always starving. I remember, the first time, when we got some food. I was raised at home to eat slowly. That is how we were brought up. But the others, who were also enslaved, they all ate so fast, and I was not at all used to eating so very fast. Now my plate was half full, and already the commander came: "Get up! Get back to work!" Even though I was still hungry, I had to leave the food on my plate and get back to work. Next day I knew better. One had to eat as fast as one could, or one would go hungry. It is not good to eat that fast, but what could we do!

Please forgive me. I cannot tell you all the horror. I don't want to explain. I am so afraid that I get a bad lapse of depression again. I do get medication for these depressions. Actually, I am a happy person who likes to do things. I do gymnastics, I do arts and crafts. I made this rose here, my gift to you. I love to do arts and crafts. But I am already eighty three years old and can't do things as I once did.

My father was not in the war because he already had lost four sons. That is why they spared him in the German military. Then the Russians came and took all German men. They brought him somewhere in Poland. They just grabbed him, and we had to watch him being taken away by brutal force. We could not say anything or do anything about it. My father was a civilian prisoner. He had to suffer a lot. While imprisoned, he was very sick. He was suffering from *Wassersucht* [dropsy], and they thought he would die any minute in that prison camp. A colleague of his told us later that my father had such immensely swollen face and legs that he could not walk any more. That was all water. Then the Red Cross brought him to Westphalia, and that was why we landed here in Westphalia. Later he got a job at the brick factory. That is when he brought mother here in 1947.

I didn't flee with my mother; she escaped alone to the West. My grandparents could not work any more. My sister married a Pole, a very good man, and she was very lucky to have found such a wonderful man. To me, it does not matter where you come from as long as you are a good person. Even though we suffered immense horror under the Poles and the Russians, there were some good people among them, like my brother-in-law.

I arrived here in Westphalia in March 1957, after five gruesome years under the Russians and seven years of brutal forced labor under the Poles. I have a very good friend named Gretel who had to escape from Poland. Both of us arrived here together. The two of us could do anything, Gretel and I. We became best friends. That is what I love: someone whom you can totally trust and who understands you, who knows what terrible things had been done to you without ever needing to talk about it, and who will be there for you, and vice versa. Gretel is such a treasure of a true friend. We are still good friends, after all these years. That is how it should be.

Yes, we had suffered not only days, but years of hell where unspeakable things happened to us. I cannot and will not talk about all the unspeakable atrocities, or I will break down again. But we also had some good days. And here I am. I am eighty three years old and still alive. My father always said, "Girl, if you wouldn't have your sense of humor, you would have been at the cemetery a long time ago." Yes, at my age a sense of humor keeps me alive. That is why I don't want to think about those years of hell. I don't want to talk or think about the part of my life that was a long, living nightmare. Please understand. I don't want to regress into deep depression. Please forgive me. Please help me not have to explain, not have to talk about it. I made this flower. It is for you.

Erna Böke, née Schlenske

"All night long we heard bombs crashing down non-stop, each following another. The entire night was lit up like daylight. It looked like the whole sky was on fire . . . The entire city of Dresden had been totally wiped out, and there was nothing left of it but rubble and ashes. We were just two kilometers away."

ERNA BÖKE

Interviewed in July 2007 in Gohfeld, Germany

I had a degree in education, and I taught sixteen girls. I always used to say, "I will stay with my people on our farm in Liegnitz." I loved it there. In January1945, before my father left our home and farm, he said to me, "We will not see each other here again." I asked, "Do you really think so?" He said, "Yes and this I will tell you: Don't stay here; see to it that you get away. Go toward the West; don't stay here." And it really happened as he had said. My mother reminded me that just in case we were unable to meet again here at home, let us meet at her parents' home in Dümmer Lake.

Eight days after my father had left, I was forced to flee from my home and farm with my two children, a four-year-old son and an infant. The women who stayed with us said, "Frau Böke, your child is only half a year old. You should drink a lot of water so that you can breast-feed him. Otherwise, you may not be able to save him through your flight." Then they also told me to take flour with me and other provisions. I asked the horseman, "How much oats do we need to take with us so that the horses will have something to eat, wherever we might land during the night?" "Fifteen Zentner," he said. I said, "All right, and let's also put the baby carriage on the wagon." My other boy was four years old. I said to the women, "Get the copper kettle ready and put carrots, peas, potatoes and a little meat in it. Twenty liters of milk will remain in the house. That way, when our workers come, they will have a plate of food and some milk to drink." We left at three o'clock at night. Oh, my goodness, all the homes we passed by were already empty. However, the cows remained in their stalls, and there would be no one left to milk them.

Everything had to happen extremely fast, and we had to leave in a hurry. Dear God! On top of it all, one of the wheels of our wagon broke down. I was so very lucky that we had such a good horseman who fixed it. It was such turbulent weather, a snowstorm with very little visibility. We didn't know whether we were on a street or in a ditch. Our horseman held on to steer the horses. Oh, how many wagons were lying broken on the way and how many dead people in those wagons and in the ditches. Our compassionate horseman jumped down from our wagon, took a cloth, covered the bodies quietly, and we drove on. The streets were paved with many dead people.

One day our horseman said, "The horses can't go on for a long time any more. One of the horses has a broken horseshoe, and we need a blacksmith to fix it." We went to an inn and asked if we could have a room until five o'clock. The inn keeper said, "Yes, the entire horse barn is open. You can tie the horses in the back, and in the front you can get straw for the horses. You can take your featherbeds off your wagon. There is an oven there; and if you want to cook something for yourselves, go ahead." I was so thankful that our workers at home had told me to take flour with me. It came in very handy now. I got the flour out and made some pancakes. The horseman said, "I think I will get some sail cloth, which is waterproof, and put it over the wagon. Then no matter how much it snows, we shall not get wet inside of the wagon."

Then came that ill-fated night which I can't get out of my mind. All night long we heard bombs crashing down non-stop, each following another. The entire night was lit up like daylight. It looked like the whole sky was on fire. It is impossible to describe that frightening thundering sound all night long and that blood-red burning sky. Whoever saw it will never forget it. Next morning, at ten o'clock, the innkeeper came to the barn and said something that I will also never forget as long as I live: "The entire city of Dresden has been totally wiped out by bombs, and there is nothing left of it but rubble and ashes."

Dresden was only two kilometers from where we were. Oh, my, what horrible news!

I remembered what my mother said, that just in case we were unable to meet again at home, we should meet at her parents' house in Dümmer Lake. That area, unfortunately, had become the Soviet-occupied zone of East Germany and later the GDR. We drove forty kilometers toward the West. My mother was supposed to have gone to her parents' home in Dümmer Lake. When we arrived there and knocked on the door, the first one who came to answer the door was my youngest brother; then my other brother. My sister said to my mother, "Henny, look, your daughter was able to keep the children alive throughout that terrible flight."

Now in the Soviet-occupied zone of East Germany, people were almost dying of hunger. What did we eat there at that time? Nettle and potato peels. My mother was an older woman. She had to flee all by herself and tolerate all the unspeakable torture and humiliations by herself. We could not flee together because I lived more than a hundred kilometers away from her. There was no way to contact her, and we all had to flee in such a hurry.

Now here in the Soviet-occupied zone with its ever present Secret Police, I had to plan another escape. I just had to try to go to West Germany, the only part of Germany that remained free. How did I escape from the GDR? We got hay for the horses. But one of the wheels of the wagon broke and I said, "Let's just leave this old wagon here and run away as soon as we can." Someone heard it and reported us. Then about two o'clock at night, our neighbor came and whispered to me, "Make sure that you leave before daybreak. The Russian police will come and get you. Don't go by bike; run through the meadow instead." In that meadow there was a long line of people walking fast. Nobody talked with anybody. And all of a sudden someone said, "Now we are in West Berlin. Now we have to make sure that we can get into a refugee camp." We had absolutely nothing; we had left with just our clothes on; we didn't take a single thing with us. We had run as fast as we could, just as we were. Later, we heard that five hundred farmers had escaped that night. There was no place for us to stay at the refugee camp. However, we were still relieved to be in the West. We did not have a place to stay, but we were free now. That was all that mattered.

When we came here to Gohfeld, I asked Pastor Pohlmann, "Mr. Pastor, if there is a God in heaven, why does he let us suffer so much?" Well, the pastor did not give me an answer. Now I am in this little room in this Senior Home in Gohfeld, all by myself, and I think about those horrible things that happened and can't stop crying.

Personal Narratives of the Flight from East Prussia, Germany

Herta Pflug, née Lorch
Born 1927 near Königsberg in the Samland, East Prussia,
Germany

"It was very scary: the fighter planes above us, the deep snow underneath us, the Russian
Red Army behind us and the lagoon in front of us."

HERTA PFLUG

Interviewed August 1, 2007, in Ingolstadt, Germany

I grew up in the countryside of the Samland, near Königsberg in East Prussia. We had a little farm which my diligent mother cared for. My father was employed with the railroad.

In January 1945 the Russian Red Army was coming closer and closer into our area. There were constant attacks on our region. There were no bunkers, but there were open ditches, and people constantly jumped into the ditches to save themselves from the attacks. Grenades were flying everywhere. My sister had many splinters in her arm from grenades, and I had splinters in my forehead. But they were, thank goodness, not so serious. I got my head bandaged.

My firm, Tengelmann, where I worked in the office, closed. I had no job. I was eighteen years old and had to enlist with the military. There was no choice; it was mandatory, or else! The military post in our region was identified as Hermann 013. I worked in the office there. My sister, who was an accountant, worked also at that post. The Russian Red Army was coming closer and closer. We could continuously hear the thunder of shots. German soldiers came day and night to our home. They were hungry, and my good mother cooked all the time so that they had something to eat. They were starved and freezing and happy to be able to sleep on the floor in our house, just to have a roof over their heads and a warm place. At any rate, my mother really took care of them. She cooked day and night to feed those poor German soldiers who ate with us. Everything was dangerously confusing in those days. We needed *Soldbücher* [soldiers' pay books]. I remember sitting at the front steps of a house and giving out pay books while fighter planes were flying above me. There I was, right in the middle of it all.

It was on Sunday, the 28th of January. My sister and I were at work in the office and heard those shots coming closer and closer. Our boss, Mr. Hauptmann, was sitting there at his desk, and he also heard those shots. So my sister and I tried to influence him to give the order that we could leave work and flee westward before the Red Army arrived. It took a long time before he was persuaded to give us the order. The temperature outside was minus thirty degrees. It was unimaginably cold and there was so much snow. We wanted to stay alive. We had no choice but to flee before it was too late, before the Russians got to us.

Now the question was what to take with us on our uncertain flight. We packed and unpacked, but we did not have much time; we had to hurry up. So we took only the most essential things to help us survive. There was a horse and a wagon waiting outside. We put our food on the wagon. We were very lucky; we at least had someone who took us with them, a family with two daughters. We passed by a ranch which was already burning. There was so much snow all around us that we could only see the black burned buildings and the black smoke in the midst of all that white snow.

I was at that time eighteen years old. Of course it was terrible for me; but for my parents it was much worse. They had to flee with us four children. In addition, there were two other parents and their daughters. So all together we were ten people fleeing, trying to save our lives. We were still able to drive all around the city of Königsberg. Oh, my God, it was awful, it was very scary: the fighter planes above us, the deep snow underneath us, the Russians behind us, and the lagoon in front of us.

Finally we arrived at Pillar. That was the harbor where people were put onto ships to cross the lagoon. However, not everybody was allowed to go on those ships because they were military ships. We begged the Marines to please allow us to be part of that ship transport. Then a marine came and announced that the ship Gustland had sunk. Upon hearing that tragic news, one man screamed out loud, "Oh, my God, my wife is on that ship!" There was great chaos; it was terrible.

Pillar is a harbor and Pillar Neutief is the passage to the sea. The passage was at some places as wide as one hundred meters. We had a little child with us, my sister's little boy. He always said, "Mama, the planes are coming, the planes are coming!" They flew so low. If they would have spotted us, nobody would have been allowed to go on that ship. It got warmer, and the ice began to melt. It was a matter of life and death. My sister took the initiative. She begged and tried her luck again to persuade a Marine to please let us on the ship to cross the lagoon. She said, "We have to get across, we just have to. Please, please let us go with you." God bless her, she was successful in her pleas, and the Marine gave the permission that we and our wagon could get on the ship to cross the lagoon.

Now we were on the ship and crossing the frozen lagoon. There was a sight that I will never forget as long as I live. So many horses with wagons that had tried to cross the frozen lagoon but had broken through the thin ice were lying dead there on the broken ice. Many a horses had only their hind legs or tails sticking out of the ice. Many people were lying there next to the horses, all dead. Above us, the deadly planes flew very low. I still see it in my mind's eye today; there were so many dead people, so many horses lying on that ice, so many bodies swimming there. Above us, the enemy planes were flying low.

How lucky we were; we made it safely across the lagoon. It was terrible. Then we continued for about eighty kilometers with our Marines and our horse and wagon. And above us were always the low-flying attack fighter planes.

We landed in Stuthof, which was known for the manufacture of planes. There was a big hall with straw on the floor where we refugees were allowed to sleep. I thought I would not do that because earlier, when we were in Mameln [city], a soldier came and called to me, "Frau Lörch, Frau Lörch!" My fiancée was on leave at that time and had somehow found out where I was. He wrote me a letter and said that I should go at once with that messenger soldier to see my fiancée. But I did not go at that time.

Well, now we were down here in Stuthof and were to lie on straw on the cement floor of that camp. I had a better idea. I was not going to lie on that cement floor. Now was the time to see my fiancée. So I tried to find a way to see him. I went to the man at the gate and asked, "How do I get to . . . ?" I can't remember any more the name of the place where my fiancée was. The man at the gate said, "It's too far. You cannot walk there, but I will give you my bicycle to get there. You will probably find your fiancée there in the inn." That place he told me was quite a few kilometers away. I started biking in the evening at six o'clock. It took three hours of constant biking until I got there. When I arrived in that town, it was dark. Thank goodness, I really did find that inn. There was a little light shining through the windows. I went inside, and there he was, my fiancé, the man whom I later married! His brother was there, too. Since it was late I was allowed to spend the night there, and I had a warm place to sleep.

The next day many people came, eager to talk with me. They wanted to know what the situation was in the Samland, our home region, and how people were able to cope. Of course I could tell them firsthand all the tragic news about the constant bombings, our jumping into the ditches and our escape crossing the lagoon where we saw so many dead bodies. I still had a bandage on when I talked with the people in that inn. But still, how very lucky we were! Unlike many, we were able to flee and stay alive.

Since I had been gone for the night without telling anyone, my sister looked for me. My fiancé was given a bicycle, and he and I biked back to the camp. Biking now in the daytime, I could see what had happened. Oh, my goodness! There were dead German soldiers hanging on trees along the streets. Every one of them had a sign hanging around his neck which read, "*Ich war feige*" [I was a coward]. It was the most horrible sight. I still get goose bumps thinking of it. Who hanged those poor German soldiers? The Nazis did that to their own countrymen, imagine that! Those men were ruthlessly hung on trees and killed because they didn't want to fight any more; they wanted to defect. Of course that was not allowed under Hitler's rule; you had to obey, or else! I had biked the night before in the dark all by myself by that gruesome sight. It was good that I did not see that there were dead men hanging in rows on just about every tree. I would have freaked out. It was such a heinous deed, such a horrible sight which I will never forget as long as I live. How can one ever forget such a thing? Last night, knowing that I was to talk with you today about our exodus from home, I thought about it again, and it seemed as if it was yesterday.

My fiancée and I biked all the way back to Stuthof. I returned my bike to the man at the gate, and my fiancé had to get back to his regiment. Our family eventually landed in Gehla, and there we intended to stay overnight. But in the middle of the night, we had to leave. The Russians were bombing the entire coast of the East Sea.

So we drove to the coal carrier on which we were to leave. Downstairs were wooden planks where people slept. We young girls made conversation with the sailors. We were allowed to go into their cabins, all of us, including my parents. Oh, and we got some food to eat, a bowl of warm soup. We were sent off to that coal carrying ship with a little piece of bread. That was all our food. I am telling you, we were very lucky. When one is young, one can tolerate a lot. It was much harder for the parents and the elderly. As young girls we had the advantage of being able to make contact with the sailors, which was not quite the case with older folks. When the sailors were working, we were able to stay in their cabins. We had a place and a bed in which to sleep. Later on we found out that in the back there was a compartment where the dead were placed. That was originally the bread storage area.

We sailed away with the ship in the midst of bomb alarms and air sirens. To tell you the truth, I didn't take the alarms too seriously. That was a good thing because otherwise I would have gone crazy. However, I was the exception. Everyone else, especially my mother, was frightened to death. But what could we do? We had no life vests, no swimming floats, nothing. We were still thankful to be alive and on that coal carrier ship. You can't imagine how many people died on that ship. There was nothing to eat, there was nothing to drink, but there were many people sick with typhoid. Typhoid reigned.

We wanted to go with that ship to Copenhagen, and were so lucky to indeed make it there. We were eight days on that ship. When we landed, a sailor said to me, "Come with us, we have leave, and we will show you Copenhagen." Explorer that I was, I went to the captain and told him that I would like to go on land. He gave me permission to leave the ship, and I spent the whole day in Copenhagen. Oh, it was so wonderful! Everything was normal there. It was like an old dream. The bakers were baking their goods, the stores and restaurants were open. There were no bombs, no dead bodies, and no frightened people. Everything was normal. My sailor friend had even a little bit of money; and he treated me to some goodies. Oh, it was so wonderful. It was as if the terrible war with all its horrors had never happened.

All of us German refugees were transported to a village called Lössling in Denmark. We were a total of sixty people, all German refugees. In that village, we were allowed to stay in a high school gymnasium which had been transformed into a refugee camp. There was straw on the floor for sleeping. The big room had a stage with a couch on it. I occupied that couch right away. That high school was transformed to a refugee camp. My two sisters were in charge of the kitchen. They cooked, and I was doing office work. Near our camp there was a neighbor who was a physician. He was Danish and married to a German. In the evening he often threw coal or potatoes or some other items across the fence for us. The man who delivered the milk gave us a little extra for my sister's little boy. It was now April 20, 1945. We had fled from our home long ago and had been on the road since January. We had no other choice but to leave our home behind and flee for our lives. We had absolutely no idea where we would land. Somehow, we just had to try to get out of that hell bombs, fire, and approaching Russian Army.

Here we landed in Denmark, and my sister and I were still wearing our German uniforms. That's all the clothes we had. But now we were in Denmark. So we took our coats, ripped them apart at the seams, colored them black and sewed them back together again, all by hand. We did not have a sewing machine. We really didn't have anything to wear. Now in

Denmark, in Rüh, I met a kind Dutch woman who knew that we had absolutely nothing. She gave me a present of four blouses, one skirt, and a pair of shoes. I was wearing boots, and it was getting quite warm in May. In the camps all the Germans were full of lice. That should not have been allowed. As soon as we found a louse in my clothes, my mother took every single piece of my clothing, put them in a pot and boiled the clothes to get rid of that louse.

The Danes were not very friendly toward us. Again and again they would stand along the street and spit at us and call us names. In the beginning we were permitted to leave the premises of our camp until the fifth of May. Then they put a Danish guard in front of our doors. We were not allowed to leave the premises any more. There were quite a few young girls in our group, and at night we sat in the yard and sang songs. The Danes passing by our camp would stand outside and listen to us sing. After that they didn't bully us and spit at us so much any more. That was a relief.

Soon the Danes wanted to get their high school back. So we were moved to the airport in Rüh. The Danes had quickly built barracks there, paid for by Germany. We were allowed to stay in those two-storied barracks. I was with my parents, my sister Erna, and her little boy. Because my sister had taken a course as a medical aid, she worked there as a physician's assistant under a female doctor. She was in a better place than the rest of us.

I also had some small personal success: I thought I was too beautiful to peel potatoes. So I went to the camp administration and said that I would like to work in the office (Of course without any pay). Now I really was able to sit there in the office during the day and did not have to peel potatoes after all. Well, why not? Whenever it was my mother's turn to peel potatoes, she took a few potatoes with her. I don't know how she managed to do that, but she did. She grated those potatoes, and from those grated potatoes she made soup. Up to this day, every time I make potato dumplings, I have to think of my mother's potato soup at that refugee camp in Denmark. We ate that soup eagerly; we were happy to have it. I mean, we did not get much food there. On Mondays we got milk soup with something in there which made quite a few of us a little dizzy. We also did

get a piece of bread and some other food which we needed
to pick up. There were two educators among us. They began
to teach classes. A lecturer from the University of Königsberg,
my hometown, started leading a choir. That was, of course, a
wonderful distraction from our plight.

Yes, we were the Germans who were interned in Denmark.
The Danes built a huge fence around the camp with big
spotlights everywhere. They lit up the entire ground so that we
German girls would not go to the Danish boys. They even built a
barracks for sentencing and imprisonment. Whenever someone
was caught leaving the premises, that person was sentenced. So
what did the girls do? They began digging a tunnel under the
ground so that they could get out. I was too scared to do that. My
sister Erna, who was working as a medical assistant, was allowed
to leave and to talk with the Danes. My other sister was a tailor.
Somehow she was also able to get out. My sister the medical
assistant knew some Danish women who needed something to
be sewn. So she was able to sew for them, not for money, but for
food. I remember one time when Erna brought us *Leber Käse*
[a South German dish] which she hid under her nurse's apron
because the German nurses were not allowed to take anything
back to the camp with them. It was strictly forbidden. We were
not allowed to speak with the Danish guards either. But we did
it anyway. Ha, ha, ha!

We were extremely lucky that we did not come across any
Russians. We really were lucky that way and cannot be thankful
enough for that good fortune. My sister, Erna, was allowed to
leave the camp because her in-laws were in West Germany. Later
on we were allowed to leave too. However, we had no papers.
All of a sudden everybody claimed to have a relative in West
Germany. One woman had a paper with the proper stamp. She
took the stamp and put it on her paper, and it seemed official.
I did the same thing because I didn't have any papers at that
time. So with the help of my stamped paper, my whole family
was able to get out too. We were lucky; unlike most families we
were always together, the whole family. Thank God for that.

We were allowed to stay together because each of us had
a different skill, a different job to do. One of my sisters was
a tailor. The other sister, the one with the child, was working

earlier in the kitchen before her job as medical assistant, and my father took care of the horses. Each of us doing different work that needed to be done. That allowed us to stay together. Otherwise, we would have been separated.

Then we had to experience another camp in Denmark, in Oxböhle. There were 38.000 refugees in that town. We were given a horse barn to stay in. There were so many bugs. Oh, my goodness, bugs, bugs everywhere! There were holes in the walls and on the ceiling. At night the bugs would come out in streams from those holes in the walls. When you put a flashlight on, you could just see the walls all black, full of bugs. It was so horrible, you can't imagine it. I still get the shivers thinking of it. My sister, the tailor, could not tolerate the bugs at all. She would sleep on the table, not on the floor. The bugs came down from the ceiling, down the walls, down at us. It was terrible.

We had no suitcases, nothing any more. So we needed to be creative. We sewed a rucksack from tent material. We also sewed blouses out of the gauze which the German soldiers had left there. We took those strips of gauze, and sewed them together by hand until we had a blouse. We ripped apart the army shirts and made socks and sweaters out of them. We had also taken the curtains off from the deserted airport and made skirts out of them. The men made wooden shoes for us. They heated up a needle and even engraved a pattern on those wooden shoes. They were elegant [big grin]! Yeah, necessity is the mother of invention.

After our two years in Oxböhle, we were allowed to leave Denmark for Germany. It was very difficult to find any housing in our war-destroyed country. Ravaged by the war, Germany simply did not have enough housing for all of those German refugees that were flooding in from the East. When we left Denmark, we could take with us the few things that we had sewn together. We took the train across the Danish/German border, and now we were in West Germany. My two big sisters went to Dortmund and later were married there. My brother, Ewald, started a shoe workshop here in Ingolstadt. It was through my sister in Berlin that we knew that my brother was in Ingolstadt. I'm telling you, those communication channels were all incredible. It was truly miraculous to be able to find out who was where. We came to Ingolstadt in 1947, two years after the end of the war.

In Ingolstadt, one of my brother's colleagues offered my parents a place to sleep. But now the problem was that they needed to have a *Zuzugsgenehmigung* [German government permission to move to West Germany], and the West German government didn't give it to us because of a lack of housing and food. So I drove with my father to Dachau. However, they did not give us the permission to stay there either. Then I finally got it at the Farmers Bureau here in Ingolstadt.

Now we were here, but my parents could not stay forever at the place of my brother's colleague. My sister lived in the same house where my brother lived. A kind family offered my sister a place to sleep, and I was offered a bed in another family's home. It was absolutely wonderful that those families were so generous and kind to us. After a while my sister found a job with a seamstress and lived with her. I found a job at the refugee office. I also found an apartment with two rooms Eventually, my parents moved into the house of my brother, who was an orthopedic shoe specialist. I continued to live in the apartment on the Milchstrasse and later moved to another apartment. Well, we did not have much money. I earned 125.00 DM a month. We really had nothing when we arrived here and needed to start all over again. It was a good beginning.

I was part of a wonderful group of former officers whose *Abitur* [high school diplomas] were not recognized because they had gone to a high school named Adolf Hitler Gymnasium. Yes, all those officers who went to that high school had to do the *Abitur* all over again here in Ingolstadt. That was the clique I hung around with. After the deprivation of the war and our flight from home, this was a great time for me. We danced, we had fun together, and I had not known what fun was like for a long time. In that group there were two brothers. Their father had arranged two girls for them to marry. The big brother always made sure that the younger brother would not come too close to me. They were to marry those two girls. When they had finished their *Abitur*, all the officers unfortunately left. That was a terrible situation for me. I had known them for a whole year, a beautiful year during which I had for the first time had fun.

You know, our whole youth was stolen from us by that senseless tragic war.

In the meantime my fiancée came. He was a prisoner of war in Russia and was released in Kiel, in northern Germany. He told me to come to Kiel, but he didn't have a place to live there. The brother of my sister-in-law was working at the police station in Kiel, and they put up beds in hallways so that they had a place to sleep. They put my fiancée up there too. My brother Ewald said, "You will not go there; let your fiancée come here, and then you can see if you still are meant for each other." Well, we actually did not match so well. We were fighting a lot.

I was twenty-one years old by now. My father said to me, "Either you marry your fiancée, or you each go your own separate ways." Well, I couldn't just leave my fiancé there in Kiel; he was very sick when he came from the Russian prison camp. I brought him to Ingolstadt where my mother took care of him. She cooked for him and nursed him back to health. In 1949 we got married. He was educated in business and began to work for Scharping as an accountant. Then one day something terrible happened. I was driving a car. My husband had no driver's license. On our way back home, we had a horrible accident on the Autobahn. My husband died instantly, and I suffered eighteen broken bones. I was not given much of a chance to live. However, my brother, who was working with the police in Munich, told the police physician about my situation. That physician said, "That is not a case for the regional hospital. She must go to Munich." That was in 1969. They got a helicopter to take me to Munich. It was April and very cold in that helicopter. When we landed in front of the hospital, my sweet brother was already there, standing and waiting for me. He was absolutely wonderful. That was my younger brother.

Unfortunately, we lost my older brother in the war. He had six children. My sister-in-law remained in East Prussia and had the misfortune of experiencing the cruelty of the Russians to whom we lost our home, our land, and all our property. After a long horrid ordeal, she and her children were finally able to escape from East Prussia and land in Leipzig, East Germany, where they heard the tragic news that her husband had died in the war. My sister-in-law and her children are now here in West

Germany and in Austria. They were able to escape from the GDR to the West before the Wall was built. Later it would hardly have been possible to escape alive. They got a job right away in Munich and in Vienna. At that time it was easier to get a job because there were very few men left in Germany. The war had swallowed up most of them.

When I got married, we had absolutely nothing. We had a bed but no bed sheets. So I bought some fabric and sewed the bed sheets and pillow covers. I wanted to make mashed potatoes, but we did not have a potato press. That is how we started, with nothing. However, I was always working. I got a job as a clerk at the *Donau Kurier* [local news paper in Ingolstadt], where I worked for ten years. After I left the *Donau Kurier*, I found a job with the army here in Ingolstadt. My first husband and I were married for 18 years. My first husband was very young when he died; he was only 45 years old. He had to endure that terrible and cruel ordeal as a prisoner of war in Russia. Many years later, in 1976, I married again. My second husband and I were married for eleven years.

We were so very lucky. When the Russian Army marched into Königsberg and East Prussia, there were so many rapes. However, we escaped that torture of the Russians in the nick of time. I don't know of any particular woman who was raped. We were very lucky to be able to escape with that ship to Denmark. Denmark saved us that way. Yes, I can truthfully say, Denmark saved the women who got across the lagoon to Denmark in time before the Russians marched into our home region of Königsberg. Even in our misfortune, we were still fortunate.

Irene Borger
Born February 7, 1940, in Gross Schöndamerau, Kreis
Ortelsberg, East Prussia, Germany

"My mother told me to climb up on her back, hold on to her very tightly, and with me on her back, we would both swim across the river. I did exactly as she said . . . And we made it safely to the other side of the river."

IRENE BORGER

Interviewed June 17, 2008, in Michigan, USA

I was born in 1940 and was not yet five years old when we had to flee our big farm early in the winter of 1945. Ever after, we were on the run. We had to find a way to be safe, look for a place to stay, and be safe and away from the Russian Red Army.

I have flashbacks, you know. These are just things that I remember. For example, I remember where I was hiding in our home. I remember things like hiding in the bunker and my mother always hiding in the haystack. The Russians would come to our farm with their spears and poke hard in our haystacks to see if anyone was hiding there. My grandmother, my mother and other German women would be on the lookout for them and quickly hide as soon as they saw a Russian coming.

We still had a few German farmers (mainly women) left in our town in 1945. There were no men at home; they had to serve in the war where many lost their lives. My mother had two brothers. Both of them were killed in the beginning of the war. My little brother, who was two years younger than I, had died of typhus. Only my grandmother, my mother and I were left at home. My grandmother was quite old by then. She had to endure much hardship, much tragedy at her advanced age, due to the war. We were not safe; we needed to escape.

Our first flight was early in 1945. I remember we got our wagon ready and took what we could. Off we went through the woods, hiding all the time. Along the way we would hide in places where nobody was living; we would stay there overnight and then quietly march on the next day. Later we did come back to our house. I guess it was still in pretty good shape. Since the Russians had some sort of headquarters in our house or they lived there, our house was more or less spared. When we came back from hiding, the Russians had already left.

The victors of WWII had decided that Germany would lose all its territories east of the rivers Oder and Neisse to Poland. Well, our home was east of the Oder /Neisse line, and it was declared that it no longer belonged to us, and that it was not a part of Germany any more. Well, what were we to now in what had all of a sudden become Poland? We would have loved to go to the West. Unfortunately, under the now-communist regime, we were not allowed to leave the communist country any more. It was strictly forbidden to escape to the West.

However, my courageous mother made very careful escape plans and took a chance to escape with me to the West. One dark December night in 1947, my mother and I left home, taking hardly anything with us. We had no horse, no wagon, nothing. I remember we walked and walked for a long time until we came to the river Oder (the dividing line between what had become now Poland and Germany). We were lucky to have a guide with us who showed us the safest way to cross the river. That good guide brought us to a particular spot and said, "This is a good spot to cross the river because the guards won't get you that easily here."

My mother was an excellent swimmer. That is what I heard from my friends from back home. I remember, clearly, my mother sat me down at the edge of the river and asked me to remain quiet. I sat there. It was night and it was dark. Not wasting a minute, my mother did a trial run swimming across the river alone. She left me behind and swam across that cold river. She barely reached the other side when she swam back immediately to get me. My mother told me to climb up on her back, hold on to her very tightly, and we would both swim across the river. I did exactly as she said. I climbed on her back and held on to her very tightly, and we made it safely to the other side.

When we got there, we were already in West Germany. The river was the dividing line. The water was ice cold. It was winter and just before Christmas in 1947. We were shivering and freezing wet when we got to the other side. That was how we swam across the river Oder to freedom. Of course we had to leave our home, our land, our streets, and our neighborhood behind. It all became Poland after the war and was German no more.

I guess we had an address of someone on the West side of Germany who would take us in. I remember a man who made *Steh-auf-Männchen* [wooden toy figures with a string to pull which would make their arms move] for Christmas. That's how I remember that it was before Christmas. I remember we stayed the night with him. The next day we were on our way to Munich, Bavaria, where my father was living. My father, who had been in the Air Force, got a job near Munich in a tool and dye shop. I went to school there until 1951 when we migrated to the U.S.A. and landed in Michigan. I was eleven years old then. I was very lucky compared to many refugees who had it much harder than we did. Compared to their trauma, we were lucky indeed.

My grandmother remained in our house in East Prussia until the people were allowed to leave the barbed-wired communist land without having to cross the border illegally. Of course our house, our property, and all the land in our region were confiscated and declared to be no longer German. Our area of East Prussia became part of Poland after the war. And that's who owns it right now, Polish people.

When my grandmother was able to come out of East Prussia after it had become Poland, she ended up in the Black Forest in Germany. Of course when we were in Bavaria, we were able to go back and forth and see her. Later she used to visit us in the United States. My grandmother would tell us about her suffering back home during the war and the years that followed after our home became Polish property. She had to endure terrible hardships and had a very hard life.

I was lucky. I was very young and don't remember the trauma that my mother and grandmother had to live through. I just wish I could have asked my mother more questions. I am so sorry to have missed that invaluable opportunity. With my mother and grandmother, a living part of history is gone. You know, you think you have so much time, but all of a sudden it's gone. You have to ask all the questions and have all the conversations when you have a chance.

There are still a lot of people that go back home. It's Poland now, but for many, the home and homeland they lost is still home in their hearts. Ten years ago I went back to see the house where I was born. We took a bus tour and spend some time there, to see where I went to school and where we lived. I was able to go inside our house. The Polish people living in our house were very nice. They let us look around and made coffee and cake for us. They even gave us a present. We had a small lake close to our property. I remember when I was a little girl, I always went to that lake. I remember my mother was afraid I would drown. So when we went back to our home, we went to that lake and took a boat ride. So many childhood memories came back. Those Polish people living in our home are quite wealthy now. They got our entire huge farm, our house and all that land that for generations was ours. It's worth a lot. It was bitter-sweet to go back to the home and homeland we lost forever.

Irmgard Pautz
Born February 18, 1932, in Willims, in the Ermland, East

"In the midst of chaos, mothers got separated from their children.
My mother always said we should stick tightly together and hold hands so that we wouldn't
get separated."

IRMGARD PAUTZ

Interviewed June 23, 2008, in Michigan, USA

All the family members from my mother's side worked at the railroad in Willims in the Ermland in East Prussia. The last months before the war were upon us, and we had to leave our house and home and flee from the rapidly approaching Russian Red Army.

It was at the end of January in 1945. Since we are Catholic, we wanted to go to the Rhineland in West Germany because Ermland was predominantly Catholic, and the Rhineland was also predominantly Catholic. But by the time the train arrangements were made to get us out, it was too late. The corridor to the West was closed, and we could not leave by train any more. Willims was a small town. At that time we didn't have any cars; people got around by horse and buggy.

I was small and don't remember how we left, but it was with my mother. We were six kids: my three older sisters, my youngest sister, my brother, and I; so including my mother, we were a sizable group of seven on our way to safety. I don't remember if we were walking or what. But we got all the way to the Kurische Meerung. From the Kurische Meerung, we somehow ended up in Danzig (now Polish Gdansk). We stayed overnight in a place with two other families. It was scary. Bombs were falling. Russians were shooting. We were in a war zone. After we were in Danzig for two days, the Caracas aid organization wanted to help us but didn't know what to do with us. So they got us into little boats. They wanted to bring us to the *Insel Rügen* [Island Rügen]. When we transferred from a small boat to a big boat, the Russians started shooting at us. They just kept on shooting and shooting. I remember the shooting went on for a long time. People screamed, and it was chaotic. A lot of people who were together before lost each other. In the chaos mothers got separated from their children. My mother always said we should stick tightly together and hold hands so that we wouldn't get separated. The family next to us had only one child. The Russian bullets hit that sweet child, and the child was killed instantly. We were right next to that child, but for some miraculous reason, the bullets missed us.

Even though the shots were flying everywhere, it was our luck that the Russians were not physically close to us. My older sisters were twenty and eighteen years old, and we were lucky that they and my mother were not violated by the Russians, unlike many other German women.

We were to go to the Island Rügen, but there they did not want us refugees. So we ended up in Kiel, Schleswig-Holstein, in northern Germany. All together I think it took about two frightful and dangerous months for us to flee from home and get to Schleswig-Holstein.

For some reason we were brought from Kiel by train to Neumünster and then to a farmhouse in a little town called Wasbak. We got a room in that farmhouse and stayed there for quite some time. The war was still going on. The fighter planes were flying above us but did not hit us in that most northern part of Germany, unlike the Eastern parts of Germany from where we escaped.

When we came to Wasbak in Schleswig-Holstein, there were many American soldiers, but they were decent. I didn't hear anything bad about them. I mean, we all were afraid; we didn't know them. The American soldiers wanted the young girls to dance with them. My oldest sister was twenty, and my other sister was eighteen. They didn't want to dance with the American soldiers, but they had to. They were afraid what those soldiers might do to them. But those American soldiers did not do any harm to them. They were not anything like the feared Russian soldiers. Thank goodness for that! I guess the American soldiers were lonely and wanted the girls to dance with them. I was too young then.

After my father, who was a prisoner of war in Russia, returned, we moved to Stuttgart. My father was a bricklayer, and bricklayers were desperately needed in Stuttgart, which was severely bombed and destroyed. I must honestly say that we were very lucky compared to the horrors that most other refugees had to endure during the war and the years that followed.

Brief History of Pomerania, Germany and the Expulsion of Germans

Some German farmers living in Pomerania can be traced back to 1173. German traders and merchants settled in the city of Stettin at that time. However, the actual settlements of Germans in Pomerania started in the 13th century at the invitation of the rulers of Pomerania and Rügen.

From the Napoleonic Wars to the end of World War I in 1918, Pomerania was administered by Prussia as the Province of Pomerania. Major industrialization happened primarily in the region around the city of Stettin. When the German Empire collapsed at the end of World War I, Pomerania was divided between Poland and Germany. After the abdication of Kaiser Wilhelm II as Emperor of Germany and King of Prussia, the western part of Pomerania became part of the Free State of Prussia, while the eastern part was annexed to Poland (Historical Exhibition, 1998). The Polish Corridor of re-constituted Poland was established from a large portion of West Prussia (Buchholz, 1999). This caused an exodus of the German population. Poland built a major Baltic port at Gdingen (now Gdynia). The city of Danzig became the Free City of Danzig (now Gdansk).

When the refugees from the East were passing through Pomerania toward the end of World War II, many Germans living in West Prussia and Danzig also wanted to flee westward. However, Hitler's Nazi Party strictly prohibited their flight and even prevented the caravans of refugees from East Prussia, the Warthegau, and other regions. As a result, the number of refugees in Pomerania increased to almost three hundred thousand. Altogether, there was a population of more than three million Germans living in Danzig and West Prussia at the beginning of March 1945 (Buchholz, 1999).

At the end of February 1945, the Soviet Army, supported by the Polish Army, reached the Baltic coast and occupied the land between the Oder and Vistula rivers. From the other side, they reached the Baltic coast through the mouth of the Oder River at Stettin. Within two weeks they took possession of all eastern Pomerania and cut off all land communication with the west (Buchholz, 1999).

Since the Russians were attacking Pomerania and West Prussia at the same time, there was a huge exodus of refugees toward the Danzig area to escape by sea. However, the sinking of many refugee ships, especially the "Wilhelm Gustloff", which departed from Danzig and was sunk by a Russian submarine on January 30, drowning about 9.000 of its civilian refugees, mainly women, children and the elderly (Höges, Meyer, et. al., 2005), frightened many from leaving by ship. Others braved to wait in vain at the small Pomeranian ports of Stolpmünde and Leba, hoping to be transported to the west. However, they became tragic victims of the Russians who occupied those ports. The sheer number of desperate refugees trying to flee by land, created such an impossible jam that soon all roads were clogged and thousands of people trapped. However, a few thousand did succeed to escape to the West. By March 10, 1945 all of eastern Pomerania had been occupied by the Red Army, with the exception of Kolberg which was occupied on March 18 (Buchholz, 1999). Those thousands of German civilians who were not able to escape were subjected to all the unspeakable horrors of the Russians, as described earlier.

PERSONAL NARRATIVE OF THE FLIGHT FROM POMERANIA, GERMANY

Frau Berghof
Born January 5, 1908, in Stettin, Pomerania, Germany

"The ones who suffer the most in any war are women, mothers and children. The crimes against them cry to heaven. I have seen it with my own eyes, heard it with my own ears."

FRAU BERGHOF

Interviewed in July 2007 in Gohfeld, Germany

I was born and raised in Stettin. I am not really a refugee because I was already in Berlin when the war started. But I experienced the deadly last years of the war in Berlin, the marching in of the Red Army and the immense terror and sorrow that followed in that once so beautiful capital city.

I had a volunteer position in that beautiful city. Then I received notice that I was to work in an ammunition factory. But I said, "No, that I will not do." I did not want to be a part of making any weapons of destruction. Then I met a community nurse and asked her if she could suggest a hospital where I could be a nurse. That was the only way to escape from having to work in an ammunition factory. The nurse told me to go to the hospital in Berlin. I did that, and they employed me right away.

Oh, those were terrible times, during as well as after the war. It was especially very difficult toward the end of the war. It was downright catastrophic. I was in Berlin, and Berlin was bombarded continuously, night and day. The Americans hit this capital city with their big deadly bombs. Every day the bombs fell, every single day. It was even worse at night. I had to study for nursing classes and had to get out every night. I was determined to finish my nursing exam and, indeed, was able to do so. At first I was working in pediatrics; then I was told by the head nurse to help in the operating room. I did not want to do that at all. I wanted to work with children. However, I was sent to work in the operating room, which was moved into the basement. Our boss said, "We will stay in the basement. If the bombs continue to fall, we may be safe there in this hospital bunker."

We served many wounded patients. One time I went to see my friend in Berlin who had to go to a clinic because she had an infection. There I witnessed, with my own eyes, what was happening in the inner city. It was literally on fire. The whole city was burning. Some people were walking on the streets, dragging a little wooden wagon in which they had put their last pieces of belongings. It was a desperate and awful situation. When I reached the clinic's location, which was right in the center of Berlin, I was told that the clinic was no longer there.

Near the end of the war, Hitler gave orders that half-grown boys were to be given a gun in their hands and were to fight. Those boys were far too young and totally without any training. They had never held a gun in their hands before. Many got hurt by simply having to learn how to use that gun. Many of them desperately called for help. I heard their cries, and I can still hear them. They called for their mothers. It didn't help; they were forced to hold those guns and shoot. One had to follow orders, follow orders or else!

There was one very young man who ran away from the military. I don't know if he took his uniform off or not. Anyway, they caught him and he begged, "I want to see my mother one more time. I want to go and see her in Berlin." The Nazis, who had forced that young boy to fight in the first place, now hanged him at the lamp post, a mere boy and fellow German, because he did not want to fight any more. Yes, such things happened too, and we saw it all. Oh, such tragedy!

When the Russians occupied Berlin, they imposed a curfew starting at seven o'clock at night. Nothing functioned any more. You could hear the Russians marching in from afar. Battalions of them went from house to house and brutally raped women and girls, some over and over again. You could hear the terrible screams of the victims. I tell you, it was so awful that I can find no words to describe it. So many of the girls died; some were barely teenagers. If there was any German man who dared to come to their defense, and there were only old men left, he was shot on the spot. Yes, he was simply shot. I saw it with my own eyes. Those Russians didn't even blink an eye. Every night, all night long, they were out hunting down females to rape and mass rape, no matter their age, whether they were eighty or thirteen years old. Oh, my God, my God, it was so unspeakably beastly and horrific.

Those brutal, barbaric Russians were, on the other hand, relatively friendly toward small children. Whenever they had something to eat, which they had, of course, stolen from us, they readily offered something to small children, but only a little bit, of course. Perhaps it was because they too had small children back in Russia. But then they could have left the women and girls in peace too. Night and day, all of Berlin was screaming from the cries of brutally violated women and girls. It was horrid, and it was truly a living nightmare to be in Berlin.

My head nurse was a very nice person. I was in contact with her for a long time after the war. She said, "When the Russians come and you think you cannot bear it any more, I will give you something (for suicide), or you take a rope and hang yourself." Well, thank goodness it did not come to that. One day when the Russians came, there was a female Russian officer among them who wanted to have a look at the operating room. My boss was very courteous and friendly toward her and showed her the operating room which was still open at that time. Then the Russians would come and throw their wounded soldiers down on the floor and leave them there without any respect, without any regard for their own fellow solders.

At night the Russians would come to our rooms and order the nurses to go with them for their "pleasure." That is when my boss said, "Now we close the bunkers and the operating room. We cannot go on like this."

Now I have a little bit of humor to share: the Russians drove around during the day wearing the shirts they had stolen from the hospital. Apparently, they did not know what was written on those shirts. On those shirts was written "Property of the city of Berlin." Ha, ha! That was again something that would amuse the Berliners who had been known for their sense of humor. But unfortunately one had to say that in such a war, it was the grotesqueness of humanity that came out of human beings. That was in Germany as well as everywhere during such a war.

When Berlin fell into the Russian hands, the Berliners said, "The Russians are coming to set us free from the very last little peace that we may still have." That was typical Berliner gallows humor. After the war, the American bombers brought us food. The Americans were the ones who supported us in West Berlin, very unlike the Russians who unfortunately were the first to march into Berlin with their unspeakable brutalities.

When the war had started, my sister and her children and my mother were still in Silesia. She never ever thought that she would have to leave her home and community that she loved so much. But that was not what happened; she was brutally expelled and had to flee. When she and her children were ordered to leave home and seek shelter in a mass refugee camp, she said, "Not with the three children and the pestilence there and all the horrible, unspeakable things that happen to women and girls. No, I will not go into such a mass camp!" Instead, she, her children, and my mother somehow managed to get on a train and get off here in Eisbergen, Westphalia, which was a small village at that time. My sister found a very old, run-down, damp building which would be considered uninhabitable now. She was happy that she had a place to stay, no matter how run-down it was. Our mother found a place to stay somewhere else. Now they were all here in the West but without any food, without any money, with nothing but their lives. They had to find a way to survive each day. In order to eat, they needed to go begging.

That was the worst for me, to go begging with my sister's children. Oh, it was so hard and so humiliating. That is where I gathered experiences in relation to people. The big rich farmers in the West whose home was not destroyed and who owned a lot of property sent their barking dogs to chase after us. The small farmers, however, who were relatively poor, they always had a heart. They always gave us something, especially when they saw the children. They would not let us go away from their doorsteps empty-handed and hungry.

I was actually the communication link for our family so that they would be informed where our family members were located. I knew that my sister was in Eisbergen. When my anxious brother-in-law came and asked me if I knew where his family was, I was happy to be able to tell him the name of the town where they lived, but I did not know the exact address. He found them eventually. But it did take a long time. He was a lawyer who had lost his position in Silesia, together with his home and everything else. When he came to Eisbergen, he helped many a people with their questions in relation to the laws in the West. In return for his help, he received some food.

After the war, Berlin was divided into four different sectors, one for each of the victors of the war. There was a Russian, an American, a British, and a French sector. We were then in the French sector. Lucky for us, we were not in the Russian sector and that the Russians were then no longer with us in our particular part of Berlin. Believe me, we had had enough taste of those Russians, more than you could ever imagine, more than we are ever able to forget as long as anyone of us who had to witness it is alive. But, in spite of all their unspeakable brutalities, one could only say, "They, too, are human beings." Wars are the most horrible things ever, bringing out the very worst in people. However, he ones who suffer the most are the mothers and the children. Yes indeed, mothers, women and children suffer the most in any war. The heinous crimes against them cry out to heaven. I have seen it with my own eyes, heard it with my own ears.

Shortly before the Berlin Wall was built, I managed to leave Berlin in a cattle-train and make it up to the border (between East and West Germany) in Helmstedt. We had to get out of the train at the border in Helmstedt and go through an awful tunnel. Then I remember going on foot through a forest. I was all by myself. Earlier I was instructed: "Just keep on going straight ahead, and then you shall be on the other side (West Germany)." Well, I had no other choice but to follow those instructions and was most fortunate to successfully escape from East to West Germany without being caught. That was very shortly before the Berlin Wall was built (in 1961). I was very lucky and happy that I was able to escape safely to the West. Later on, it was impossible to escape alive from Russian communist-ruled East Germany to free democratic West Germany.

After successfully escaping to the West, I was again very lucky. When I arrived, exhausted at the West German border, someone gave me a ride all the way to Rinteln (a town in Westphalia). I don't usually go in strangers' cars, but I was too exhausted. The driver said, "Where are you going?" I said, "I have to go to Eisbergen." He replied, "Well, hop on in!" That man had such a commanding voice. Later I found out that he was a physician who helped people by bringing them very much needed food. He brought me to the police station in Rinteln and said to the policemen, "Drive to Eisbergen and take her with you!" Imagine that! Those policemen were not too happy about that, but they did it for him. Once again, luck was with me when that physician came my way. Exhausted, I lied down on a bench at the police station and fell immediately asleep. The policemen had to wake me up. They said to me, "It's time to get up; we are now off to Eisbergen." Yes, that is how I remained somehow safe. That is what you call lucky, indeed.

In Eisbergen my sister was not so very happy to see me. She had a hard enough time feeding her own children, and now I was another mouth to feed. I had to try to find a place to work. I did not get paid much; but I did work and got a little bit of money. My brother-in-law found that job for me. He knew a professor of medicine in Holzhausen, and that professor gave me a job. I was working there at the lowest nurse's rank. The professor had lost the nuns who were his nurses. Those nuns belonged to a diocese and were placed somewhere else. The professor said, "Would you have the courage to manage the operating room?" I replied eagerly, "Oh, yes, I have that courage. I have worked long enough in the O.R. in Berlin." So now I had a job there as a nurse in the operating room.

Later we moved to Minden, Westphalia. From there I moved to Bad Oeynhausen. My sister advised me, "Don't work in a private clinic; go to a bigger institution and you'll get a better salary." So I tried here in Bad Oeynhausen to get a position in an operating room. There I was told, "I am sorry, we have nothing open in the O.R., but I can offer you a position in another, smaller department." I took that position and had really not much experience or knowledge about the work in that department. But there was another nurse, and she taught me a lot of things. Unfortunately, she was leaving the hospital. She said, "If I would have known that you were to come, I would have stayed here."

I worked in that hospital in Bad Oeynhausen for many years until I got hepatitis. One of the attending physicians told me, "I want to tell you something: you better file for retirement. You will not be able to get your strength back with this hepatitis." I said, "What? I only have half a year to go until I am sixty years old, and by then I will be fit again." He said, "Well, go ahead if you wish." But he was absolutely right. I was so weak, too weak to continue working. So I filed for retirement, became a retiree, and now I live in joy and peace.

However, there are these singular, powerful experiences that one remembers vividly and can't ever forget. But it is also wonderful that one is able to forget some things. That is actually very good. One can no longer think of all that immense, unspeakable sorrow and suffering. There is no way to comprehend it. There is no way for someone who has not experienced such unspeakable atrocities to begin to imagine them. I suppose that is why many women do not want to talk about it and prefer to push it aside as much as they can.

I think that especially many women who survived the brutal multiple Russian rapes deal with their trauma silently by themselves.

I tell you, the tragedy of the Second World War was the unspeakable agony of the women. But, about thirty years earlier, during the First World War (1914-1918), my grandmother lost many children. She was in agony. Her beloved children had become that war's canon food, just like those millions of mothers who lost their children during and after World War II. What madness! What living hell! What for? When will it ever end?

POLAND

BRIEF HISTORY OF THE WARTHEGAU, POLAND

The Warthegau or Warthegau region in Poland (currently known as Wielkopolskie) is located south of the Silesian-Polish border along the river Warthe (now called Warta). The Warthegau region was a part of Poland until 1772 when Poland was partitioned out to Russia, Prussia, and Austria. Then it became a part of Prussia (i.e. Germany) until 1919 (see Map of Germany 1914). After World War I ended, Germany lost the Warthegau territory to the newly re-formed independent country of Poland (see Map of Germany 1950), except for a brief period during World War II when Warthegau was re-incorporated into the German Reich after defeating the Polish Army in 1939 (Historical Exhibition, 1998; Magocsi, 2002). When German forces gained control of the region, the Warthegau was inhabited mostly by Poles with a significant German minority of 670.000 (Schieder, Vol. 1, p. 27E, 2004). Most of the German population (about 30 percent) lived in the western part of the Warthegau in the Province of Posen, especially near the old German borders. The Province Posen (now Poznania) is located east of Berlin and north of Breslau. It is on trade routes from Western Europe and Scandinavia to Russia.

Flight and Expulsion of Ethnic Germans

The Russian front offensives in January 1945 were so unexpectedly fast that by January 20, the Warthegau region was already closed and the Germans in the Warthegau trapped. In fact, as early as January 18, no trains were running west since the Russian troops had already reached Lodz, and the train lines of Lodz-Posen and Kutno-Posen were not running either. There was no other mode left for the Germans to flee but by horse and wagon on the frozen streets during one of the coldest winters in recorded history. While the fleeing treks in East Prussia and Silesia lasted for a period of four months, the sudden panic-stricken flights of the Germans in the Warthegau took place in just fourteen days (Schieder, 2004, Vol. I, p. 27 E). German women, children, and the elderly were desperately trying to escape the Russian Army by means of horse and wagon which were plundered and taken away from them by Poles. Battling snow storms and deep freeze during one of Europe's coldest winters, they had to march two hundred kilometers to the river Oder to be able to cross over to Germany. Thousands did not survive this dangerous odyssey. Many froze to death or were murdered by plundering Russian or Polish partisans. When the refugees came face to face with the Russian Army or Polish partisans, especially in the Kalisch-Konin area of the Warthegau, the women of all ages and even very young girls became victims of the most heinous crimes of mass rape and murder in the most sadistic ways (Kahl, (2004, pp.348-350). Small children were torn away from the arms of their mothers, their heads banged to death at sharp edges of trucks and their grief-stricken mothers taken away (Jesko, 1951, p. 350-351). Those refugees who found it hopeless to make it all the way to the German border tried to return home. There they found that all their property had already been confiscated by the Poles. They were forced to do hard labor for the Poles, while suffering hunger pains and humiliation, years after the war was over. Many of them were beaten and killed (Buchholz, 2004, p. 347; E.L. 2004, pp. 364-365). Thousands of ethnic Germans were brought to forced labor camps. One of those camps was in Potulice where 24,000 Germans, including 6,000 children, were brought in 1947. The records of the Polish camp administration reveal that 3,500-4,000 found their death in that forced labor camp (Cwikla, 2008, p. 137).

For immediate identification, Germans were forced to wear white arm bands (Meyer, 2005, p. 156). The German language was forbidden to be spoken in public and any written German words were removed from signs and cemeteries. German music was not allowed to be played. The wealthy Germans, or even those who were employed by Germans, were killed or slowly tortured to death (Buchholz, 2004, p. 348).

Leokadia Wenzel, née Kühn
Born September 30, 1911 in Konin, Warthegau, Germany
(now Poland)

"Whenever you think you can't go on any more, there comes from somewhere a little light showing you the way."

Excerpts of a Personal Narrative of the Flight from the Warthegau, Poland

LEOKADIA WENZEL

It was in the heart of that bitter cold winter of January 1945 when the devil ruled our region of the world and tore it into pieces. He swallowed our loved ones, our home, land and all. We had to leave everything behind, for there was no more place for us, nothing. The Russians and Poles got the right to what once was ours. That month and year still brings ice-cold shivers down my spine. Polish men came storming into our farm. They took our horses, except for two that were in another barn. Oh, we had such beautiful horses, Papa's pride and joy. They took our cows, put them on a truck and drove them away. The dogs were barking loudly. The men simply shot those poor dogs. I can still hear the sounds of those guns, terrible, terrible.

Then some Polish men came into the house looting and screaming, "Out, out, you Hitler folk. You have no place here anymore!" I ran to hold you and to keep you quiet. You were just a baby. Your terrified sisters, nine year old Sophie, eleven year old Lilli, and twelve year old Edith were shaking with fright. Oh, how much I feared for their lives! Two of the Polish men went to the bedroom while others continuously pointed their guns toward us and yelled swear words at us.

Finally they left. We all huddled together. I fell on my knees and cried bitter tears. Still, I had to be thankful that they did not kill us, that they did not violate our bodies. After all, we were all female and German. Any German female was defenseless and easy prey at that time in that part of the world. What were we to do? We had to flee, but where to? That was our home. If we were not safe here in our own home, how safe would we be on the streets, the streets leading to God knows where?

A German leader of the village hurriedly knocked on our door and advised us to flee as quickly as possible. A German man riding on a horse screamed loudly while passing by, "the Russians are coming; the Poles are looting; run, run for your lives!" Oh, my God, where shall I run with four children, one of them a little baby? What about my dear mother and grandmother who lived about thirty kilometers away? How will I know what happened to them? There was no telephone, no way to contact them. What shall I do?

A week before getting that advice to flee, my dear mother, your grandmother, Oma, had sent us Anton, whom she had taken care of since he had lost his parents when he was very young. Anton was about thirty nine years old now and mentally challenged. Since he was male and strong, he came to protect us. It was lucky that Anton managed to hide in the attic when the Polish men broke in to loot. Thank God they did not find him or they surely would have killed him on sight. Yes, any German man was simply killed on sight. Since all the German men, including thirteen year old boys, were forced to fight in the war, there were only defenseless women, children and old folks left at home on the farms. Anton was spared to fight because he was mentally slow. Somehow Oma was able to spare him from being killed by Hitler's Nazis who did not tolerate any mentally unstable German or anybody voicing any disagreement with Hitler's regime.

Anyway, Anton crawled down from his hiding place. There was no time to lose. We got some featherbeds from the attic. Anton packed some hay for the horses. Edith and Lilli hurried to bring the only two horses left in the barn to pull the wagon; one of them was a pregnant mare. Hurriedly, I loaded the wagon with meat, bread, and the feather beds to keep us warm in that bitter cold winter. We had to flee as fast as possible, leaving our home behind to escape from the approaching Russian Army and the Poles who had seized neighboring German homes, farms and property. Worse, there were reports that Russian soldiers mass raped and killed German women and young girls wherever they found them. With our layers and layers of clothing under our coats, we climbed quickly on the wagon and left our beloved home, our land, our neighborhood, our church, and our familiar surroundings forever.

Anton was sitting in the driver's seat. I sat in the back of the wagon with all the children, tightly holding you, the baby, in my arms. I had a long look at our home and farm that I was never ever to see again. I looked at our beautiful lake across the street. It was all frozen now in the bitter cold winter. I still have the picture in my mind's eye. We left everything, everything behind. My only hope was to save my children and to be able to keep all of us together. I prayed very hard, "Dear God, please, please, keep us together and show us the path, for we don't know where to go and how to be safe. Our destiny is in your hands. But please, whatever you do, dear God, please keep us together through thick and through thin. Please, don't let any one of us be separated."

On the road, we saw many wagons with people like us, fleeing for their lives. A young German man, riding on a horse, raced as fast as he could to the front of a memorial in the city square. In a desperate voice, he called out loud for all the wagons not to go in the same directions if we wanted to stay alive. Pointing in different directions, he called "Ten wagons here, ten there, ten there!" He urged all of us, all refugees, to split up our wagon trains in order to save our lives and prevent a mass killing by the Russian Red Army that was marching in our direction and had already killed many fleeing German civilians in similar wagon trains.

Hearing that terrible news, we followed the direction which the rider pointed for us to take. We drove without stopping almost the whole day, resting the poor horses only when absolutely necessary. On the road, oh, my God, we saw the most gruesome sights. I wished we would have never had to see what we saw. I wished my poor innocent little girls would have never had to witness those most horrible sights. There were bodies lying on the roadside, bodies of women, children, and old folks. Oh, my God, my God, the women's coats and dresses were lifted to their midriffs; their bodies exposed from waist down; their legs apart; their blood covering the white snow. Oh, what a horrible sight! What heinous crime, what terrible death happened to these people! Oh, my God, my God, how those poor women could be so brutally violated and then killed in cold blood. The white snow was red from their blood and that of their innocent children. My heart nearly stopped. Anton and I looked at each other. We didn't say a word. I drew each child closer together and held you tight in my arms. I felt thankful to have Anton with us. He climbed out of the wagon to see if any of the victims was still alive. They were all dead, all shot dead. Anton climbed back up on the wagon and led the mare forward. My mind was filled with worries and questions. "Oh, dear God, where are we going? What is yet to come? I must hold my tears back and concentrate on the immense challenges of the moment."

In the evening, we stopped near the woods at a road side; hungry, freezing, afraid, and forlorn. I began to fetch some food that we had brought along. However, it was so bitter cold that all the food was frozen and hard as stone. There would have been no time to eat anyway, for we heard voices and sounds of horses approaching.

All of a sudden three Russians stood in front of us. They got off from their horses and shouted, "What do we have here? Look at that, an entire German family!" They went straight to Anton. One of them immediately put his gun at Anton's throat. Poor Anton, he was so scared, he shook like tree leaves in high wind. The Russian spit in Anton's face and yelled, "You Hitler," followed by a Russian swear word, and kicked him with his gun right in the face. I ran toward him and said, "No, he is not my husband; he is my helper who has the misfortune of being mentally ill. He does not know what is going on. He is like a child!" The Russian yelled, "Oh, a child, eh, a child of Hitler! You, *niemka* [German woman], watch what happens to a child of Hitler! Men, what shall we do with a Hitler?" They spit at Anton and laughed as one of them said, "Watch *niemka*, watch!" He took a step back, aimed his gun at Anton and shot the poor man in cold blood. One shot followed another, and another, and then yet another. After that cold blooded murder, they kicked Anton's poor body again and again.

We stood there in horror. You, my little baby, cried so much. You couldn't stop crying. All I could do was to hold you and huddle all of you near me. My God, at that most horrible moment, I did not want any attention drawn to you children, especially to Edith who was already developing into a budding teenager. "*Cholera* (swearword) *niemka,*" one of the men yelled. Then he kicked poor Anton's bleeding body again and again and laughed. "There, *niemka*, there is your husband!" We stood frozen and petrified. You would not stop crying. One of the men came toward us. I was holding you tightly in my arms. As he approached, I thought my heart would stop beating. He touched your cheek, looked at you, and murmured something. Then another man called him back. They all left on their horses, laughing. They had just killed poor Anton in cold blood and left laughing. Yes, they left laughing!

What to do now? Poor Anton laid there on the snow covered ground in his own blood, so horribly brutalized. Was there no end to suffering and pain? Was there no end to human brutality? We tried to bury him. But the ground was frozen, and we had no shovel. We covered him with snow and some tree branches. I tried desperately to sing a hymn, but no sound came out of my mouth. The tears running down my cheeks froze into ice. We managed to make a cross out of two tree branches, knelt down and prayed, and we cried bitterly. That was our poor Anton's funeral. Oh, if my dear mother would have known that, her heart would have broken. . . . . .

We did not get very far when Russians came and took one of our horses away from us; but they left us untouched. They took Edith's favorite horse, the white pregnant mare. She loved that horse. Trying to soothe her pain, I pulled poor Edith close in my arms, asking her to be brave and to be thankful that we still had one of our horses and the wagon, and most of all, we had each other, alive and together. In spite of having lost Edith's favorite mare, in spite of having lost dear Anton, in spite of the freezing cold, in spite of our hunger pains and our days and nights on icy roads, we must go on. We must not give up. Cuddling up against each other in the wagon, we continued onward.

We came upon a battlefront. There they were, right in front of us, the German and the Russian soldiers fighting each other. Oh, God, what a sight! More scared than ever, I took you in my arms and held you close to me as we all climbed out of the wagon with trembling knees, and hid underneath it. We sat close together under the wagon, quiet like mice, not making the slightest of noise and afraid to breathe. That battle was indeed a living hell. Bodies were laying all around us, everywhere blood; the freshly white fallen snow had turned into a red field of blood.

After the shooting stopped, we quietly crawled out from under our wagon. Some men approached us and took our horse and wagon away from us. They were Polish men. First it was the Russians that took our horse, now it was the Poles. What's the difference? Since I could speak Polish, I begged the Poles to please let us take some of the pitiful bundles on the wagon. "Sure," said one of them. He climbed quickly on the wagon and threw some of our things at us. The other man was already at the horseman's seat. He whipped our horse, commanding it to leave fast, and away they went.

Here we all stood in the bitter cold, our bundles lying on the icy road. Heartbroken, each of us took whatever we could carry and walked with the bundles on our backs. Edith and I took turns carrying you and our bundle. Lilli carried a heavy backpack, and Sophie carried a bundle. With our bundles on our backs and even heavier bundles of fear in our hearts, we moved on forwards in the heavy snow, ever so slowly.

A Polish man on a horse and wagon passed us by. "Here, let me help you," he said. Would you believe it, that man took all of our bundles away from us and threw them on his wagon, all our feather beds, our blankets, our little bit of provision. Even worse, while he was taking our things away from us he grinned and murmured that it would be much better for him to take our stuff than the approaching Russian army.

We had lost absolutely everything. However, a Polish man still found something they could take. I was wearing a pair of tall leather boots, a sheer necessity for the bitter cold winters in that Eastern part of Europe. He tore the boots from my feet and left me barefoot in the snow and the minus twenty some degrees Centigrade deep freeze (minus four Fahrenheit). Still, I had to be thankful that none of them tore the shoes off my children's feet.

Now what to do, where to go and how to walk without shoes on the icy roads? I had no choice but to wrap my scarf around my feet and go on in the snow. Every step hurt. I tried not to feel the sharp pain on my freezing and wet bare feet on that icy road. My poor feet were full of white blisters. I could hardly feel them any more. I tried to put pain out of my mind and to concentrate on you. It began to snow harder and harder. It was too hard, too painful to walk. My feet were numb. We were hungry, exhausted, and oh, so forlorn and hopeless. My heart was broken, my spirit smashed into pieces. I was on my very last rope. "Dear God, if you are there, please give me a sign, a direction to go on, and how to go on barefoot in that bitter cold snow."

I looked at you all and thought of the children who were separated from their mothers during their frightful flight. Even in our most miserable condition, we were still blessed. We were still together even though, day and night, we lived in fear, and were hungry and shivering in the bone chilling deep freeze of winter. I thought of the small children and the elderly whose bodies we saw frozen to death on the roadside. I looked at you and worried. No matter how much you were bundled up, your little baby feet were ice cold. Later I saw they were stiff, frozen and blue (that is why you could not walk for a long time). I thought of my dear mother who was a woman of faith and who taught me to pray. In my desperation, I folded my hands together and cried, "Oh my God, my God, have pity upon us. Where shall we go? What shall we eat? Here in the street, we will freeze to death. Where shall we find any shelter in that bitter cold? Where will we be safe from Russian and Polish soldiers?"

A woman, who saw me and took pity upon me, gave me a pair of old wooden shoes. She was a Polish woman with a kind heart. Her wooden shoes didn't quite fit me, but they were a relief from walking barefoot in the snow. However, the snow was very high; the wooden shoes were too big and always getting lost in the deep snow. Each step was a pitiful struggle. We met another kind Polish woman on our way who exclaimed, "Oh, *Matka Boska* [Holy Mother], you poor folks; you are half frozen and blue. Maybe you can take shelter in that dairy farm over there."

Totally exhausted, we finally reached a barn at that dairy farm. We went inside the barn and fell exhausted to the ground. We remained there quietly over night, our empty stomachs growling with hunger pain, my poor feet blue, blistery and numb. Next morning, I took my heart in my hands and walked into the farm house. Every step hurt. Before I left, I gave each of you a big hug and told you where I was going, in case I would not come back. My heart racing and my body shivering with fright, it took every ounce of my courage to knock on the door and ask the people in the house if they could use some help in exchange for food.

So we cleaned and worked very hard; but we did not get a single bite to eat. They just laughed at us. One man, however, handed me a handful of dried peas. We chewed on those uncooked dried peas. Oh, yes, hunger hurts. Those who have never known hunger pain will never know how very much hunger hurts. Oh, and seeing your children starving, hurting due to hunger, is a matter all together too painful for a mother to take.

After having worked very hard at the dairy farm, it didn't seem unreasonable to ask for a small amount of milk, especially for a little baby. So I asked for some milk for the children. The people got very upset and their angry outburst is still ringing in my ears: "For Hitler's kids we have not a single drop of milk! But wait, you like the peas so much!" He came back and handed me a bowl of peas. They were mixed with feces. Yes, you heard me right, feces. He gave it to me and laughed. Then someone screamed, "Out, you Hitler folk, out this instance!" We were thrown out of the barn. Here we were, exhausted, hungry, thirsty, cold, no food, no blanket to keep us warm, and no bed; and to top all that, we were humiliated. However, we still were together and that was reason enough to be thankful and to go on.

Exhausted, humiliated, and hopeless, we left the dairy and walked toward Budziszewko, one kilometer away. On our way, another German woman, Mrs. Wendland, joined us with her two children. I was happy to have the company of another woman. When we arrived in Budziszewko, we heard four shots. It was snowing, our lips were blistered, and our bodies hurt from frost bites, our stomachs growled for hunger. I looked at Mrs. Wendland, thankful to have another adult with me and said, "Mrs. Wendland, someone will surely shoot at us Germans." A Polish woman was passing by and called out, "Oh, *Matka Boska*, where on earth are you going! Look at you. You are already frozen blue, every one of you. I just saw four German soldiers who were shot. One didn't want to die. So, they took him and beat him to death." Mrs. Wendland and I looked at each other. My knees were shaking. I looked at the frightened faces of my children and it seemed as if my heart stood still. Here I was, with my four little frozen girls. Were we walking toward death? Standing there in the snow, I folded my hands and prayed with all my might. "Dear God, lead us wherever you need to lead us, but please don't let me lose a child. Lead us all together wherever we must go, but keep us together. Please, I beg you, keep us together."

Our pitiful little group walked on slowly. In Budziszewko, we ran into that Polish woman again, the one we had seen the day before. She looked at us and exclaimed, "Oh, *Matka Boska*, you are still all frozen blue!" I said, "Beyond being frozen and blue, we are starved."

She brought us to her house. There she had a whole room full of German uniforms and coats. I was stunned and frightened. What had we walked into? We quickly saw that she was a poor woman who lived with her mother in a tiny one-room house. She warmed up milk for us and gave the children some bread to eat. Her kind, aged mother asked Mrs. Wendland and me to please feel free to eat too. Here were those two women, themselves poor, sharing with the poorest of poor. My child, remember this, "Whenever you have hunger pains and nothing to eat, go to the poor. They will always find something to share with you." I replied to that kind woman who was poor herself, "Mrs. Czaczka, we thank God that you gave us milk and each child some bread to eat, and that you gave us a place to rest in this warm room, if only for a short while." There were many piles of clothes spread around the room and laundry to be ironed. So, I offered to help with any sewing, ironing or whatever needed to be done. She was so very happy for that help, and I was thankful for not having to accept my children's food from people who were poor without doing something in return.

We sorted and ironed the clothes. I opened the sewing machine and started fixing some clothes. The two women were very happy. After about two hours, the Polish owner of the farm nearby, Mr. Tumczok and his wife came to visit the two women. They started talking about German women fleeing with their children from their homes. Mrs. Tumczok said, "If I would meet a German family here, I would kill them all!" We all looked at each other (we were all in the same room). We looked down to the floor without saying a word, without making a sound. The man replied, "Anna, those Germans are people like anyone else." A moment later, the words of our host, Mrs. Czaczka, nearly killed me. I was so frightened when I heard her say, "I have here two German families." My knees shook. Mrs. Wendland and I looked at each other. Had this woman, whom we thought to be kind and trustworthy, betrayed us? We held our breath fearing the worst. Then Mrs. Czaczka continued, "You, Mr. Tumczok, are a clever man. You would be smart to take on some Germans to work for you and run your entire farm for free. We will be taking on Germans ourselves to work hard for us without any pay." Mrs. Tumczok pointed at Frau Wendland and said, "That woman looks strong and healthy, I would take her to work for me for free. The other one, however, she could not be good for anything, she is far too small and weak; just look at her small frame and tiny hands. What could she ever do?" Frau Czaczka replied, "It is those tiny hands that did most of my work in the last two hours." Mr. Tumczok suggested in a mild manner, "Anna, take both women to work for you. It doesn't cost you anything, and if you don't like their work, you can always send them away. Take both of them; they will work for you for free. There is nothing to lose." I liked his words because we simply could not go on like this. We had no roof over our heads in that bitter cold winter. We were frozen and hungry. Homeless we were exposed to all dangers in the bitter cold, not only from snow storms and ice but worse, from the Russian army. Anna, replied, "No, that weak one (pointing at me) with four mouths to feed, I don't think so. There are just too many mouths eating my food!" Our kind hostess, Mrs. Czaczka, said, "look, two of her children are capable of doing some work for you, and the third one can always do something like tending the geese and the chickens." She persuaded Mrs. Tumczok to take us on as her free laborers to do whatever needed to be done. Well, I was not afraid to work. I was young and healthy, and all of us were very hungry. No, I was not afraid to work for our safety from the cold, the streets and the Russian army.

Mrs. Tumczok asked us to get straw and lay it on the floor of an old shack near her house. That was to be our place to sleep. With no sugar in her voice she told us that she would call all of us early in the morning to work. Now we were in servitude of that woman. It was late evening, and we were hungry, but we cuddled together, thankful that we were still together and that we had at least a roof over our heads, even though it was a cold shack with holes in the walls and roof. We huddled close together and cried and cried, and cried ourselves to sleep.

It was eleven o'clock next morning and Mrs. Tumczok still didn't call any of us to work, and there was no sign of any food or drink for us. As I was about to leave our straw covered shack, I could not close the door; my heart pumped so much. I came back, gave a big hug and kiss to each of my beloved children and said, "If I do not come back, then you know where I am." Knowing that Mrs. Tumczok could do with us whatever she pleased and remembering her terrible threats the day before, I needed to be very careful not to make her mad. So, I got an idea. I still was wearing, under many of my layers of unchanged clothing, a beautiful lace blouse that my brother, Arthur, had brought me as a gift from Paris, France. That blouse was my pride and joy and the only connection with my family members. For the first time since we left our home, I took off my layers of clothes. The first layer, close to my skin, was my precious lace blouse. I took it off. Oh, how I shivered in that cold shack. I quickly put back on all the other layers of clothing, caressed my precious blouse, gave you all a big hug and left our straw covered shack.

Bravely, I walked to the main house with my treasured blouse in hand and rang the door bell. My poor heart pumped so fast that I was afraid it would stop of fright. The door opened and Mrs. Tumczok stood in front of me. I said, "Good morning Mrs., Tumczok. I will give you this fine lace blouse from Paris, France, in return for warm food and drink for my poor children. They are so very frozen and hungry, and so am I." She looked at the beautiful blouse, took it out of my hand, smiled and said, "Oh, I totally forgot about you. Why don't you call the other strong woman, and the two of you do some cleaning up first."

Relieved to see the woman smiling, I went back without my precious blouse and told Frau Wendland that we were both to clean the main house. Reluctantly we left all our six children alone at the straw floor in the shack. That was the first time I left you all alone since we fled from home many days ago. Mrs. Tumczok called another German woman, Frau Gross, who came from the Ukraine and who had also four children and was in servitude there. A lot of work was divided among the three of us

After finishing all my work, I went to Mrs. Tumczok and asked her if it met with her approval. She was pleased with everything I had done. I was glad but exhausted and painfully starved. After all, I had not eaten for days. It was lunchtime and you children had not eaten since Mrs. Czaczka had given you that milk and bread the day before. I simply had to ask Mrs. Tumczok for food for all of us. Before doing so, however, I quickly hurried back to you, to see how you were doing. There I learned that our brave and starved eleven year old Lilli had taken matters in her own hands. She had gone behind the shack where she found buried a pile of potatoes and rutabaga. She brought a few of those frozen rutabaga, cleaned them with the straw on our floor, and gave every one a piece of the rutabaga to chew on, to reduce the hunger pain. With tears in my eyes, I hugged my incredible child. I too chewed a piece of the hard, cold rutabaga.

Then I left you children again and found the courage to tell Mrs. Tumczok, "We simply have to eat, we are weak, we have done the work, the children are starving and we all have not eaten since your friend had given the children milk and bread." I also asked her whether she liked her new lace blouse. She simply said, "Yes", and asked me to go and cook something myself, all the while watching me. I asked, "What shall I cook?" "Whatever is fastest," she replied. So, I quickly looked what I could find. I peeled some potatoes, put them in a pot, mixed them with grits, added milk, and cooked them. I did not want to be greedy and cook anything too valuable that might make her mad. After my pot of potatoes and grits was cooked, I called the children to come and eat. That humble meal tasted so good, better than any fancy banquet. It was the first warm meal we had eaten since we fled from our home. Mrs. Tumczok ate it too. She liked it, and even smiled.

That smile gave me the courage to ask her if we all could wash up somewhere to be more presentable. We had not been able to wash up since we left home. She pointed to the well outside and a bucket in the kitchen and said annoyed, "I know four lousy kids would be four too many, don't you take too much water now!" I took the bucket, went to the well, took a big pot, warmed the water and asked politely for a towel or two. She gave me one kitchen towel. All of us washed up in our straw covered cold shack with that one pot of water, and dried up with that one little kitchen towel. Oh, but how good it felt to clean ourselves for the first time with the sheer luxury of that bit of warm water, and to have a roof over our heads, no matter how humble, and no matter how cold the shack!

I went back to work. There was a whole big pile of laundry that needed to be washed, all by hand of course. There was no washing machine. I put on a whole big pot of water on the stove, cooked the white linen in it, washed everything by hand, wrung them out by hand and hung up to dry. There was also a big pile of laundry to be ironed. The irons in those days were different from the ones we have today. They were heavy. You needed to warm up pieces of brick and put those hot bricks inside the iron. Then you needed to press that heavy iron on the clothes to be ironed. You had to be very careful not to burn the clothing.

It was very hard work. My hand and wrist hurt from holding and pressing that heavy iron. My feet hurt from standing all day long, but I worked and worked until late evening.

The next day, Mrs. Tumczok called all of us three German women who worked for her and asked which one of us would bake the bread. There was a huge old oven and a lot of bread needed to be baked regularly for about twenty eight people. That required a lot of strength. Nobody volunteered. Now Mrs. Tumczok got very angry. Her fist thundered on the table as she yelled, "I will not bake bread for you, Hitler women!" I thought my heart had stopped. My knees were trembling again so much that I could hardly stand. Well, there was nothing left for me to do but to raise my hand and to volunteer baking bread. All of a sudden she laughed like crazy and yelled, "Mattheus, now I have seen everything. The *marna* [little weak one] wants to bake all the bread!" Mr. Tumczok came out of the dining room, grinned and asked me how on earth I was going to do that. I told him, "I can bake either sour dough bread or wheat bread", and explained how I would do it.

After all the dinner dishes and all the cleaning was done, I worked as long as it took to make everything ready to put eleven loaves of bread in the oven for early next morning when I get up. Yes, you heard right, eleven loafs of bread. In the wee hours, next morning, I got up to bake all those loaves of bread. I moistened each loaf with water and sprinkled dill over it. Dill gives such a wonderful baking smell. After putting all eleven loaves in the oven, I had to hurry up as fast as I could to make breakfast for all the Polish people in the household and their guests. That household always had to have a hot and hefty breakfast. By the time they got up, I had already put in a good hard day's worth of work.

From now on my work place was both in the kitchen and in the house. I was to do all the cooking, all the bread baking, all the laundry and ironing, as well as tending to the whole household. I got up every day at three o'clock in the morning, seven days a week, to start baking eight to ten loaves of bread. That was a large household. Exhausted, I would drop on the straw covered floor every night at about midnight, rest for a few hours, only to get up three hours later. I was still working when everyone was already asleep and got up when they were still sleeping. So, basically, I got three hours of sleep every night. There was just too much work, and it all needed to be done on time if I wanted to avoid the wrath of Mrs. Tumczok.

One day, a group of Russians arrived on horseback with their guns and weapons. I thought, "This is surely the end of all of us." Yes, I was afraid especially after Mr. Tumczok introduced me as his German housekeeper. The Russians had brought many bottles of vodka. I had to cook for them and set the table for them in the dining room. They got drunk, came into the kitchen and spoke Russian with me. I told Mr. Tumczok, "Please, tell Mrs. Gross that I will do all her day's work for her tomorrow if she would talk with those Russians. She speaks excellent Russian and is a good conversationalist." He called her and she sang Russian songs with the Russians; drank and ate with them and had a good time. Meantime I did her chores in the dairy department. I was exhausted after doing mine and her work all day and all evening long. Now, Mr. Tumczok came and said to me, "*Gospocia*, [house keeper] now you better hide. The Russians are drunk and are looking for German women."

I rushed immediately to our straw-covered room in the shack where a Polish woman (whose husband was in the war) was also living with her child. Two Russians came into my room and the Polish woman cried out loud, "Oh, *Matka Boska*, now your life is over, and the children, the children!" Her words rang in my ears as the Russian men were grabbing me and dragging me upstairs. There was a lamp up there, but no light bulb in it. Perhaps the dear Lord wanted it that way. I somehow desperately freed myself and tried to escape down the ladder. Unfortunately, I missed a step, fell down and sprained my ankle. But I still ran as fast as I could to Mr. Tumczok in the main house and exclaimed breathlessly, "Mr. Tumczok, please hide me; the Russians are after me. I barely escaped."

In the corner of the living room was a closet. The good Mr. Tumczok moved the tall closet and I hid behind it all night long. I was afraid for my girls. You were all lying together on the straw floor in that shack. I prayed, "Dear God, please, don't let anyone harm them. I will work even harder; I will do anything, but please, God, don't let anyone harm my little girls."

Next morning, Mr. Tumczok relieved me from my hiding place. I was a bundle of fright. My feet were so stiff; I could hardly walk. My swollen sprained ankle hurt. But that was nothing compared to the fear I had to face those two Russians whose rape attempt I barely escaped. I was so sure that if those Russian men would see me, they would shoot me immediately, and my poor four children would be all alone. Those worries about my children occupied my mind while I was making breakfast with such a heavy heart. Yes, I had to make breakfast for the same Russians that tried to rape me the night before. Not only did I have to prepare breakfast for them, I had to set the table for them and serve them. I had to face them. Oh, how my hands shook, how my hear beat, how I avoided looking at them. The Russian men ate, thanked me for that good food and didn't seem to remember a thing about the night before.

One day, two policemen came and reported that two German soldiers lay dead on the road next to the cemetery and that they had to be put under the ground. We German women were ordered to dig two graves for those bodies. Then we had to carry each body by hand and put it in the grave. I put my hand into the coat pocket of one of those dead men to get his papers, so that I could perhaps somehow inform his family of the death of their loved one. Oh my, those two policemen saw that I was trying to get his identity papers and started screaming at me. They held their guns at me and at the other women and threatened to kill us if we didn't throw the bodies into the graves immediately without looking into anyone's pocket. We quietly put the heavy bodies into their graves and buried them, all the while feeling the sharp edges of the policemen's guns in our backs. I patted the graves tightly after all was finished and drew a cross with my fingers on each of them. "*Cholera niemka!*" [swear word preceding 'German woman'] screamed one of the policeman with great contempt and spit on the floor.

On Sundays, during a free hour, we would go to the "cemetery" to visit our two German soldiers whose graves we dug. We looked how they were lying there, wondered who they may be and who may be worried about them. That cemetery hour on Sunday was our rest. We looked up to the sky and hoped for a miracle to appear and free us all from our misery.

After a while, we were not even allowed our Sunday visits to "the cemetery" any more. We Germans had no place where we could talk together alone any more. In some ways, we were worse off than slaves; we were hated like the pest. The children also had to work very hard all that time. Edith and Lilli had to feed all the cows and a very dangerous bull. One Polish man remarked that the bull had killed the man who previously had Edith's job of feeding him. Now I was afraid for Edith and Lilli's lives. I had no moment of peace, only fear, fear, and more fear. Fortunately, all went well with the feeding of that dangerous bull. Yes, all three children, Edith, Lilli and Sophie had jobs to do and were not allowed to leave the premises.

I was also worried about Oma [my mother] and Uroma [my grandmother], and tried very hard to find out if they were still alive, where they were, and how they were doing. However, I had to be extremely careful in getting that information. No one at the farm could ever know or suspect that I was seeking that information. Mrs. Tumczok would have made my life miserable. Many Polish and Russian people in influential positions used to visit the Tumczok's. One of those visitors was a Polish physician who arranged for me to meet with a kind Polish driver, Mr. Kanczurzewski who was now working at Oma's farm. He discretely told me that my mother's farm, the home where I grew up and where all my brothers and my sister grew up, was taken over by a Polish family now. My poor mother and grandmother were now held in servitude in their very own home. Imagine that!

With the help of the kind Mr. Kanczurzewski, I learned that a Polish major now occupied a big farm near my mother's place. One day, the major's wife arrived riding on her impressive carriage driven by six horses. She was accompanied by my mother. Oh, it was so wonderful to see my sweet mother again. But we were to act as if we were strangers and did not know each other at all. Well, they both entered the house. Mrs. Major was impressively well dressed and extremely assertive. She waved her document that stated that I and my children were hers from now on and that she would take us with her. When the Tumczok's refused to give us up, she shouted in a loud voice, "Mr. Tumczok, not only can I take these Germans away from you, but I can take this entire farm away from you!" Well, there was no question that

that woman had a lot of power. The Tumczok's lost. Mrs. Major
commanded us to get on the carriage right away, and away we
drove toward my hometown, Mostki, where my dear mother
and grandmother were still staying, but now in servitude.

We may have been near Mostki, but we came from the frying
pan into the fire. Now our problems got much worse. We were
closer to my mother, but the farms were very far apart, too far
to go and see her. A young German man, Helmut, who came
from Litzmanstadt (Lodz) and was working at the farm where
we now were, murmured to me (in German), "Frau Wenzel,
what have you done? You and your children will hunger and
work yourself to death here." He was right, that young man. All
of us, the children and I worked from dawn to dusk for two days
in a row without any food. We were starved and exhausted. We
were indeed overworked and severely underfed. The children
cried of hunger and were too weak to continue their hard labor,
much harder than at the Tumczok's.

After the second day without food and exhausted from the
hard labor, I went to the major and said, "Mr. Major, we have
been here now for two days. The children who are so young
and small have to do hard labor. They do the job of grown-ups.
They are dangerously overworked, exhausted and weak. They
are suffering from starvation, and so am I. We have not gotten
a thing to eat since we came here, and hunger, it hurts." He
got very angry and screamed, "*Niemka*, if you don't like it here,
I'll get rid of you by sending you to the forced labor camp in
Siberia. There you'll get 150 grams of bread each day to feast
on. I'll keep the children here to work. You'll never get the
children back. You'll never see them again. There, do you like
that better?" Oh, my, what had I done? That was far worse than at
the Tumczok's. I went indeed from the frying pan to the fire.

One day, I asked for a piece of bread for Mr. Müller who was
starved and freezing after working outside all day. A policeman,
a friend of Mrs. Major, came storming out of her room and
demanded that Mr. Müller take off his pants. That police man
hit him fifty two times with his police stick until poor Mr. Müller
was all black and blue, and bleeding. And I, who asked for a
little bread for him was also hit six times with that hard stick.

It was not the first time that cruel policeman beat me. I will never forget the first time that frightful man beat me half to death. It was the time when I refused to give you up to be adopted by the major's mistress whom we addressed as "Frau Major." You were by now three years old, and cute as a button. You had long blond hair, and your blue eyes sparkled, especially when you sang, and you liked to sing. You spoke Russian and Polish and sang Polish songs. The major's mistress, who had no children of her own wanted to adopt you so badly. She already had the adoption papers and demanded that I sign them. I refused. Then she tried persuading me by saying how much better off you would be with her. After all, what could I offer you? I was merely her German slave and was penniless and homeless. She, on the other hand, was well off and would raise you as her very own daughter. No one would ever need to know that you were not her own Polish child, and after a little while, you would even forget all about me. Oh, my God, my God, what have I done to deserve such ultimate cruelty? Did I try to keep you alive and all of us together for it to come to this? I fought with all my might against that awful adoption plan of hers. I would not let her tear you away from me.

Oh, was she angry! Oh, was she mad! She spit in my face; she yelled and screamed, calling me all kinds of unspeakable names. Then she called for that cruel police man to come and "punish me for my crime." That police man rushed toward me with a horse whip in his hand, screaming, "*Cholera niemka!*" He commanded me to lie on the floor, face down. I was so struck with fright; I could hardly move. Then I felt the sharp whip. Like a long sharp knife, it split up my back, one sharp whip following another. I thought my back would surely break. Oh, that sharp, excruciating pain, I can still feel it. I surely felt my skin open up and blood spraying out. I thought that would surely be my end. Then I would be dead, and they could take you for sure. I kept thinking about all of you children. I heard you all cry so bitterly, and tried to hold on, tried to be strong for you all. Yes, I needed to remain strong for you, my four poor sweet innocent children who had to witness all that unspeakable cruelty. For sure, Mrs. Major wanted me dead and out of the way, so that she could adopt you. I could not let that happen. I could not let them beat me to death. I had to be strong.

Then the whipping stopped. He shoved that piece of paper in front of me and the pen in my hand, forcing me to sign that paper. I would not do it. I closed my hand to a tight fist and would not open it to sign that paper. What would become of your sisters, Edith, Lilli, and Sophie, with me gone? What would become of you? I had to be strong for all of you. I had to be stronger than that blade-sharp whip. Again the whip came crashing on my back, each stroke harder than the other. My entire back burned like a flaming fire. I felt the blood running into my clothes, sticking. Still, I tried to hold on, tried to remain conscious. Your bitter cries gave me strength to pray for God's help. I thought of Jesus being whipped. That Polish police man whipped and whipped, and whipped me until I was unconscious, until I literally could not hear his hateful screams any more or feel his sharp whip crashing down on my back, or feel his brutal and big calloused hand that shove pen in my tightly closed fist while I refused to open my fist to hold that pen. I don't know what happened afterwards. I was told he just left me there lying unconscious on the ground. My poor children carried me to our room and took care of me. Oh, my God, my God, was there no end to this slavery, to the torture and cruelties which we had to endure and which you children had to witness at such an innocent young age?!

It took two days before I was able to get up again. My back felt literally split open and burned like fire. I could hardly move. The pain was too excruciating. However, I heard the stern voice of Mrs. Major demanding, "Lazy *niemka*, get up and work!" What was a poor homeless German woman with four children, all enslaved to the Poles, to do? *Ja, ja,* [yes, yes,] work slave, work for the master, until you drop! But each time I looked into the sad blue eyes of my girls, my heart melted. I could not give up; I could not despair. I needed to try not to think of my pain and deep wounds that traumatized me and my children. Somehow I found the strength to get up and work for that cruel woman who had me whipped half to death and now demanded to "get up and work" for her.

Remember this, my child, whenever you think you can't go on any more, there comes from somewhere a little light showing you the way. One dark night in autumn 1947, as per Oma's careful planning, the good Mr. Augustinus Kanczurzewski helped all of us escape from slavery and brought us to Stettin. Two days later, at dawn, all seven of us, Uroma Oma, and the five of us were standing in a long line at the main refugee camp. We were waiting for a chance to be transported by a freight train to the border of what still remained German ground. Even though it was now the Russian occupied communist zone of Germany, it was still Germany; and we longed to be free to be able to speak our own language again. We were all starved because there was nothing to eat or drink. You were small and cried. Great grandmother was eighty years old and frail. But we had hope; hope to be able to escape from our miserable existence under Polish servitude. Even now, no matter how hard I try to forget, I can't stop thinking about those terrifying experiences of our flight and the years of enslavement. They haunt me like a bad nightmare. Sometimes at night, the nightmares we lived through come to torment me, and I have to live through it all over and over again.

We were like run-away slaves who had to escape their miserable condition, afraid to be caught. When the long awaited train that was to bring us to the border arrived, we all hurriedly climbed in, hoping not to be noticed. It was a train on which cows and cattle had been transported. Oh, the compartment smelled so bad! However that did not matter. What mattered was that we were not caught as run-away slaves and that the train would get us close to the border.

The next day, we took another train. It was so overcrowded, we were packed like sardines. People were pushing and shoving, trying to get on that train. We were all holding on tightly to each other, as tight as we could, not to be separated, and stay together. Even after the train started, people ran along side of it, trying to get on. People held up their hands, some got on, even as the train was accelerating. After we crossed the border, all of us knelt on the ground of our compartment and thanked God that we were on German ground. It was a jubilation unsurpassed!

The entire compartment was filled with great relief and tears of joy.

It had taken us about a day to get to Dessau. However, in Dessau, there was typhoid; there was disease all around us. Many people were dying or had already died. I became violently ill. My whole body shook; I had diarrhea and suffered from severe dehydration. Many believed I would surely die. All around me, many children and grown-ups were dying. They were falling like flies. There was no room at the refugee camp. One person was squeezed right next to the other. There was simply not enough space for all those people. There was also nothing to eat but two dried up potatoes per day which were rationed carefully for each person. Some people could not tolerate the potatoes and got sick. We lived under those miserable conditions in the camp for about four weeks. We survived.

From Dessau we were told to go to Klein Rosenburg in Sachsen Anhalt in the Russian occupied sector of Germany where its mayor found a room for us to stay upstairs in a bombed and ruined castle. That village was full of ruins and rubble. All of Germany had been bombed so severely that there were piles of bombed rubble everywhere.

One thing, however, was clear; we could not stay there very long. There was no future for you all in that "Ostzone" (East Sector of Germany); no freedom under the communist, Russian occupied regime. We heard from the grapevine that each day people got shot because they tried to escape to West Germany. With each passing day it was harder to escape. Even though we were so happy to speak German again, we had to be very careful what we said. We were not free to speak our minds. One had to be very careful because the Secret Police was everywhere. They were just watching and waiting for any sign of escape attempts or any criticism of communism.

For the complete personal narrative of Leokadia Wenzel, see Vora, E. (2010). *The will to live: A German family's flight from Soviet rule.* Bloomington: Xlibris Corporation.

AUTHOR'S NOTE

Thanks to the ingenious planning of my mother and grandmother, we risked our lives and courageously fled, one by one to West Germany in the darkness of night. After my oldest sister Edith escaped safely to the West, my sister Sophie ventured to escape as well and joined Edith in Westphalia. With every year, the escape from East Germany was getting more and more dangerous. After my great grandmother died at the age of eighty two, my sister Lilli, who was very close to her, risked her life to escape with the help of a good man, named Demann. Finally, on a dark and rainy summer night in 1950, my mother and I crawled through bobbed wire and escaped to the West. My mother kissed the ground and twirled me around. In response to my question, "Mom, is this really the Golden West?" she said, "Yes, yes, my child, we are in the West and its gold is our freedom!"

EPILOGUE

The purpose of this book was to share the experiences of a few of the millions of Germans who were expelled, deported, imprisoned, and killed at the end of WWII and the years that followed. It was not written to point fingers at perpetrators of horrors during and after WWII. The thirty three survivors in this book who coped silently with their trauma for more than sixty years finally broke their silence. They wanted to speak for the millions of German WWII victims, mainly women, children and the elderly who cannot speak any more. With this book, the hope is that their stories will be a lesson for history and that their suffering shall not be forgotten.

Where are the survivors who shared their narratives in this book now? All of them currently live in Germany, Austria or the United States. The Banat Swabians from Romania and Yugoslavia live in Ingolstadt, Germany. Most of them live in the Nieschbach Senior Home for Banat Swabian deportees where they all share a common, tragic history. Some of them live nearby and regularly partake in the weekly, monthly, and yearly memorial celebrations of their Banat Swabian Association at the Nieschbach Home. For example, every week, there is a meeting; every month a birthday celebration with song and instrumental music to honor those members who were born that month. Once a year, in January (that fatal month when they were force deported to Russia) they partake in a memorial that reflects their life as Banat Swabians through their traditional costumes, dances and folk songs.

The survivors from Czechoslovakia and East Prussia live with their families or by themselves in Ingolstadt, Germany, with the exception of one who lives in Austria and four who live in Michigan, U.S.A. The women from Silesia and Pomerania live in an assisted living facility of a nursing home in Gohfeld, Germany, except for one who lived in Ingolstadt. The survivor from Warthegau, Poland, my mother, lived with her family in Gohfeld, Germany.

Even though all of the survivors interviewed can never forget their traumatic experiences more than sixty years ago, and relive them through nightmares, not even one survivor seems to have contemplated suicide. That shows their strong spirit and zeal for life in spite of all they endured. These survivors bent like a branch of a tree in a terrible storm, and seemed to have adjusted to life the best they could.

The endurance, strength, courage, and sometimes faith of these survivors are awe-inspiring. What is remarkable is that the flaming hatred of their perpetrators who committed unspeakable brutalities and gross human rights violations against them, is absent in their victims. These German survivors who had endured unspeakable atrocities showed no hatred or malice toward their perpetrators, only immense sadness and deep wounds of painful memories which will never heal. They truly follow Mahatma Gandhi's words in his non-violent struggle against oppressive British rule, "An eye for an eye will make the whole world blind."

REFERENCES

Annabring, M. (1955). *Volksgeschichte der Donauschwaben in Yugoslawien*. Stuttgart, Germany: Verlag Südost-Stimmen.

Anonymous (2003). *Eine Frau in Berlin*. Frankfurt am Main, Germany: Eichborn AG.

Bade, K. J. (2000). *Europa in Bewegung. Migration vom 18. Jahrhundert bis zur Gegenwart*. München, Germany: C.H. Beck.

Barcan, M., & Millitz, A. (1977). *Die deutsche Nationalitäten in Rumänien*. Bukarest, Romania: Kritorion Verlag.

Barwich, L., Binder, F., & Beer, J. (1993). *Weissbuch der Deutschen aus Jugoslawien: Erlebnisberichte 1944-48*. (Vols. 1-2). München, Germany: Universitas Verlag.

Bobango, G. (1979). *The Emergence of the Romanian National State*. New York, NY: East European Q.

Bosch, H. (2005). *Das Banat – Gross Tetscha*. Unpublished document. Ingolstadt, Germany: Nieschbach Home.

Breslau, (1950). Breslau 1945: Schicksal einer Stadt. In *Breslauer Nachrichten, 1950, Nr. 29 – Nr. 34*, Breslau, Germany.

Broszat, M. (1968). Deutschland—Ungarn—Rumänien. Entwicklung und Grund-Faktoren nationalsozialistischer Hegemonial—und Bündnispolitik. *Historische Zeitschrift, 206, 552-553.*

Buchholz, M. (2004). Vergebliche Flucht.. In T. Schieder (Ed.), *Die Vertreibung der deutschen Bevölkerung aus den Gebieten östlich der Oder-Neisse.* (Vol. I/1, pp. 129-130). München, Germany: Deutscher Taschenbuch Verlag GmbH & Co. KG.

Buchholz, W. (1999). *Pommern.* München, Germany: Siedler Verlag.

Bundesministerium für Vertriebene, Flüchtlinge und Kriegsgeschädigte (1957). *Dokumentation der Vertreibung der Deutschen aus Ost-Mitteleuropa: Das Schicksal der Deutschen in Rumänien* (Vol. 3). Augsburg, Germany: Welt-Bild Verlag.

Carpathian German Home Page. *Carpathian German History.* Retrieved June 10, 2002 from http://www.geocities.com/yertmr/hist20096#History.

Cwikla, I. (2008). Wir lagen uns in den Armen und weinten. In S. Dreher, M. Kröpelin, & O. Teichert (Eds.), *Treibgut des Krieges: Zeugnisse von Flucht und Vertreibung der Deutschen.* Kassel, Germany: Volksbund Deutscher Kriegsfürsorge e.V.

Davies, N. (2007). *Europe at war 1939-1945: No simple victory.* London, UK: Pan Books.

De Zayas (1994). *A terrible revenge: The "ethnic cleansing" of the East European Germans, 1944-1950.* New York, NY: St. Martin's Press.

Dwinger, E. (2000). *Der Tod in Polen: Die volksdeutsche Passion.* Scriptorium..

Ehm, A. (2004). Die Austreibung der Bevölkerung von Komotau und Ermorderung während des Fussmarsches zur sächsischen Grenze. In T. Schieder (Ed.), *Die Vertreibung der Deutschen Bevölkerung aus der Tschechoslovakai.* (Vol. IV/2). München, Germany: Deutscher Taschenbuch Verlag GmbH & Co.

E.L. (2004). Flucht in Richtung Czarnikau, Überrollung und Rueckkehr. In T. Schieder (Ed.),

Die Vertreibung der deutschen Bevölkerung aus den Gebieten östlich der Oder Neisse. (Vol. I/1). München, Germany: Deutscher Taschenbuch Verlag GmbH & Co. KG.

F.B. (2004). Erlebnisbericht eines Prager Deutschen in den Tagen des Tschechischen Aufstandes. In T. Schieder (Ed.), *Die Vertreibung der deutschen Bevölkerung aus der Tschechoslovakai,* (Vol. IV/2). München, Germany: Deutscher Taschenbuch Verlag GmbH & Co. KG.

Freihoffer, H. (1981). *Sklaven im Bărăgan.* Deggendorf, Germany: Self-published.

Frommer, B. (2004). *National cleansing: Retribution against Nazi collaborators in postwar Czechoslovakia.* New York, NY: Cambridge University Press.

Geier, C. (1994). Bărăgan—der Rumänische Gulag. *Banatica,* Vol. 3, Freiburg, Germany.

Ghyka, M. (1941). *A documented chronology of Roumanian history from prehistoric times to the present day* (F.G. Renier & A. Cliff, Trans). Oxford, UK: B. H. Blackwell, Ltd.

G. F. (2004). Leiden der zurückgebliebenen Bevölkerung durch Gewaltakte russischer Soldaten. In T. Schieder (Ed.), *Die Vertreibung der deutschen Bevölkerung östlich der Oder-Neisse.* (Vol. I/1, pp. 452-454). München: Deutscher Taschenbuch Verlag GmbH & Co. KG.

Glassheim, E. (2000). National mythologies and ethnic cleansing: The expulsion of Czechoslovak Germans. *European History,* 33 (4), 463-486.

Glotz, P. (2003). *Die Vertreibung: Böhmen als Lehrstück.* Berlin, Germany: Ullstein Verlag.

Glück, A. (2004). Räumung der Stadt Filehne und Flucht im Treck bis in die Westprignitz. In T. Schieder (Ed.), *Die*

Vertreibung der deutschen Bevölkerung aus den Gebieten östlich der Oder-Neisse. (Vol. I/1). München, Germany: Deutscher Taschenbuch Verlag GmbH & Co. KG.

Gollancz, V. (1946). Die Vertreibung. In P. Glotz (Ed.), *Die Vertreibung: Böhmen als Lehrstück.* (pp. 48-68). Berlin, Germany: Ullstein Verlag.

Grothe, H. (1932). Grothes kleins Hardwörterbuch des Grenz-und Auslandsdeutschtums. München, Germany: Verlag R. Oldenbourg.

Grube F. & Richter, G. (1980). *Flucht und Vertreibung: Deutschland zwischen 1944 und 1947.* Hamburg, Germany: Hoffmann und Campe Verlag.

Hamberger, J. (2004). The debate over Slovak historiography with respect to Czechoslovakia. *Studia Historica Slovenica, 4*(1), 165-191.

Heimatsortsgemeinschaft Jahrmarkt, (1995). Deportation 1945. *Jahrmarkter Heimatblätter* Nr. 2. Waldkraiburg, Germany: Druckerei Keller.

Hillgruber, A. (1954). *Hitler, König Carol und Marshall Antonescu. Die deutsch-rumänische Beziehungen 1938-1944,* Vol 5). Mainz, Germany: Institute für Europäische Geschichte.

Historical Exhibition in the Deutscher Dom in Berlin (1998). *Questions on German history: paths to parliamentary democracy.* Berlin, Germany: German Bundestag.

Höges, C. et. al. (2005). Die verdrängte Tragödie. In S. Aust, & S. Burgdorff (Eds.), *Die Flucht: über die Vertreibung der Deutschen aus dem Osten.* München, Germany: Deutscher Taschenbuch Verlag GmbH.

Hoffmann, G. W. & Neil, F. W. (1962). *Yugoslavia and the New Communism.* New York, NY: Prentice Hall.

Hughes, S. (1961). *Contemporary Europe: A history.* New York, NY: Prentice Hall.

Institute for Research of Expelled Germans (2012). The removal of Czechoslovakia's Germans through expulsion and discriminatory laws. Retrieved July 17, 2012 from http:// expelledgermans.org/sudetengermans.htm.

Istrati, P. (1987). *Die Disteln des Bărăgan.* Leipzig, Germany: Verlag Reclam.

Jesko, S. (1951). Greueltaten bei der Überrollung durch russische und polnische Partisanen, Rückkehr ins Heimatsdorf, und die Leiden der Deutschen in der ersten Zeit der Besetzung. In T. Schieder (Ed.), (2004), *Die Vertreibung der Deutschen Bevölkerung östlich der Oder Neisse,* (Vol. I/1, pp. 81-87). München, Germany: Deutscher Taschenbuch Verlag GmbH & Co.KG.

Jungk, R. (2002). Aus einem Totenland: Polen 1945—Eine historische Reportage. In S.Aust, & S. Burgdorff (Eds.), *Die Flucht: Über die Vertreibung der Deutschen aus dem Osten* (pp. 21-28). Hamburg, Germany: Spiegel-Buchverlag.

Kahl, I. (2004). Flucht bei Kalisch, Überrolung durch die Russen, Rückkehr und die ersten Erlebnisse in der Heimat. In T. Schieder (Ed.), *Die Vertreibung der deutschen Bevölkerung östlich der Oder-Neisse.* (Vol I/1, pp. 348-350). München, Germany: Deutscher Taschenbuch Verlag GmbH & Co.KG.

Kaltenegger, R. (2001). *Titos Kriegsgefangene: Folterlager, Hungermärsche und Schauprozesse.* Graz, Austria: Leopold Stocker Verlag.

Kann, R. (2000). *A history of the Habsburg Empire, 1526-1918.* Berkeley, CA: University of California Press.

Kent, M. (2003). *Eine Porzellan Scherbe im Graben.* Bern, Switzerland: Scherz Verlag.

Kleindienst, J. (2007). *Nichts führt zurück: Flucht, Vertreibung, Integration—Zeitzeugen Erinnerungen 1944-1955*. Berlin, Germany: Zeitgut Verlag GmbH.

Kleindienst, J. (2001). *Von hier nach drüben: Grenzgänge, Fluchten und Reisen im kalten Krieg 1945-1961*. Berlin, Germany: Zeitgut Verlag GmbH.

Kibelka, R. (1999). *Wolfskinder: Grenzgänger an der Memel*. Berlin, Germany: Frauenverband im BdV e.V.

Klier, Freya (1996). *Verschleppt ans Ende der Welt: Schicksale deutscher Frauen in sowjetischen Arbeitslagern*. Berlin, Germany: Frauenverband im BdV e.V.

Knopp, G. (2004). *Die grosse Flucht: Das Schicksal der Vertriebenen*. München, Germany: Ullstein Buchverlag GmbH.

Kopeczi, B., (Ed.). (2001). *History of Transylvania*. New York, NY: Institute of History of the Hungarian Academy of Sciences.

Landsmannschaft der Banater Schwaben (1983). *Der Leidensweg der Banater Schwaben im zwanzigsten Jahrhundert*. München, Germany: Landsmannschaft.

Lay, H. (1995, May 1). Die grösste Tragödie unserer Geschichte: Die Zwangsverschleppung der Romaniendeutschen in die Sovietunion. *Banater Post*, p. 1.

Lemberg, H., & Franzen, K. E. (2002). *Die Vertriebenen. Hitlers letzte Opfer*. Berlin, Germany: Ullstein.

Liddell, H. (1973). *History of the Second World War*. London, UK: Pan Books.

Lukes, I. (2000). Strangers in one house: Czechs and Slovaks 1918-1922. *Canadian Review of Studies in Nationalism, 27*(1-2), 33-43.

Lumans, V. (1982). The ethnic German minority of Slovakia and the Third Reich, 1938—1945. *Central Europe, 15* (3), 266-296.

Mackintosh, M. (1963). *Rumania.* London, UK: University Press.

Magocsi, P.R. (2002). *Historical atlas of Central Europe.* Seattle, WA: University of Washington Press.

Marinessa, M. et.al. (1996). *Die Deportation in den Bărăgan, Schicksale—Dokumente-Reportagen.* Temeschburg, Romania: Mirton-Verlag.

Matley, I. (1970). *Romania: A profile.* Prague, Czechoslovakia: Präger Publishers.

Meyer, F. (2005). Hass auf Befehl. In S. Aust & S. Burgdorff (Eds.), *Die Flucht: Über die Vertreibung der Deutschen aus dem Osten,* (pp. 22-28). München, Germany: Deutscher Taschenbuch Verlag GmbH & Co. KG.

Meyer, F. (2005). Hohn für die Opfer. In S. Aust & S. Burgdorff (Eds.), *Die Flucht: Über die Vertreibung der Deutschen aus dem Osten,* (pp. 30-36). München, Germany: Deutscher Taschenbuch Verlag GmbH & Co. K.G.

Mühlfenzl, R (1981). *Geflohen und Vertrieben. Augenzeugen berichten.* Königstein im Taunus, Germany: Athenaeum Verlag.

Mükusch, H. (2004). Die Austreibsaktion in Jägersdorf und Fussmarsch der Ausgetriebenen. In T. Schieder (Ed.), *Die Vertreibung der deutschen Bevölkerung aus der Tschechoslovakai.* (Vol. IV/2, pp. 363-373). München, Germany: Deutscher Taschenbuch Verlag GmbH & Co.KG.

Münz, R. (2000). Das Jahrhundert der Vertreibungen. *Transit: Europaische Revue, 23,* 132-154.

M.v.W. (1951). Death march to Pohrlitz. In W. Turnwald (Ed.), *Documents of the expulsion of Sudeten Germans,* (pp. 2-12). Report Nr. 8. München, Germany: Association for the Protection of Sudeten German Interests.

Nagy-Talavera, N. M. (1970). *Green shirts and others: A history of fascism in Hungary and Romania.* Iaşi, Romania: Center for Romanian Studies.

Naimark, N.M. (2001). *Fires of hatred: Ethnic cleansing in twentieth-century Europe.* Cambridge, MA: Harvard University Press.

Neumeyer, I. (1981). Der Brünner Todesmarsch nach Pohrlitz. Mai/Juni 1945. In R. Mühlfenzl (Ed.), *Geflohen und vertrieben: Augenzeugen berichten* (pp. 47-57). Königstein im Taunus, Germany: Aethenaeum Verlag.

Pridonoff, E. L. (1955). *Tito's Yugoslavia.* Washington D.C.: Public Affairs Press.

Reuth, R. G. (2007). *Deutsche auf der Flucht.* Augsburg, Germany: Verlagsgruppe Weltbild GmbH.

Rozumet and Zdenek (1951). The expulsion. In W. Turnwald (Ed.), *Documents on the expulsion of the Sudeten Germans,* (pp. 20-31). Nr. 4. München, Germany: Association for the Protection of Sudeten German Interests.

Scherer, A., Straka, M., & Nijemacal, K. (1999). *Abriss zur Geschichte der Donauschwaben.* Graz, Austria: Leopold Stocker Verlag / Zagreb: Pan Liber.

Schieder, T. (1961). *Documents on the Expulsion of the Germans from Eastern-Central-Europe.* (Vol. II). Bonn, Germany: Federal Ministry of Expellees, Refugees and War Victims.

Schmider, K. (2002). *Partisanenkrieg in Yugoslawien 1941-1944.* Hamburg, Germany: Verlag E. S. Mittler & Sohn.

Schmidt, K. (1957). Evakuierung, Internierung und Abtransport der deutschen im Fussmarsch nach Prag. In T. Schieder, (Ed.), (2004), *Die Vertreibung der deutschen Bevölkerung aus der Tschechoslovakai*, (Vol. IV/2, pp. 37-45). München, Germany: Deutscher Taschenbuch Verlag GmbH & Co.KG.

Schmidt, S. (1991). Die Zweite Deportation von Banater Schwaben—Bărăgan 1951-1956. *Donauschwchwäbische Forschungs—und Lehrblätter*, Heft 3, München, Germany.

Streibel, R. & Alexander, M. (1994). *Flucht und Vertreibung: Zwischen Aufrechnung und Verdrängung*. Wien, Austria: Picus Verlag.

Sunic, T. (2002). *The destruction of ethnic Germans and German prisoners of war in Yugoslavia, 1945-1953*. Address at the 14th IHR Conference, on June 22, 2002 in Irvine, CA.

Sunic, T (1995). *Titoism and dissidence: Studies in the history and dissolution of communist Yugoslavia*. Frankfurt, Germany: Peter Lang.

Ther, P. & Siljak, A. (2001). *Redrawing nations: Ethnic cleansing in East-Central Europe, 1944-1948*. Lanham MD: Rowman & Littlefield.

Teutsch, G.D. (1907-1926). *Geschichte der Siebenbürger Sachsen für das sächsische Volk*, (Vols. 1-4). Hermannstadt, Germany: Krafft.

Von Darnstädt, T., & Wiegrafe, K. (2002). Lauft, ihr Schweine! In S.Aust, & S. Burgdorff (Eds.), *Die Flucht: Über die Vertreibung der Deutschen aus dem Osten*. Hamburg, Germany: Spiegel-Buchverlag.

Vora, E. (2010). *The Will to Live: A German family's flight from Soviet rule*. Bloomington, IL: Xlibris Corporation.

Vucinich, W.S. (1952). Soviet Rumania: 1944-1951. *Current History*, *22*, 85-91.

Weber, W. (1988). *Und über uns der blaue endlose Himmel: Die Deportation in die Bărăgan-Steppe Rumäniens 1951*. München, Germany: Eigenverlag Landsmannschaft der Banater Schwaben.

Weidner, I. (2008). Vergewaltigungen. In *Treibgut des Krieges: Zeugnisse von Flucht und Vertreibung der Deutschen*. Kassel, Germany: Volksbund Deutscher Kriegsgräberfürsorge.

Wheeler, C. (2002, 3 December). Czechs' hidden revenge against Germans. *BBC News*. Retrieved July 18, 2012 from http://news.bbc.co.uk/2/hi/europe/2536261.stm.

Wildmann, G., Sonnleitner, H., & Weber, K. (1998). *Verbrechen an den Deutschen in Jugoslavien 1944-48: Stationen eines Völkermords*. München, Germany: Donauschwäbische Kulturstiftung.

Wildman, G. et. al. (2001). *Genocide of the ethnic Germans in Yugoslavia, 1944-1948*. Santa Ana, CA.: Danube Swabian Association of the USA.

Zatschek, M. (2004). Erlebnisbericht. In T. Schieder (Ed.), *Die Vertreibung der deutschen Bevölkerung aus der Tschechoslovakai*. (Vol. 2, pp. 438-455). München, Germany: Deutscher Taschenbuch Verlag GmbH & Co. KG.

Zentner, C. (1989). *Drittes Reich und Zweiter Weltkrieg*. Köln, Germany: Tigris Verlag, GmbH.

Zentrum gegen Vertreibung (2012). *History of the German Expellees and their Homelands*. Retrieved July 18, 2012 from http://www.z-g-v.de/english/aktuelles/?id=56

APPENDIX 1

Slave Song 1

Wo die Landestiere fahren durch die Welt,
Wo die Welt mit Bretter zugenagelt ist,
Wo man unter Tränen Mais und Mobel frisst,
Wo man weder Tische oder Stühle sieht,
Und . . . sein Quartier bezieht,

Wo die Landestiere fahren durch die Welt,
Auf den Bahnen's wagen, so lang der Tag anhellt,
Über Weg und Strassen,
Über Stock und Stein,
Gibt's für unsere Kehle weder Bier noch Wein.
Wo die grünen Zelte? und das Wasser knapp,
Wo man nichts zu essen und auch nichts zu trinken hat,
Wo man nichts kann kaufen und auch nichts erhält,
Muss man Not getrieben sparen all sein Geld
(weil wir ja nichts gehabt haben)
Wo man Hauser baut aus lauter Lehm und Dreck,
Wo man bis zu Knien in schwarzer Erde steckt,
Wo aus jedem Ritze kriechen Wanzen raus,
Ist der Läuse Heimat und auch mein Zuhaus.

Slave Song 2:

"Wenn man sich hinlegt und alles schläft so still,
Kriechen aus allen Ecken Wanzen raus.
Manches Mädel sitzt gallant
Mit dem Schuckel in der Hand
Und dann geht das Knacken los,
Ei, wie knackt es im Kolchos.
Und die Nacht geht schnell vorbei
Mit der Wanzen Jagerei.
Wo ein neuer Tag einbricht
Und dann kommt 'ne neue Schicht.
Ja, das ist der Tages Lauf.

Bei der grossen Wäscherei,
Ich höre ein Geschrei,
Wenn der Hahn nicht abgedreht,
So dass das Waschen mit Spucken geht.
(Ja, da war ja kein Wasser!)

Dann ist Kucken wieder da
Dann ess auch schnell,
Ein Brocken Brot und zwei Löffel Supp,
Das ist unser ganzer Club.
Und das Brot war klitschenass,
Ausgesehen wie Schweinefrass.
Und was ist denn schon dabei,
Mittags kriegen wir dafür Brei.
(Aber der Brei war ja nur zwei Löffel voll
Und da waren auch noch Würmer drin.)

APPENDIX 2

Map of Romania

Map of Germany 1914

Map of Germany 1950

MAP OF ROMANIA

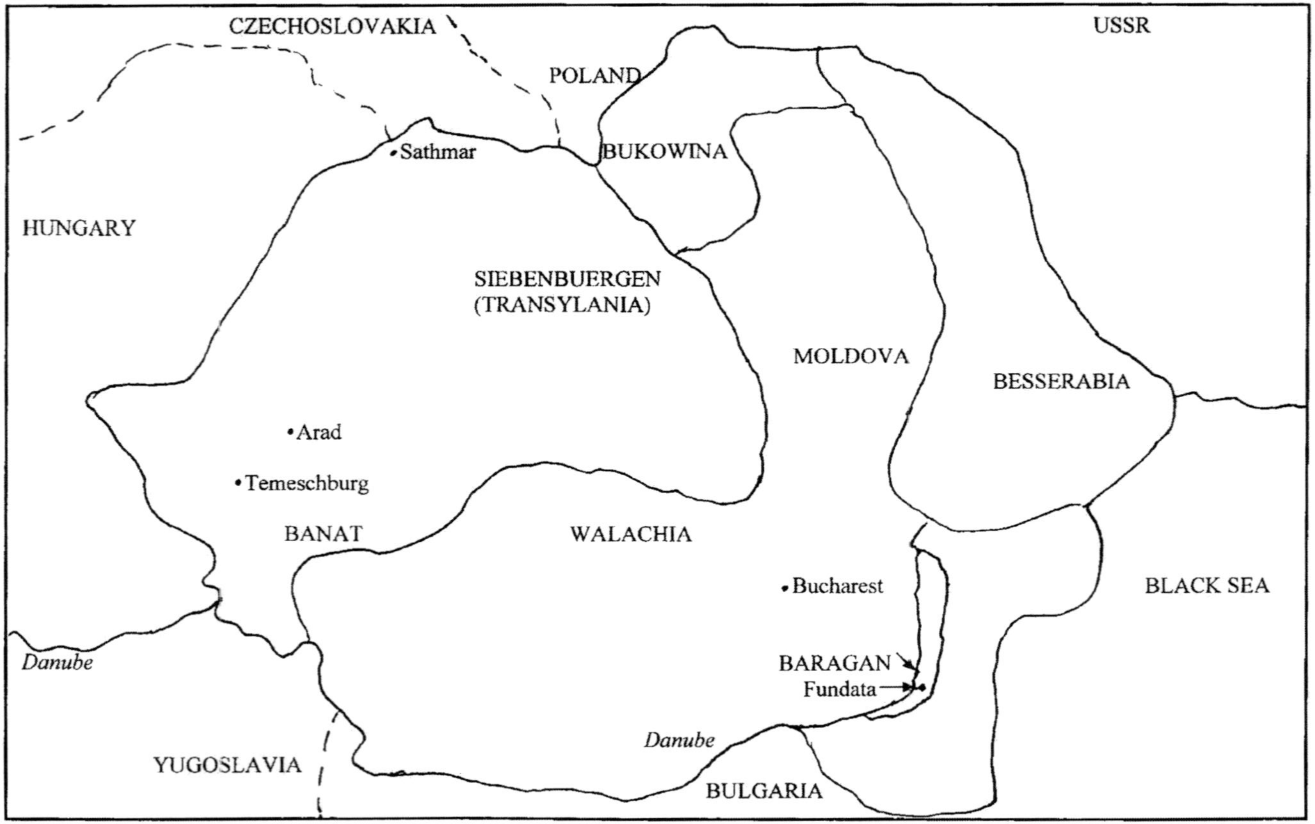

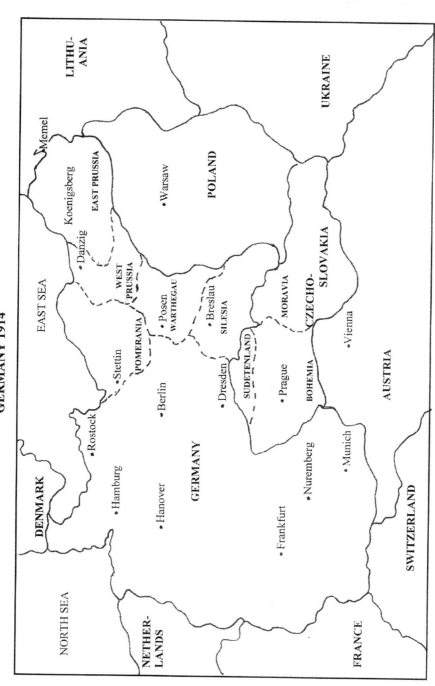

GERMANY 1914

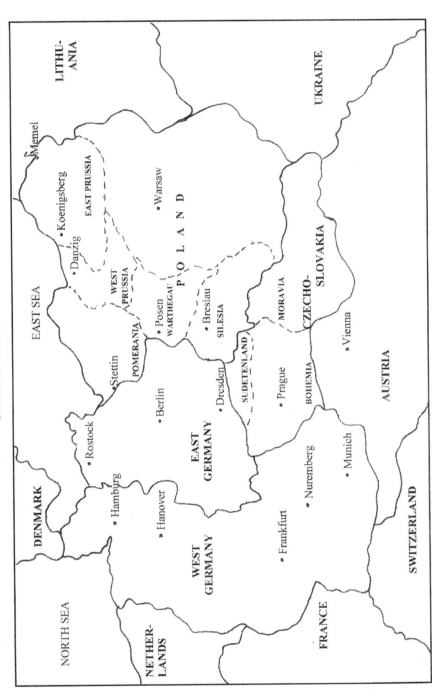

GERMANY 1950

CPSIA information can be obtained at www.ICGtesting.com
Printed in the USA
BVOW081130210413

318709BV00003B/178/P